BEDENKLICH HAPPENINGS
AND MORE, VOLUME II

Copyright © 2016

by

Levi L. Fisher
5780 Buena Vista Rd.
Gap, PA 17527

Printed 2016
Masthof Press
219 Mill Road
Morgantown, PA 19543-9516

Bedenklich Happenings

AND MORE

VOLUME II

compiled by
Levi L. Fisher

TABLE OF CONTENTS

Dear readers and all,

Due to the *Aufnam* and interest shown to the *Beden-klich Happenings* book in 2013, it gave me courage to keep right on going, which I am doing and hope it will be enjoyed by many. *Un Mir Vella Gott da eir geva.*

- Levi L. Fisher

The mountainous region of Ararat is approximately midway between the Black and the Caspian Seas. Mount Ararat is a name associated with the double-peaked mountain in the background of this photograph. The higher peak is nearly 17,000 feet above sea level.

*And in the seventh month,
on the seventeenth
day of the month, the ark rested upon
the mountains of Ararat.*
GENESIS 8:4

as a cross between a dog's bark and the bray of a donkey increased a thousandfold and can be clearly heard for ten miles. A St. Bernard in Lebanon, MO, had 23 puppies in 1975. A kangaroo, while being chased in Australia made a jump of 42 feet long.

-Jonie Esh

AMAZING ANIMALS

A female blue whale was caught in 1947 that was ninety feet long and weighed 109 tons. The longest one ever recorded was 110 feet. Newborn calves are over twenty feet long and weigh over six hundred pounds. The highest giraffe was almost twenty feet high in a zoo in Britain. The cheetah can run sixty miles per hour on level ground. The elephant is the biggest land animal. A bull was shot in 1974 in Angola that was thirteen feet high and weighed thirteen tons. The noisiest animal is the howler monkey. Their screams have been described

DON'T JUDGE BY SIZE!

The wonderful things in nature are the smallest.

A flea leaps 200 times its length. A man would have to jump 1,200 feet to equal this proportionately.

The housefly takes 440 steps to travel three inches, and does it in a half second—corresponding to a man running 20 miles in a minute.

An ant lifts a load many, many times its own weight—a man would have to lift a diesel locomotive and carry it on his back to compare with that of the ant.

Elephants

Elephants—the word conjures up pleasant childhood memories of circuses and zoos, playful antics with their agile trunks, gentle giants whose memory is legendary. And . . . team players?

In recent experiments, elephants have shown an amazing capacity to recognize when cooperation is essential to reach a common goal. And then, as a team, they quickly learn how to get the job done.

The experiments, originally designed for chimpanzees, were conducted on Asian elephants at an elephant conservation center in Thailand. A table holding a tasty snack was placed in a separate enclosure from the elephants. A rope was then attached to the table. By pulling on the rope, a single elephant could drag the table close enough to his pen to claim the treat.

But then the researchers changed the setup. They wove the rope through loops around the table—like a belt through belt loops—then dropped both ends of the rope in the adjoining elephant enclosure, attached to nothing. Now if a single elephant dragged only one end of the rope, the rope would move freely through the loops, but the table wouldn't budge.

Teamwork was needed. Two elephants dragging both ends of the rope could pull the table toward them, but neither could do it alone. Each elephant adapted quickly to this need, even waiting patiently for the second elephant to enter the pen before they began to pull.

Overall, the elephants performed as well as chimps, and they learned more quickly than chimps to wait for a second helper. These extraordinary findings confirm what scientists have long believed: that elephants are among the most intelligent and socially adaptable animals on the planet.

The amazing teamwork and intelligence of these remarkable creatures also give us a glimpse of their Creator. He has not restricted special abilities to a lucky few at the top of some imaginary evolutionary chain. Instead He has distributed amazing abilities freely among all His creatures, each according to its need to survive and adapt in a complex and changing world—whether dancing bees or nesting birds, chattering chimps or lumbering elephants.

This article originally appeared in Answers magazine, copyright ©2011/2014 Answers in Genesis. The article is reprinted here by permission of Answers in Genesis.

-Melinda Christian

CAMELS

Did you know a thirsty camel can drink up to 50 gallons of water on one trip to the water hole? Imagine a 50-gallon drum of water, what a stomach they must have!

Camels are very useful animals, but they can also bite like a horse and kick like a mule. They can go for weeks without food or water. They carry their built-in food supply in their humps on their backs. If they go a long time without food the hump disappears. In the 1850s the US Army brought 80 camels from Africa and Asia to carry cargo from California to Texas. Then the trains came along and took over. Some camels have one hump and some camels have two. The ones with two are used for riding and racing. Others are used for carrying cargo. Some were used to pull farm equipment. Camels are also used for food. Their meat tastes like veal. They melt the fat from the camel's back and use it for butter. They drink camel's milk and make cheese of it. Their milk is very rich. Enough about camels for this time.

-Yonie Esh, 2014

THE INVISIBLE VISITOR

This area over in southwest district had an invisible visitor recently. At the supper table at Willie J. Petersheims somebody knocked on the door. As they opened the door nobody was there. On down the road at Elmer W. Millers somebody rapped hard on the door at the time of their evening devotions. Upon checking the door, again nobody was to be found. Back over at Ben Beachys he saw a man walking east with something on his back but as a car came along Ben could see no sign of the man. Over at Abie J. Bontragers they woke up to the sounds of somebody being in their house.

Fear set in, Abie kept his eye focused from the bedroom door to their desk in the living room. Their little one in the baby bed asked if Mom is out there. Abe sh-sh her down. It appeared the intruder may have slept in the living room. When he left he rattled on the door latch a good while before leaving. Abies had only one door not locked and had the clothes dryer rack standing in front of it. The next morning the clothes dryer was still there and nothing missing. Hmmm, any explanation?

-Herman E. Stutzman, Feb. 2011

A LOT OF BULL

Another item found in the Lanc. paper shows the wastefulness and thoughtlessness of people today. A massive bull charged at the truck driver, when he was transferring him from his truck to a pen (at a butcher shop). He slammed the door on him but the bull knocked it open and got away. City Policeman John Ulrich said eight cruisers were needed to keep the bull penned in the 400 block of W. Vine St. Two schools kept their children almost 30 min. overtime for safety's sake. The bull wandered up and down the block occasionally looking into front doors and windows greatly scaring people. An employee from Lanc. Stockyards was called with a rifle that fired special darts containing an animal tranquilizer. Two massive doses were shot into him. So Capt. Ulrich ordered his men to shoot the bull. They fired 10 shots from their 38 cal. revolvers before he finally collapsed and died. (Sounds like a lot of bull, doesn't it?) After he died he was loaded on a truck and taken to a local rendering works. This seemed very wasteful to me, what would have been wrong with that meat and who stood the loss?

-1978

CREATION WONDERS

How lovely to think about the way our Creator God planned everything so carefully and perfectly, everything with a plan. As His highest creation, 'we are fearfully and wonderfully made.'

God's accuracy may be observed in the hatching of eggs.

For example:
- The eggs of the potato bug hatch in 7 days;
- Those of the canary in 14 days;
- Those of the barnyard hen in 21 days;
- The eggs of ducks and geese hatch in 28 days;
- Those of the mallard in 35 days;
- The eggs of the parrot and the ostrich hatch in 42 days;
(Notice they are all divisible by seven.)

God's wisdom is seen in the making of an elephant. The four legs of this great beast all bend forward in the same direction. No other Quadruped is so made. God planned that this animal would have a huge body, too large to live on two legs. For this reason He gave it four fulcrums so that it can rise from the ground easily.

The horse rises from the ground on its two front legs first.

A cow rises from the ground with its two hind legs first.

How wise the Lord is in all His works of creation! God's wisdom is revealed in His arrangement of sections and segments, as well as in the number of grains.

- Each watermelon has an even number of stripes on the rind.
- Each orange has an even number of segments.
- Each ear of corn has an even number of rows.
- Each stalk of wheat has an even number of grains.
- Every bunch of bananas has on its lowest row an even number of bananas, and each row decreases by one, so that one row has an even number and the next row an odd number.
- The waves of the sea roll in on shore twenty-six to the minute in all kinds of weather.
- All grains are found in even numbers on the stalks. The Lord specified thirty fold, sixty fold, and a hundredfold—all even numbers.

ANIMAL HOUSE

In Ephrata a man pleaded guilty to endangering a child and three adults, to have 105 animals in the house, including twenty-five chicken peeps, twenty-one chickens, fifteen parakeets, ten doves, seven ducks, four ducklings, four dogs, four pigs, three turtles, two ferrets, two quail, two cats, two rabbits (one dead), one iguana, one parrot, one chinchilla and a cockatoo. I'll not write the conditions of the home as it was written, just use your own thoughts, the home was eventually condemned. The man told the judge he planned to buy a farm and was temporarily housing the various animals in the mobile home.

by Ben & Lydia King, 2013

"Please Let Me Stay"

The following touching story is based on real-life incidents, but some details have been altered to protect the identity of "W.M."

May it help readers to appreciate more fully the blessings of home, family, and church, and of a Christian upbringing.

-By W.H.

AS THE SNOW FALLS gently, my spirit soars to new heights. I savor the warmth of the stove, the comforts of home, and the peaceful feeling in my heart. The lantern casts a soft glow over the calm setting as my mind races backward to days long gone. I reflect on the past events of my life, having rehearsed them again and again to my children at Christmas time.

Last year, sixteen-year-old John said, "Daddy, you must write down your story so your grandchildren can read it after you are gone." So after much thought, I sat down with pen and paper and wrote out by hand, word for word, the following account. I seek no acclaim for myself, for I truly understand, I believe, the grace of God.

I WAS BORN on the south side of Chicago on November 10, 1960. "Home" was a word I knew belonged to the English language, but I did not understand what it really meant. I lived on a street whose name I do not remember, in one of the row houses with numbers beginning with 205 to 210. All the houses were the same. Each one had a small living room, one bathroom, a tiny kitchen, and three bedrooms. The rooms were always cold in the winter. The old steam radiators hissed and sputtered but never put out enough heat to keep us warm.

Each bed was full every night and sometimes the living room floor held the overflow. That is why I said that I lived from house #205 to #210.

Each night I would go to one of the houses until I found a place to lie down. I always began with #206, because it was there that I kept my hidden treasures. I soon learned that if I began early enough in the evening, I had a greater chance of finding an empty side of one of the beds.

I knew who my mother was, but I rarely saw her, and I do not remember having much feeling for her. I did not know if I really had any brothers or sisters. I think I had two half-brothers and three half-sisters. There was coming and going all the time. No one ever said to me, "This is your daddy."

I am not sure even yet as to what my last name is. My mother (or "Mom" as I called her) told me that my last name was *Larkin*, but when I started to school they enrolled me with a last name of *Jordan*. I never liked my first name, but once you acquired a street name, it never went away. Mom said my name was "W.M." but I was never told what it stood for. It didn't take long until all the boys on the street shortened up the initials of "W.M." to "Dumb." They would say, "Dub-ul-u-um" and then shorten it to just the first and last sounds which came out like "D-u-m." So it stuck. I was called "Dumb."

But I wasn't really dumb. I made B's and C's in school. In math, I sometimes dropped to a D. I found out that if your grades were too good, they took notice of you, and that was not good for a boy who came from the south side.

I was always hungry. Each of the row houses had a refrigerator, though it seldom worked and there was never much food. We never sat around a table to eat. No one ever fixed a meal and said, "Let's sit up and eat." Each one took what he could. There were some unwritten rules about the food, especially for little boys. We never ate the last bite of anything. It was truly "survival of the fittest." I don't know who supplied the food, but I know my mom and other mothers brought in food from time to time.

My main staple was peanut butter. I ate many peanut butter sandwiches, that is, if I could find any bread around. I learned how to cut a banana in half and fill it with peanut butter. The bananas were usually overripe. I had learned early that if there was only one banana left, you always cut it in half and left a little for the next person. It was not acceptable for a little boy to clean out the last of the peanut butter, for that would bring a smack on the head from the big people.

I was glad when I was old enough to go to school. They had a program for children who were poor to arrive early and get something warm to eat for breakfast. It was usually a milky soup, sometimes thick and sometimes watery, with chunks of egg and bits of bacon in it. It tasted so good at first even though eventually I did get tired of it. But it was hot and it was nourishing.

With the exception of an occasional hot dog, the only other warm meals we ever ate were at the Soup Kitchen that had free meals once or twice a year at the Salvation Army building during the Thanksgiving and Christmas holidays. We had to wait in long lines for our turn to eat. As we would get closer we would hear words like, "We're about out," or "We'll need to stretch a bit," or "Make the servings smaller." In all my childhood in Chicago, I do not remember ever eating until I was full.

I don't remember many events that took place, but I do recall one. I had a place where I hid my treasures—things that I had found, and I must confess, some things that I had taken. I never thought of myself as a thief. I was just surviving. I would bring home rubber bands from school and hide them in my secret place. I would find some coins on the street, or if money was lying out in the open, I would take it and hide it.

There were about fifteen children who lived in the row houses from #205 to #210, and we all learned to keep our eyes open for any kind of plastic. You see, the plastic would be wrapped over our shoes and then we would place rubber bands over the top of the plastic, and around our ankles. This kept out the Chicago snow so that our feet did not get wet. We never had boots, and the shoes we wore were either too big or too small. You claimed anything you could get your hands on that was in the closets of the row houses.

But back to the event I was telling you about. When I was about seven, a big man started to live in our row house units. The problem was that he was mean. His big hands could smack your head quickly. I had learned to stay out of his way, but it didn't always work. One day, when no one else was around, this big man took me by the neck with his big hands and started to squeeze.

"Tell me where you have your stash hidden!" he demanded. I told him. He took my trinkets, left the rubber bands, but of course, took the little bit of money I had. It had reached the sum of $12.26. I remember crying, since I would now have to start all over. He no longer showed up at the row houses after that. I heard from some of the other children that he had done the same thing to them.

I HAD ONE PASTIME. I loved to read. My second grade teacher, Mrs. Misner, introduced me to the world of books. I read all the books she had in the classroom, which were not many. She then took me down to the library that was five blocks away. It was not on the way home from school, yet not too far out of the way. She helped me get a card, taught me how to check out and turn in books, and where the books were that she knew I would like.

I liked stories that were about happy families, with warm houses and plenty of food. It didn't make much sense to me when I read about a mother and a father, for I knew nothing about a home like that.

During the month of November, I checked out a book that contained a story about an Amish home that had all the family together on Christmas day. I read it again and again. The birth of the Baby Jesus had never been explained to me, and meant nothing to me. True, we sang Christmas carols at school, but no one bothered to explain what they meant.

What really caught my attention in this story was the glow on the faces of the children in the pictures, and the excitement I could read in the words. Family . . . family. Then I began to dream. If only . . . if only I could live in a home like that. If only I could live there. A foolish thought came into my head. Why not?

I asked Miss Mikesell, the librarian, if there were real people like those in the book. She told me she knew that a group of them lived east of Chicago in northern Indiana about a hundred miles away. "Why not . . . why not . . . why not?" The thought kept going around in my head until I could think of little else. So I decided, "Over Christmas time, I am going to an Amish home just like those in the book."

I checked how much money I had hidden again, and it came to $14.52. I had no idea how far that would take me, but maybe someone would give me a ride. I didn't know exactly where I was going, but I knew the name of the town where the Amish lived close to, and it was east of Chicago. I had become streetwise and knew which way was east, and how to ride the city transit system for very little money.

I left the row houses of Chicago on December 22, 1969. Dear reader, you probably cannot relate to this, but I left with very little emotion or regret. I did not feel any bond with Mom and there was no one who really seemed to care about me. My clothes were too small and my shoes were too big. My coat was patched but warm. I wore no boots, by covered my feet with plastic held by

rubber hands. I took the bus east through Chicago as far as I could. I tried to act grown-up and like I knew what I was doing, so I would not attract anyone's attention.

I spent the first night at the bus station, pretending that I was going to take the bus the next morning. My plan was to get a ride with a trucker that was going east. In the morning I asked the attendant at the bus station where there was a truck stop. He gave me directions on a piece of paper. I set off walking the ten blocks.

Now what? I had no idea. Should I outright ask a trucker to take me? That didn't seem like quite the thing to do, for I figured that if I could not answer all the questions he would ask, I would be taken right back to the row houses. I finally made up my mind to go as a stowaway on one of the rigs.

It had begun to snow and the temperature was well below freezing. I arrived at the truck stop, cold and hungry. I now had $10.22 left. I bought a hot dog and warmed up by sitting in one of the stalls in the rest room. Finally, I went outside to pick a truck in which to stowaway. There were many trucks in a row. Some had their engines running, and some did not. I concluded that there was a driver inside if the engine was running, so I did not try to get in one of those trucks.

Oh, the disappointment because door after door was locked. At last, one was unlocked. I hurriedly crawled into the big rig and made my way into the area behind the seat. I hadn't known they made these things this big. It had a bed with blankets. I made myself as small as I could and waited and waited and waited until I fell asleep.

THE NEXT THING I remember is the gentle sway of the rig and the noise of the engine. How long we had been driving, I did not know. I was so hungry, but I did not dare call out. At least the truck was warm. Finally we pulled off the highway and I hoped we were going to another truck stop. I knew I had to make my getaway as soon as the driver left the rig.

After he left, I counted to fifty and then worked my way to the door on the right. There were so many gadgets and the steering wheel on the left. As soon as I opened the door, I could tell it was snowing hard and had gotten colder. I had to hurry for I didn't want to get caught, but I hurried too fast. When my foot landed on the second step, I slipped and fell.

It happened so fast that I really don't know what happened. When it was all over, I was upside down with head, shoulders, and arms in the snow, and my left foot caught on something on the passenger side of the truck. What was I to do? What if the driver came back out and took off, dragging me along in the snow with my head and shoulders bouncing on the road? What if no one found me? Would I freeze to death? It was so cold, I began to shake and tremble, both from fear and from the cold. I called out, "Please, someone help me!" But the wind muffled my cry.

I started to dream about a warm stove, hot food, laughing children, and happy sounds. Somewhere in my dream I faintly heard sirens and felt myself being lifted onto a bed with voices asking, "Who is he?" Another said, "This is my truck, but I never saw the boy before."

I heard them ask me, "Who are you?" All I could think to say was, "Amish . . . Amish . . . Amish."

As I slowly woke up, I was aware of the activity around me. I was in a bed with things hanging over my head, and people at the foot of the bed. I pretended to still be sleeping but opened my eyes just a tiny little bit so I could see what was going on. I saw a tall lady at the foot of the bed, talking to a lady dressed in white who must

have been the nurse. "We do not know who he is. As he was being brought to the hospital, he kept saying, 'Amish.' We have called for some Amish to come to see if we can unravel this mystery. Oh, here they come now."

I could not believe my ears. The Amish were here. Two men walked in and they looked just like those in the pictures in the book. The tall, well-dressed lady walked up to the two men and shook their hand. "Hello, I am Mrs. Joyce Barr, social worker with the state of Indiana. This lad was found with his foot caught on the step of a semitruck and he was very cold. We do not know who he is, but he kept saying, 'Amish' while being transported to the hospital in the ambulance."

I opened my eyes a slight bit wider so I could take in the scene. The two men looked at me as they stroked their beards. "I do not think we can help you," said one of the men. "We are not missing anyone."

Mrs. Barr shook her head in bewilderment. "What are we to do? Our agencies close down over the holidays, and the hospital administrator wants the boy discharged as soon as he wakes up. There is nothing wrong with him, and no one to pay the bill. He is physically okay. We may have to place him in a foster home until we can determine what is to be done with him."

Oh, no! A foster home, what was that? Foster sounds close to frost and frost is cold. I had enough of being cold. Please, don't send me to a foster home.

Mrs. Barr continued, "Mr. and Mrs. Henry Yoder are approved for foster care, and they are Amish. Do you think they would take the boy until we can decide what to do?"

The one bearded man said, "Yes, I believe they would be willing. I happen to know their family is coming home for Christmas, but I don't think they would mind having this lad."

Now they noticed that I was fully awake, and Mrs. Barr began to question me. "What is your name?" she asked.

"W.M." That was all I could say.

"What does W.M. stand for?"

"I . . . I do not know," I answered.

On and on they asked questions that I could not answer, but really, questions that I did not want to answer. I wanted to go to the Amish home so badly that I just quit answering their questions.

MRS. BARR TOOK ME to the Henry Yoder home in her car. What happened the next few days seemed like a whirl in my head. Some of it I cannot remember, for the sounds, smells, and sights overrode the ability of my tired head to grasp it all. By now it was the 24th of December. I barely remember eating supper. The table was spread with food. They told me they were going to pray before we ate, but I had no idea what they meant. They told me to fold my hands and close my eyes.

I could hardly get the food past the big lump in my throat. I watched a lot and spoke very little. The chatter and the love filled my very being with emotions I never had before. It was just too much for this boy from the south side of Chicago.

That night I slept on a cot in the hallway next to Eli's room. Eli was six months younger than I. Soon I was fast asleep from exhaustion because of all that had taken place.

We woke up early on Christmas day. They fit me into some of Eli's clothes, and asked me if I wanted to help him do his chores. It was all fun to me—new sights of cows, pigs, chickens, and milk. Breakfast was a repeat of supper the night before, with plenty of food for everyone. I could eat a little more since the lump in my throat was smaller.

The morning was spent getting ready for the family to be together. The children were excited and bubbling over with anticipation for the company that was to come. The table was stretched out long and another table was placed up against it to make room for the family. I never saw such a big table. And the food! You cannot imagine the emotions I felt as I saw the steam coming off the mashed potatoes, and it looked like there was going to be enough for everyone. Children were laughing and everyone was polite and considerate as they waited on each other to sit at the table. There was talk of the activities planned for the afternoon. They couldn't wait for Grandpa to tell them a story of when he was a boy.

Again, Henry said we would bow our heads in prayer. This time we would each pray silently as we thanked our Lord for the blessing of Jesus' birth. I bowed my head in prayer, not knowing for sure how to pray. My prayer went something like this, "Dear Lord, please let me stay. Please let me stay here forever."

It was just too much for this heart of mine. I began to cry . . . and not just cry, but to sob and shake. I was told later that all heads came up and everyone looked at me. Henry got up from his chair, came over to mine and picked me up with two strong arms and carried me to the rocking chair by the stove.

While holding me, he began to rock slowly, and with his deep voice he said, "Family, sing 'Joy to the World' as W.M. settles down." So they did. As they sang, Henry continued to rock and hold me tight. After the last verse, Henry said, "It just dawned on me that W.M. must stand for 'wise men.' I believe W.M. is like the wise men of long ago who came from far away in search of Jesus, and found Him."

THAT WAS NOT THE END of the story. Christmas was over and we had to return to the question of what was to happen to me. Mrs. Barr came two days later and took me in to the city that was nearby. They got all the information they could about me so they would be able to make contact with agencies in Chicago. They were never able to find where I came from. Maybe today, with the computer networking they have, they would have been able to locate my mother. I have never been back to visit Chicago.

Henry Yoder and his wife adopted me two years after my arrival. It took quite awhile to get all the paperwork processed. I always felt it a privilege to be a part of their family, and I was determined to never cause them any trouble. They gave the name of William Melvin Yoder to me. The years have rolled along and I am now in my 50's. I married an Amish girl named Miriam and we have five boys and two girls. Of course, we named our first boy Henry and our first girl Mary.

Today, as a father and grandfather, I feel a great burden as we live in this modern world with all the many choices we have to make. I'll finish this story with a question that you, dear reader, may be able to answer for me. Many years ago, as a little boy, I left the south side of Chicago in search of a better life. Tell me, please tell me, why do the boys and girls of our Plain churches leave their Anabaptist heritage in search of a worldly life in places such as the south side of Chicago? I sob at times, as I did that day many years ago, when I think about what they are throwing away.

I pray that when I leave this earth and am ushered into the presence of our Lord and Saviour, Jesus Christ, that He will honor my request when I ask of Him, "Let me stay, dear Lord, please let me stay."

P.S. W.M. was 9 years old when he left Chicago and 11 years old when he was adopted.

The Value of Onions

I have a lot of faith in cutting up onions and laying them around to gather up flu germs and also if one of the children are stuffy and can't breathe well. I like to wait till they're asleep then lay an onion cut in half or quarter on their pillow or very close to them and I do believe they sleep better. It doesn't always prevent a Dr. visit but worth a try. My mother used to do and still does this every winter. Following is part of an article that was in "Die Botshaft" several years ago.

Quote: A friend of mine told me a story of when he was a kid, he was in the hospital and near dying. His Italian grandmother came to the hospital and took a large onion, sliced it open and put a slice on the bottom of each of his feet and clean white socks to hold them on. In the morning when he woke up they removed the socks, the slices of onion were black and the fever was gone.

In 1919 when the flu killed 40 million people there was a doctor that visited the many farmers to see if he could help them come over this. Many of the farmers and their families had contracted it and many died. He came upon a family and to his surprise everyone was healthy. When asked what they were doing the wife replied that she had placed an onion in a dish in all rooms of the house. The doctor couldn't believe it asked for 1 of the onions and placed it under a microscope and he did find the flu virus in the onion. It obviously absorbed the bacteria, therefore keeping the family healthy.

Still quoting: a hairdresser said several years ago many of her employees were coming down with the flu and many of her customers also. The next year she placed several bowls with cut up onions in her shop. To her surprise none of her staff got sick. End of quote.

I think if a person was totally faithful in keeping fresh onions in each room all winter we'd be amazed how much it would help, yes it would smell up the house, oh well! And yes, it would take lots of onions but if it would prevent even 1 doctor visit it would be worth the effort and the few dollars for the onions.

TALLEST MAN ON BIRTHDAY

Robert Wadlow, 21 years old, height 8 feet 8½ inches, had to bend down a good deal to get out of an elevator in the courthouse at St. Joseph, Mo., where his libel action against Dr. Charles Humberd of Bernard, Mo., was in progress. Spectators stood aside in awe as the Alton, Ill. giant hove into view.

11TH HR. RETURNS

David Stoltzfus, Gap, PA, left the Amish church in his youth and joined the Mennonite church. He was there 70 years or close to it. In 1997 or 1998 he came back to the Amish church again. He was a faithful member again but he only lived long enough to be daby one time Gross Gmay.

Another man from Lanc. Co. left his family and was out in the world 29 years but he also came back about 2002 with a change of heart. He also died soon after he bame back.

-LF

Robert Wadlow, proclaimed by doctors, world's tallest human at 8 feet 8½ inches, celebrated his 20th birthday in his home at Alton, Ill. The 460-pound boy holds a cake his mother baked for him. On the right sits a friend of average size.

STRONG JACOB YODER

Born in 1700's, married to an Anna Beiler, moved from Northkill to the Conestoga in 1767. He was very strong I was told. They were building a stone wall for a building and they needed to put a big stone above a window, but decided to wait till after dinner. Then Strong Jacob put the stone up all by himself. He sweated so much from working so hard, that he jumped into the creek to cool off and didn't live very long after that. Before this a strong man of Virginia heard of Strong Jacob and went on horseback to go see Jacob. When he got close to Jacob's place, he talked to one of Jacob's neighbors and told him he wanted to test Jacob's strength. The man told him Jacob was a man of peace, and he would better leave him alone. The man got to Jacob's home after dark and made a lot of noise on Jacob's porch. When Jacob opened the door the man got hold of him, but Jacob put the stranger to the floor. Someone got a rope and Jacob tied him and laid him beside the fireplace. The next morning Jacob sent the stranger home.

PIONEERS OF THE 1940's

Can you believe before 1940 no Amish existed south of the Mine Ridge? This would include Nickel Mines, Georgetown, Nine Points, Kirkwood, etc. areas. In 1940, Enos Petersheim and Levi Esh were the first to make the move. In 1941 and 42, six more families made the move. My parents moved here to Nickel Mines in 1943. If I remember my dad saying there were thirteen families that moved south of the Mine Ridge that year. This was from Nickel Mines south to Nine Points. This area was considered by some as a "romote area," towards the productive well-kept farms north of the Mine Ridge. Most farms were not "kept after" as some of the natives had good jobs at the factories during the war which was war related. The soil was poor on many. The first year, Enos Petersheim got two loads of loose hay from 20 acres. Wide fence rows, 8 to 10 feet high with brush and trees up to 5 feet high. This is an example of one farm. This farm consisted of 102 acres and had to pay a total of $7,500. In the early forties, wheat was a good cash crop and helped to make payments. One farmet had 15 acres of wheat giving him a check of $2,000 which was a lot of money those days.

Up 'til 1944, Intercourse, Georgetown area was one church district, probably a spread of 15 miles. Lots of dirt roads back then. The first place of church was at Enos Petersheims. When the people of Intercourse came over the ridge some saw turkey buzzards flying around and joked that maybe some horses dropped over dead before reaching their destination.

This was considered not a wise move by some, but somehow they survived. Some said they will never make it and come back hungry. At the present, the Mine Ridge is considered the halfway mark. One half of the Amish population on the north side and other half on south side.

Many of the Amish congregations in Adams County, Indiana, do not permit any use of motors or engines. Animal-powered devices such as this are still common there. These devices may be used for such purposes as pumping water, powering a washing machine or turning a lathe.

CIVIL WAR 1863

The people were warned that the war could come into Lancaster County the next day. It is said, an Amish boy went to bed one night at nine o'clock, and his parents were praying. That night at twelve o'clock he woke up and they were still praying. He woke up again at two o'clock, and his parents were still praying. That night the Columbian Bridge was burned down, and kept the war from coming over here.

It is said, the day they thought the war was coming over here, a young Amish farmer was plowing with a walking plow, and his wife was walking with him all day, so she would be with him when the war comes through.

My Granddad went to fetch tobacco plants one day before the Civil War was over. He got as far as Molasses Hill, this side of Bird-in-Hand, then he was told that the rebels are coming. He turned around and came home as fast as he could. But then the Columbia River Bridge was burned down, and they came no further. Some people had hidden their horses already, as the rebels took the horses as they went.

-Susie Lapp

Reminiscences From By-Gone Times

by John Y. Schlabach
Written on December 23, 1993, in his 98th year.

When my grandfather, John Yoder, died in June of 1909, my brother Simon moved to the farm in 1911. He farmed for grandmother until her death in 1923. Grandmother Susan Mast Yoder was born on December 29, 1826 and died on December 9, 1923 at the age of 96 years, 10 months, and 10 days. Her grandmother lived to the age of 101 years. My wife and I, with son Levi, moved to the farm in February of 1924. Simon then moved to the Snyder farm.

When grandmother was a little girl, they had no apples, and the stars fell from Heaven in 1833. About 1830 to 1840 a shoemaker went from house to house to make shoes. Hogs were dressed and taken to Massillon and sold for $2 to $2.50 per hundred pounds. The pay was partly in cash and the remainder in merchandise, such as salt. Eggs were three cents per dozen and butter five cents per pound. Cows were worth from eight to twelve dollars per head.

Farming implements were a wagon, a wooden plow and a shovel plow. Plows had wooden moldboards up to about 1860. They may have had spike tooth harrows. Father related how they used a bushy tree for a harrow. They had log houses with no basement, and but one room for the first floor. They smoked their meat in the attic. Travel was by horseback or they walked. Cook stoves were introduced about 1848. Buggies were scarce before 1850. Reapers were first used in Ohio in 1860. My grandmother Schlabach showed us scars on her left wrist that she had gotten from harvesting grain with a sickle. Her son, Crist, was a frail child, and she said that she cooked many a meal for the harvest hands with Crist tied to her apron strings. They began to use oil lamps about 1860 and began to can fruit about 1865.

Threshing machines formerly had web stackers. Father told how it took five men to take the straw away from the web stacker and to stack the straw. I helped thresh when one man cut bands with a knife and another fed the bundles into the machine by hand, and threshing machines were driven by steam engines. Grandfather used his horse-power to run the threshing machine. Steam engines were dependable power, and steam whistle messages were convenient. A half dozen short toots of the steam whistle when the water supply in the steam engine was getting low told the water tank man to hurry. Two long, a short, and a long toot indicated travel on the road, which was usually given when they were on top of a hill. A number of long toots told the neighborhood that help was needed. Brand names of steam engines were: *Reeves, Peerless, Gaar Scott, Huber, Russel* and *Aultman Taylor*. Walter Burkey bought a gasoline tractor about 1920. Soon there were many different makes and some of them were of light weight.

Aaron Yoder of Kansas related that a well-broken team of oxen were a good and handy team to plow with. I began plowing with a walking plow with a lead horse that was broken to the use of a single line. He could be guided with the single line without saying a word: a steady pull on the line would turn the team **haw** and a few short tugs on the line was the signal for the **gee** turn.

About 1855 cream was sold by the inch. The butterfat testing of milk and cream was not then in use. Cheese factories operated mainly from April to November. A good grade of cheese required having cows on pasture because the rennet they had then did not make good cheese when the cows were on winter rations. There were no milk trucks nor feed trucks in 1924 when we moved onto the farm. In springtime father sold hay that was baled with a baler powered by three horses. One man was needed to feed the baler, two men tied bales with wire, and one man weighed and stacked the bales of hay.

In 1899 and on to about 1907 my father had walls built of sandstone. The sandstone were split in the woods and then hauled home. Then the stones were dressed by a mason. With a hand-operated crane they were lifted and placed on the wall. The first cement wall that I saw was made in 1909.

Can we appreciate the ease and short time that is needed at present to build a house or a barn, with power saws, etc.? I was told that it was considered to be usual for a man to hew a log for a barn timber on one day. Our former Holmes County Auditor, H. Gray, said that his grandfather had a stone house built under contract. The mason and carpenter work cost $105.

In father's time it was not unusual for a man to do feeding in winter for board and lodging. About 1910 the Berlin-Millersburg road was partly graded and hard surfaced. Farmers helped to grade and limestone was crushed and shipped to Millersburg and hauled with horses and wagons to the roadway. Main Street in Millersburg was not paved. In 1900, in case of illness, a physician would see the patient in their home. Office calls were about 50 cents. Generally livestock that was sold was taken to Millersburg then shipped to Cleveland in freight cars.

Hillsboro, WI
by Ruben Yoder, 2011

Here are more reasons to be thankful. As I recently read in an article, and I would like if someone could prove it right or wrong, but there are seven billion people in the world today. One billion of these seven live on a dollar a day. Two more billion live on two dollars a day. Which means nearly one half of the people struggle to find enough food to eat. Every day 29,000 children die of starvation, or preventable diseases, brought on by contaminated water, infections, and the like.

Every year American Christians spend $21 billion on soft drinks, and another $5 billion on bottled water. These same people will spend $100 billion on Christmas gifts. Can we say we are Christians if we pay over $100 for a pair of sneakers when we already have six pairs of shoes? Is Lazarus lying at our door? Something to ponder on.

Legend of Dogwood Tree

Now that the Easter holidays are over we see the Legend on the dogwood trees to remind us of the crucifixion, the blossoms are the form of a cross, 2 long and 2 short petals. And in the center of the outer edge of each petal are nail prints, brown with rust and stained with red. Center of flower a crown of thorns. All who see it will remember. I once read the dogwood tree had been the size of oak or other large trees that it was chosen for the timber of the cross, but after being used for the crucifixion never again will the tree be large enough to be used for a cross but hence forth it shall be slender and bent and twisted. So still today we call it the legend of the dogwood tree for us to remember the cruel suffering for us.

Circle of Faith

by Dick Eastman

Little ten-year-old Maria lived in a rural village in central Chile.

When her mother died, Maria became the "woman of the house," caring for her father who worked the night shift at the local mine. Maria cooked and cleaned and made sure her father's lunch was ready when he left the house for work each evening.

Maria loved her father and was worried by how despondent he had become since her mother's death. Maria went to church on Sundays and tried to get her father to go with her, but he refused. His heart was too empty.

One evening, as Maria was packing her father's lunchbox, she slipped a gospel booklet inside that she had received from a missionary worker who had been distributing them home to home in the area where they lived. Maria prayed that her father would read the booklet and find the comfort she had found in God's great love.

It was 1:10 a.m. when Maria was suddenly awakened by a horrible sound—the emergency whistle at the mine was blaring through the darkness, calling the townspeople to come running with shovels and willing hands to help dig for miners caught in a cave-in.

Maria made her way through the streets to the mine in search of her father. Scores of men were frantically pulling debris away from the collapsed tunnel where eight men were trapped. One of the men was Maria's father.

Emergency crews worked through the night and finally broke through to a small cavern where they found the miners. Sadly, they were too late. All eight men had suffocated.

The rescue workers were devastated, but as they surveyed the scene, they noticed that the men had died, seated in a circle. As the workers looked closer they discovered Maria's father was sitting with a small gospel booklet in his lap opened to the last page where the plan of salvation was clearly explained. On that page, Maria's father had written a special message to his daughter:

My darling Maria,

When you read this, I will be with your mother in heaven. I read this little book, then I read it several times to the men while we waited to be rescued. Our hope is fading for this life, but not for the next. We did as the book told us and prayed, asking Jesus into our hearts. I love you very much, Maria, and one day soon, we will all be together in heaven.

How Many Is One Billion?

More than a billion people live in China. One billion is a very hard number to imagine. Most of us can understand a thousand for we can count to a thousand in a few minutes. A million is a thousand thousands. A billion is another way of saying a thousand millions.

If you could line up a billion marbles four to an inch, the line of marbles would stretch almost the length of the border between the United States and Canada. If a billion people could stand in a line, the line would reach around the world fifteen times!

Could you count to a billion? Never! You could need to count over 1,100 every hour, every day, for over 100 years!

Earthly Angels Pay a Visit

It was Christmas Eve 1949. I was 15 and feeling sad because there was not enough money to buy me the dress that I wanted. We did the chores early that night, so I figured Pa wanted a little extra time for us to read the Bible.

After supper, I took off my boots, stretched out by the fireplace and waited for Pa to start reading. I was still feeling sorry for myself and, to be honest, wasn't in much of a mood to read Scriptures. But Pa didn't get the Bible; instead, he bundled up again and went outside. I couldn't figure it out because we had already done all the chores.

It was a cold, clear night, and there was ice in Pa's beard when he came back in. "Come on, Elizabeth," he said. "Bundle up. It's cold out."

I was upset. Not only wasn't I getting the dress, now Pa was dragging me out in the cold. I put on my coat and boots, and Ma gave me a mysterious smile as I opened the door. Something was up.

Outside, I became even more dismayed. There, in front of the house, was the work team, already hitched to the big sled. Whatever we were going to do wasn't going to be a quick job.

I reluctantly climbed up beside Pa, the cold already biting at me. We pulled in front of the woodshed, put on the high sideboards and started loading wood—the wood we spent all summer hauling down from the mountain and all fall sawing into blocks and splitting.

Finally, I asked, "Pa, what are you doing?"

"You been by the Widow Clark's lately?" he asked.

Mrs. Clark lived about 2 miles down the road. Her husband had died a year before and left her with three children.

"Yeah," I said. "Why?"

"I rode by just today," Pa said. "Little Jake was out digging around in the woodpile trying to find a few chips. They're out of wood, Elizabeth."

That was all he said, and we loaded the sled so high that I began to wonder if the horses would be able to pull it.

Pa then went to the smokehouse and took down a big ham and a side of bacon, telling me to go load them. He returned to the sled carrying a sack of flour over his right shoulder and a smaller sack of something in his left hand.

"What's in the little sack?" I asked.

"Shoes. They're out of shoes. Little Jake had gunnysacks wrapped around his feet when he was out in the woodpile. I got the children a little candy, too. It just wouldn't be Christmas without candy."

We rode the 2 miles to the Clarks' place in silence. I tried to think through what Pa was doing. We did have a big woodpile, meat and flour, so we could spare that, but I knew we didn't have any money. Widow Clark had closer neighbors than we did; it shouldn't have been our concern.

We unloaded the wood behind the Clark house and went to the door. We knocked. The door opened a crack, and a timid voice said, "Who is it?"

"James Cotton, ma'am, and my daughter, Elizabeth. Could we come in for a bit?"

Mrs. Clark opened the door and let us in. She had a blanket wrapped around her shoulders. The children were huddled beneath another blanket, sitting in front of a small fire in the fireplace. Widow Clark fumbled with a match and lit the lamp.

"We brought you a few things, Ma'am," Pa said and set the sack of flour and meat on the table. Pa handed her the other sack. She opened it hesitantly and took out the shoes, one pair at a time. There was a pair for her and one for each of the children—sturdy shoes that would last.

She bit her lower lip to keep it from trembling as tears filled her eyes and ran down her cheeks. She looked at Pa as if she wanted to say something, but it wouldn't come out.

"We brought a load of wood, too, Ma'am," Pa said. He turned to me and said, "Elizabeth, go bring in enough to last awhile. Let's get that fire roaring and heat this place up."

I wasn't the same person when I went to bring in the wood. I had a big lump in my throat and tears in my eyes.

We soon had the fire blazing, and everyone's spirits soared. The kids giggled when Pa handed them each a piece of candy, and Widow Clark looked on with a smile that probably hadn't crossed her face for a long time.

"God bless you," she said. "I know the Lord sent you. The children and I prayed that He would send one of his angels to spare us."

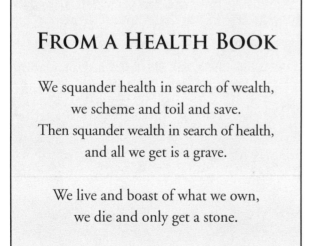

FROM A HEALTH BOOK

We squander health in search of wealth,
we scheme and toil and save.
Then squander wealth in search of health,
and all we get is a grave.

We live and boast of what we own,
we die and only get a stone.

THOUSANDS OF FOSTER CHILDREN

"In thee the fatherless findeth mercy."
Hosea 14:3

The very air was tense with fear in the city of London, England in early September 1939. Those days may have been largely forgotten by the rest of the world, but for those who experienced the trauma, they are deeply etched in their memory.

In mainland Europe, just across the narrow English Channel, Hitler's German troops were conquering one nation after another. The English knew they would be next. Already German planes had begun dropping bombs on London. Surely there would be worse to come.

On September 1 the government of England took drastic action, seldom matched in the history of mankind. Hundreds of thousands of children in London made their way to the nearest railway station. There, trains moved them out into the country where they would be relatively safe from bombing. In the rural areas, families were asked to open their homes to theses foster children. What a confusion this caused as these school age children settled into makeshift homes. Many of them stayed for years before they were reunited with their parents. Some of them never were.

As is usual in wartime, the women and children were the greatest victims. Some of these transplanted children were placed in good homes where their physical and emotional needs were met. But others were mistreated and were very unhappy in their foster homes. Some were little better than slaves, often abused or neglected. And yet, by comparison with the children of Germany these children in England probably fared well.

Indeed, war is always cruel and heartless. In Old Testament days war seems to have been a common occurrence. That is still true today. Jesus said, "Ye shall hear of wars and rumors of war..." (Matthew 24:6).

Both Canada and the United States have been involved in several major wars in the past century. But the actual battles were fought overseas. We were very fortunate to have been spared from warfare in our homelands.

Somehow, when we think of the great suffering in war-ravaged nations, it does not seem quite fair that we have been thus favored. Do we realize how greatly God has blessed us by giving us peace in our time? Do we realize how quickly this could change?

Can we visualize the trauma if suddenly our children would be taken from our homes and sent to live with total strangers, as were the children of London in 1939. I am thinking that we as Christian parents would not give our consent. Perhaps we would choose to remain together as a family, and suffer whatever fate might bring. Or maybe we would choose to relocate as a family in a safer location.

Still, those options were hardly available. Most of the residents of London were not financially able to pick up and move to a rural area. To have bombs come shrieking down out of the night skies was not a nice prospect either. Because we loved our children, we might have welcomed any plan that would have removed them from that danger.

We do not know what we would have done had we been there. But we do know that many thousands of parents bade good-by to their children and allowed the government to place them in foster homes. As we try to imagine those scenes of parting, let us count our blessings and thank God for letting our families live happily together. Let us not take this wonderful privilege for granted.

1958 RECORD BREAKER SNOWSTORMS

The first months of 1958 gave a series of snowstorms that will long be remembered. In January a blizzard came from the eastern seaboard that would stand out in memory if two more severe storms had not followed, one in February and one in March.

A newspaper account, (The associated press) goes on to say that; The winter of 1957-58 goes down in history books as the time when snow fell on the streets of New Orleans. From Texas to Florida and up to Maine the land was swept with snow, hail, sleet and raging winds.

Already late in November, lower west central Texas was paralyzed with a 14 inch snowfall. Florida was hit by a freeze in December. Tornadoes swept Illinois, Missouri, Indiana, and Arkansas the same month.

In January a mid-west blizzard put six foot drifts across roads in Kansas City.

Suddenly without warning, says a newspaper clipping, the storm came on Feb. 15, 10:00 a.m., Saturday morning, it started to snow and snowed till Monday morning, blew till Wednesday morning. February's storm brought 18 inches of snow with severe cold and 35 mile per hour winds, drifts 20 ft. high were reported.

While the good old fashioned snowstorm brought joy to the hearts of youngsters, reality brought hardships to follow. Transportation was practically at a standstill for a day or two, suddenly we realize how much our daily life is geared to public and private transportation. The milkman, the baker, the fuel man, the doctor, now came into our life as a necessity, but could not be reached for a few days, at some places for half of the week.

Accompanying the deep snow was the frigid air that caused the mercury to dip to sub-zero temperatures that stayed there for five days. Even with heavy snow moving equipment that existed many rural roads were shoveled open by hand, especially in emergencies, when a doctor or hospital was needed. Many volunteers boarded together to dig out a snowbound home that was in need of aid.

Practically all roads including railroads, were blocked somewhat at one time or another. Two Amish funerals in Lancaster County were delayed for a day or two and then only the near relatives and a minister or two followed the bobsled hearse to the brief burial rites. Some snowbanks remained almost for 5 weeks just before the next snowstorm came.

On March 19, came the trailblaze in history, which brough the deepest heaviest snow in Lancaster County history. It started to snow around noon on Wednesday and snowed until early Friday morning giving an accumalation of 38 inches in eastern Lancaster County and 48 inches were reported in the Morgantown area. Besides being the deepest snow it was also the heaviest. A soggy snow that appeared to be full of water, clung to telephone and electric wires that played havoc with many lines. According to news reports 80 percent of the county was without electricity. Fortunately mild weather followed the snow with many homes without heat, hundreds of people would likely have froze to death, with no heat in their homes and no place to go.

The heavy snow caused many line poles to snap off under pressure of the overloaded wires. A scene is remembered along a secondary state road, where electric line poles resembled toothpicks sticking out of the snow. Along a two-mile stretch, only 8 poles were counted to be standing.

Besides poles, many roofs of buildings were damaged or completely demolished by the weight of the heavy snow.

All around it was an unusual snow. After the sun came out to shine on the new snow, a reflection of pure whiteness shone so bright that it was at times more than the eye could bear. An array of bluish white sparked in the snow.

With this clipping I want to share our experience from the February snowstorm of 1958. February 15, Saturday morning it started snowing and snowed till Monday morning. Dad needed feed for the chicken and cows, so we hitched 2 horses in bobsleds and went out to Gap Walker Feeds where Sam J. now is (Lanchester Gas). Thursday morning the Township Supervisors asked for help to open roads. They couldn't handle it all with the equipment they had. Buck Jake Davy, David Beiler and I worked together. We started at 340 and worked in Millwood Road. The second day we met a crew coming in the other way. We had a lot of fun. A healthy job and we could keep warm by keeping at it. We were paid $1.00 per hour. On Gap Hill, Rt. 30 trucks were lined up one after the other. They were stranded. The kind neighbors took food to the truckers.

-written by Levi Fisher
(Happened at 19 years of age.)

A Nice Day

Many years ago there was a man that whenever he was asked about the day he would always say it's a nice day. He would say that when it was a sunny day or a rainy day. When he died, the day of the funeral was rainy and it was a very miserable day. His friends wondered if he would still be here if he would also call this a nice day. Then came a voice saying, *this is a nice day*.

March 1958 Snowstorm

Mrs. Moses Smucker
January 24

I read a story to the children yesterday that Aaron Lapp Jr. wrote in his book *Weavertown Church History* of a funeral in the snowstorm of March 1958. Mose and I both remember this storm even though we were only eight and six years old. I could still see my Dad struggling through the drifts to go feed his chickens and milk cows. The following is what Aaron wrote.

Amos and Lindy Zook lived on a farm in Ninepoints area. Their son Samuel died suddenly while helping his Dad do chores. He slumped over a bale of hay he was carrying and died on his 13th birthday. It was Sunday evening March 16, 1958. Amos called the funeral director Al Furman and requested the funeral for Wednesday. Furman already had two funerals for Wednesday so they planned it for Thursday.

Snow started falling on Wednesday. The viewing was held at the Zook home on Wednesday evening. Travel was difficult preventing some people from attending.

Thursday morning while Furman was on the phone with Amos, the phone went dead and that would be the last phone call for days. The snow kept falling until Friday noon. Snow covered the 46-inch high fence around Amos' barnyard. Electricity was cut off from downed wires. There was no water; livestock must have water. Amos set a steel barrel on concrete blocks. He built a fire underneath and shoved snow into the barrel. One bucket of snow does not make one bucket of water. It takes many buckets of snow to get even one bucket of water. Just one cow needs 10 to 20 gallons of water a day. Where does one get wood to build a fire and keep it going when one has four feet of snow covering everything? Up in the barn were some old hand rails used by a previous farmer to hang tobacco. Amos started sawing. How much wood does it take to melt enough snow for water to satisfy 15 cows, livestock and 500 chickens? A good bit when you realize Amos had no power saw, no chain saw and only a carpenter's saw.

Lindy helped Amos. The cows had to be milked by hand. Other extras had to be done. There were children to be cared for in the house and their son lay in a coffin awaiting burial. By Thursday afternoon both of them were too tired and stressed to walk, sit or even lie down. They were totally exhausted and it soon would be time again for feeding and watering.

Early Friday morning three carloads of men met at Kauffman's Fruit Farm to organize attempts to reach Amos Zooks. They could not realize the impossibility of their mission, nor how God could and would indeed give His help. These men only knew they must try. Their area only had three feet of snow.

Friday night came, the Zooks went to bed after another exhausting day. Amos could not sleep. This night was even longer. All at once he heard an engine at work. A snowplow came into their lane with church men following the plow. It was 2 a.m. Saturday morning. Several hours later 15 men returned to do chores. Jacob Glick who had a water delivery service sent a tanker of water. By noon the work was done and the Zook family was on their way at long last to Weavertown Church for the funeral of their beloved son. The pallbearers could not come, many relatives could not come, and many people were still snowed in. The funeral director was not there. 185 people came, many of them not knowing whether a funeral would be held.

Later, neighbors to the Zooks told Amos they tried to come to their aid but the snow was up to their armpits and it was humanly impossible.

The effects of the snowstorm were felt for quite some time. Seven local barns collapsed under the weight of snow. On a six-mile stretch of Route 772 between Intercourse and Gap, 85 percent of the telephone poles were snapped off.

THE INVENTION AGE

Once upon a time,
some over a hundred years ago,
The Devil aware of his work
progressing too slow,
Counseled with his demons,
which weren't just a few,
Concerning the matter to see
what they could do.
Says the Devil: —You know,
ever since the creation,
There always have been some
seeking their Salvation,
We need to invent something
different and new,
To blind their eyes and
confuse their minds too.

In the beginning when God
created Man and Beast,
He created a balanced system,
to say the least.
Man made good use of these Beasts,
taking for granted,
It's the perfect work of God
and were contented.
So now I've got an idea,
I know just what we need,
It will be called modernism,
and will prosper indeed.
Because nothing is more attractive
to the heart of man,
Then modern inventions,
which we'll make as we can.

We will make beasts of Iron
to replace those of God,
For to till the earth with
and turn over the sod.

They will not eat the produce
of the acre of grain,
But a special invented fuel,
all serving to my gain.
They will do the work
of a hundred men or more,
Creating independency and
unemployment galore.
The poor will be forced to a
life of grime and misery,
As the rich overtake their farms
with modern machinery.

The main and most highly esteemed
of all in the deal
Is my ever craved for invention,
the "automobile."
The majority will fall for it,
running about so quick,
Justifying their guilt,
as to better care for the sick.
Many at first being doubtful,
with conscience burning,
Will sit behind the wheel as they start turning,
But they will overcome it,
and also we must teach,
There's no scripture against it
even if some so preach.

Once we get started
on this new invention craze,
It'll be easy to keep the people excited
and in a daze.
The more new gadgets we make,
the softer they'll get,
Bound as slaves to modernism,
as they shy from sweat.
We will invent machines both great and small,
To deceive the whole World,
and prepare for their fall,

The more they get,
the more they'll want of this treasure,
Forgetting God by living in
abundance and leisure.

It will be the most successful trick,
every heard from me,
So attractive and alluring,
that it will work perfectly,
To undermine the Church
in a round about way,

That even the Leaders
will be easily led astray.
Throughout all History
there never has been a time,
Of such leisure and luxury
or of violence and crime.
The softer and easier they live,
the harder they'll fall,
And as you know I, the Devil,
am the Author of it all.

-A.S.G.—Paraguay

THE "MOVINGEST" AMISHMAN

Jacob K. Miller, the oldest man of the Amish settlement at Salinas, California, has the distinction of having moved a greater total of miles than any other Amishman. Following is an account of the places where he moved and the distance he traveled to get to each. This does not include any miles he traveled on trips taken to visit friends or relatives. It is the distance he traveled when he moved. Also, to determine the distance he moved each time, a U.S. map was used and a ruler and mileage scale. Since a ruler measures mileage "straight as the crow flies," it is quite likely the distances Jake K. Miller covered were more than what is shown here. But we didn't want to exaggerate, so we figured the mileage at the minimum.

Jacob K. Miller was born in 1852 in Somerset County, Pennsylvania. At the age of 13 he moved with his parents to Arthur, Illinois—a total of 550 miles. In 1873 he married Elizabeth Yoder. Then in 1879 he moved to Needy, Oregon—2,000 miles. Within Oregon he moved to Hubbard and later to McMinnville—a total of 50 miles. In 1903 he left Oregon for Geauga County, Ohio—2,200 miles. Several years later he returned to Oregon—2,200 miles. In 1913 he moved 650 miles from Oregon to Salinas, California. In 1914 he moved 2,550 miles across the nation to Norfolk, Virginia, where he rented a house for three months before moving to Dover, Delaware—200 miles. In 1918 he was scared out of Delaware by World War I and moved West again—this time 1,700 miles to Glendive, Montana. From there he again moved to Oregon—900 miles. Then in 1921 he moved for the last time—2,600 miles back to Dover, Delaware. Altogether he moved a total of 15,600 miles and had lived in eight states in his lifetime. All of it was done by train. Having lived in Oregon three times, Jake became known throughout the rest of his life as "Oregon Jake Miller."

Noah and the Flood

The story of **Noah** and the **flood** is probably a very familiar one. Most of us as young children learn about the animals coming onboard the great ark "two by two." We see pictures of doves, rainbows, and Noah, smiling next to his wife when the sun comes out.

These are indeed great points of the story to remember. But there is so much more to think about than just the happy ending. Consider with me the reason behind the flood. It says in Genesis 6:5–6 that "the Lord saw that the wickedness of man was great in the earth…" and that "He was grieved in His heart." The Bible says that God was so sorry His creation had become evil that He decided to destroy it all. Except, and this is the good part, "Noah found grace in the eyes of the Lord…Noah was a just man, perfect in his generations. Noah walked with God." (Gen. 6:8–9)

Including the 40 days and 40 nights of rain, Noah's ark was tossed and carried in the waters of the Great Flood for almost a year.

Noah is a great example to us of a man with profound faith. Hebrews 11:7 says of him, "By faith Noah, being divinely warned of things not yet seen, moved with godly fear, prepared an ark for the saving of his household, by which he condemned the world and became heir of the righteousness which is according to faith." And the result of his godliness was that the human race and the living creatures on the ark were saved from destruction!

You see, the Bible says that the flood was so bad that "all flesh died that moved on the earth … All in whose nostrils was the breath of the spirit of life, all that was on the dry land, died … Only Noah and those who were with him in the ark remained alive." (Gen. 7:21–23)

When did Noah enter the ark? The Bible says Noah was 600 years old when "the flood of waters was on the earth." (Gen. 7:6 and 11) Counting genealogies in the Bible, we believe it was **2349 B.C.** when the flood started. How long did the flood last? Well, this part can be confusing. The Bible tells us that it rained for 40 days and 40 nights, but the flood lasted much longer than that. It took a long time for all that water to subside and allow dry land to appear. Noah and his family were on the ark for over a year! (With all those animals, it probably smelled.)

Our Earthen Vessel

Insomnia

There are some individuals who can lay their heads on their pillows and be asleep in two minutes. Other normal people require nearly half an hour. The average is about eight minutes. One common problem is that although sleep comes on promptly, after a certain amount of time spent sleeping, the individual begins to enter lighter and lighter sleep until he enters a very superficial level of sleep, immediately becomes wide awake, and being now rested, cannot return to sleep. The other common type of sleep disorder is that the person dreads to go to bed, as he knows he will be tossing and turning for an hour or two before sleep will come. There are special things that should be done for those two types of sleep disorders.

For the person who goes to sleep promptly, but cannot stay asleep for the full length of time needed for refreshment, several things may be helpful. The first thing is that upon awakening, instead of thinking about the trials of the day and the duties of tomorrow, the person should begin immediately to take deep breaths, making certain that the room is filled with fresh air. Sleep is a positive action of the mind, not an absence of mental activity. Often the person tries to lie entirely immobile, even rigidly motionless, becomes anxious about the anticipated sleeplessness, and is soon in no state to go back to sleep. One should not fear a bit of moving around; in fact, tensing and relaxing successive muscle groups, beginning with the facial muscles and progressing to neck and shoulders and so on, is a good way to go back to sleep.

Have at the beside a cup of catnip tea which may be taken to give a little sedation. It is entirely innocuous and leaves no hangover. Catnip tea may also be taken in the evening to induce sleep soon after going to bed. One should spend the time that one is awake contemplating the eternal virtues such as goodness, humility, love, patience, temperance, carefulness, care taking, faithfulness to duty, and loyalty. There is a peace-giving quality to this category of thoughts. One should not waste one's time on senseless thoughts such as counting sheep or picket fence slats.

For the second kind of insomnia, the inability to get to sleep at night, among the best things that can be done is physical exercise during the day, at least one hour being spent out-of-doors in some kind of brisk labor or sports. A second thing is to avoid the taking of a heavy, late supper. It is best for everybody to eat only lightly in the evening, and especially for the insomniac. If anything is taken it should be only whole grain breads or cereals, and simple fruit.

One should never take sleeping pills, as to do so merely borrows sleep from the future which must all be paid back with interest. An often overlooked cause of insomnia is the use of stimulating beverages. All caffeine-containing drinks such as coffee, tea, colas, and chocolate should be avoided in the evening. The nervous system is pharmacologically stimulated by these drugs, and can cause sleep to flee.

-Adapted from Dr. Thrash's
Health Counseling Library;
used by permission.

IN 1900'S

English ladies all wore dresses.
Folks only bathed once a week.
Head washed once a summer.

There are 300,000 Amish Living in the U.S.

* A New Amish Community is formed, on average, every 3-1/2 weeks.
* The Amish population may exceed 1,000,000 by 2050.
* The Amish population doubles every 20 years.

■ ....Amish
▢ ....No Amish

TWELVE LARGEST SETTLEMENTS, 2015

AREA	STATE	DISTRICTS EST.	POP.
Lancaster Co.	Pennsylvania	204	34, 070
Holmes Co.	Ohio	257	33,410
Elkhart/LaGrange	Indiana	168	23, 015
Geauga Co.	Ohio	115	17,020
Adams Co.	Indiana	57	8,275
Nappanee	Indiana	42	5,755
Arthur	Illinois	30	4,200
Daviess Co.	Indiana	29	4,570
Mifflin Co.	Pennsylvania	28	3,360
Allen Co.	Indiana	21	3,045
Indiana Co.	Pennsylvania	21	2,795
New Wilmington	Pennsylvania	19	2,415

NOTE: Settlement and district statistics were updated as of May 2015. The number of people in a church district varies by settlement. For example, there are approximately 167 people per district in the Lancaster County settlement versus approximately 130 per district in the Holmes County settlement.

2015 AMISH POPULATION GROWTH REPORT

November 2015, Submitted by Young Center for Anabaptist and Pietist Studies
at Elizabethtown College, Elizabethtown, PA

STATE	SETTLEMENTS	DISTRICTS	ESTIMATED POPULATION
Arkansas	2	2	270
Colorado	3	5	675
Delaware	1	10	1,500
Florida	1	1	75
Idaho	1	1	75
Illinois	18	52	7,280
Indiana	22	364	50,955
Iowa	23	61	8,785
Kansas	7	15	2,025
Kentucky	43	86	11,010
Maine	5	5	675
Maryland	3	11	1,485
Michigan	43	109	14,495
Minnesota	23	36	4,535
Mississippi	1	2	150
Missouri	43	96	11,230
Montana	4	4	540
Nebraska	5	6	810
New Brunswick	1	1	20
New York	52	128	17,280
North Carolina	1	1	135
Ohio	54	513	69,255
Oklahoma	3	6	810
Ontario	16	38	5,130
Pennsylvania	54	465	68,820
South Dakota	1	1	95
Tennessee	9	22	2,750
Texas	1	1	75
Vermont	1	1	15
Virginia	6	8	1,080
West Virginia	3	3	225
Wisconsin	50	138	17,665
Wyoming	1	1	75
Total	501	2,193	300,000

New Era photo by Ed Sachs

In this early 1950s photograph, Amish men leave the prison where many were jailed for lawbreaking.

Amish went to U.S. Supreme Court, and to jail, to keep their children out of public schools

THE 1952 SCHOOL CASE ABOUT THE 14 YEAR OLDS

Some Amish children went to a two story school at Gap at southwest corner of Rt. 30 and 897, in 1930s and 1940s.

In 1952 the English school board wanted to make the Amish children go through the nineth grade and to high school. The Amish wanted to keep their 14 yr. olds that were through the eighth grade at home from school. The school board arrested the Amish and put them in jail for not sending their 14 yr. old to school...and not paying their fine.

I understand about the worse years were 1952 and 1953 and 1954. I once read in a book that this case lasted five years.

Johns Benuel Stoltzfoos along the Newport Road told me that he was in jail five times over that case. He said he doesn't think he had a hired man and had no boys at home from school and they were busy. When they were in jail they didn't hear anything from home. There were a number of Amish men in jail. Once or so, some of the English people bailed them out.

Gid King's mother was a widow, and an English man said he can't see a widow go to jail for that reason, and paid her bail so she didn't have to go to jail.

Over one Sunday a number of Amish men were in jail. There was a church district, that had church that day. The older people in that district think this was before preacher Levi King was ordained on Oct. 22, 1954.

They think preacher Henry Lapp still lived and was not in jail but was not able to be in church.

Their other two ministers were in jail. Church in that district was at Bennie Zook's along Musser School Road, and "Dad" Abram L. Beiler close to Spring Garden went there to church, as his brother Jakes lived in the other end of Bennie Zook's house. When they got there to church, their three preachers in that district were not there. Deacon Bennie Lantz of that district was there in church. Dad Beiler was the only preacher there so dad had the *anfang* and the main sermon and Bennie Lantz read the scripture.

In *Amish History of Southern Lancaster County* it says, in 1953 and 1954 the school board kept prosecuting the Amish with some being arrested four or five times. Often times their fines were paid by unknown friends.

In 1956 the school officials and the Amish agreed on a Vocational school plan which is still in use.

-Ira Stoltzfus

My dad was also in jail a few days as he kept me home from school at 14 years old. He came home hungry. He said food was scant in there.

-Levi Fisher

AN ANSWER TO PRAYER
A True Story by Harvey S. Ruth

A man who had buried his first wife took to drinking, and had fortune to marry for his second wife a good Christian woman. In time, they were blessed with four children, three boys and one girl.

This man did not like his wife's Christian attitude, and so he tried to offend her in every possible way, and live an ungodly life and enjoy life as he desired, but she was steadfast to her faith.

One day as he was sitting in his house, he took his little son, about two years old, between his knees, and wanted to teach him to repeat profane words. This the child tried to imitate as best he could. The father uttered another big curse word. The child tried again to imitate. By this time, the mother's heart was breaking and she wept. She could bear no longer the cruel training of her dear little boy. However, it pleased the father to see her weeping. To crush her heart still more, he said to his wife, "Now I am going to Hellertown" (to his drinking post). He went out, hooked up his little horse to a two-wheeled sulky, and started out for this place where he had gone many times.

While he was driving away, his wife went to her secret closet and prayed to God that He should stop him, for she could not. This she asked the Lord many times before, but her prayer had thus far not been answered.

For a short distance, he went on the straight road that went to another town. The Hellertown road joined this road with a turn to the right and this little horse took him to Hellertown many, many times. But today the horse would not make that turn to the right; it went straight. This surprised him. He turned the horse around and when they came to the same road, the horse ran straight toward home. He could not understand this, but turned around again and said, "Nancy (which was her name), now we want to go to Hellertown." But when she came to that road, she went straight again. The man looked around to see if there might be something somewhere to frighten Nancy, but he saw nothing. Well, once more he tried, took a good grip at the line to make her go his way, and at the same place she made a leap for home. Then he said, "Nancy, if you do not want to go to Hellertown, then go home."

When his wife saw him return she was wondering why they were back so soon. He drove to the barn, unhooked Nancy, who went to her stall to eat the small portion of hay which was his custom of giving her upon their return. When this man put his fork back in the hay, he himself fell down—not being unconscious, but he could not move. He was entirely helpless. He could not move his hands or any part of his body. He could not get up. There was nothing left for him to do but call his wife—the one whose religion he condemned and whom he tried to abuse with insults. He called and called; finally she heard and responded to his calling and found him lying on the hay, conscious but helpless. He could talk and told her what happened. Then she knelt down beside him and prayed. She thanked Him for answering her prayer and said, "Now Daddy, let us go into the house." She took him by the arm and led him to the house. After that there was no more drinking. The wife's prayer had been answered. The husband changed his attitude toward her and toward God. He became a staunch Christian, and they lived together happy thereafter.

This is a true story. It was told by the man himself to me, the writer of this article. I have driven this little Nancy and passed this place many, many times. He says the angel Gabriel must have stood in the road that led to Hellertown, and the spot has become very sacred to him. Little Nancy saw the angel, but the man, like Balaam, did not see him. God moves in a mysterious way, His wonders to perform.

Woman Dies, Leaves 90 Cats in Her Home

1991 - Anchorage, Alaska (AP)—Lyda Scott loved cats, and when the 49-year-old woman died accidentally last summer she left 90 of them, each with a name and no place to go.

Now the Alaska Humane Society, a veterinarian and Scott's daughter are trying to find them new homes.

"It got out of hand," daughter Nadine Scott said. "I tried to tell her that we had too many, but she kept picking them up in parking lots."

70 Years

If one lives to be 70 years of age and is the average person he spends:

23 years sleeping

19 years working

9 years playing

6 years traveling

6 years eating

4 years sick

2 years dressing himself

1 year in the house of the Lord.

-Selected

A lady was mailing a gift of a Bible to a relative. The postal clerk examined the heavy package and inquired if it contained anything breakable. "Nothing," the lady told him, "but the Ten Commandments."

Wanted—A Worker

God never goes to the lazy or to the idle when He needs men for His service. When God wants a worker He calls for a worker. When He has a work to be done, He goes to those who are already at work. When God wants a great servant, He calls a busy man. Scripture and history attest this truth.

Moses was busy with his flocks at Horeb.

Gideon was busy threshing wheat by the press.

Saul was searching for his father's lost beasts.

David was busy caring for his father's sheep.

Elisha was busy ploughing with twelve yoke of oxen.

Amos was busy following the flock.

Nehemiah was busy bearing the king's wine cup.

Peter and Andrew were busy casting a net into the sea.

James and John were busy mending their nets.

Matthew was busy collecting customs.

Saul was persecuting the friends of Jesus.

Food for Thought

It is illegal to read the Bible in the public schools of Illinois, but a law requires the STATE to provide a Bible for every convict! Don't worry, kids, if you can't read the Bible in school, you'll be able to when you get to prison!

-Baptist Beacon

What a Small Boy Missed

A small boy found a bright copper cent glistening in the grass. He seized it eagerly; it was his, and it had cost him nothing.

Thereafter, wherever he went, he walked head downward, eyes glued to the ground, searching for further treasure. During his lifetime he found 313 pennies, 61 nickels, 22 dimes, 14 quarters, 7 half dollars, and one lonely paper dollar—a total of $16.38.

The money cost him nothing—except that he missed the fiery splendor of 25,550 sunsets, the glow of millions of stars on innumerable nights; the singing of the birds in the trees; the smiles of friends he could have had if he had not passed them by.

How many people do the same? How often do men and women become so occupied with the business of living that they fail to appreciate the beauty of nature, the love of family, and the companionship of friends?

Amish Population Growth in Lanc. and Chester Co.

1843	3 districts
1900	6 districts
1945	19 districts
1977	57 districts
2000	126 districts
2010	170 districts
2015	194 districts

87 Districts stem from Lancaster Co. from 1967 on to now 2015.

A Direct Sign From God

There's proof that God still gives signs. A story in the *Johnstown Tribune* tells how a Bible was found on Sept. 11 at the Flight 93 crash site near Shanksville. About 15 yards from the main crater or hole the aircraft had made when it hit the ground. It appeared to be an older Bible, you could tell it was used a lot. Only the cover was singed a bit. Pages as white as snow in the burned area. It was lying face up, open to First Kings Chapter 13 to 15, which tells of Solomon's kingdom being divided. One must recall the big 200 ton jet was demolished to dinner plate size in the crash and horrible fire.

The writer Tom Lavis says many Bible scholars agree the Bible was a direct sign from God. Rev. Dimetrus Dunn, Latrobe, Pa., says God's word will prevail even if earthly things are destroyed. Tom Shoffer, Shanksville Fire Dept. chief, personally saw the Bible, said there was definitely a feeling God's hand was present.

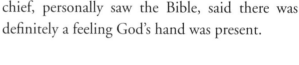

A Thanksgiving Prayer
by Samuel F. Pugh

O God, when I have food,
    help me to remember the hungry;
When I have work,
    help me to remember the jobless;
When I have a home,
    help me to remember those who have no
    home at all;
When I am without pain,
    help me to remember those who suffer.

WATER OR COKE

by John O. Mast
346 Denson Rd, Lawrenceburg, TN 38464

I found this information in a chiropractor's office and thought it would be of interest to some of our readers.

WATER—

1) 75% of Americans are chronically dehydrated

2) In 37% of Americans, the thirst mechanism is so weak that it is often mistaken for hunger

3) Even mild dehydration will slow down one's metabolism as much as 3%

4) One glass of water will shut down midnight hunger pangs for almost 100% of the dieters studied in a University of Washington study

5) Lack of water is the number one trigger of headaches and daytime fatigue

6) Preliminary research indicates that 8-10 glasses of water a day could significantly ease back and joint pain for up to 80% of sufferers

7) A mere 2% drop in body water can trigger fuzzy short term memory trouble with basic math and focusing on a printed page

8) Drinking 5 glasses of water daily decreases the risk of colon cancer by 45%, plus it can slash the risk of breast cancer by 79%, and one is 50% less likely to develop bladder cancer

Now for the properties of COKE—

1) In many states (in the USA) the highway patrol carries two gallons of Coke in the truck to remove blood from the highway after a car accident

2) You can put a T-bone steak in a bowl of coke and it will be gone in two days

3) To clean a toilet, pour a can of Coca Cola into the toilet bowl and let the "real thing" sit for one hour then flush clean. The citric acid in Coke removes stains from Vitreous China

4) To remove rust spots from chrome car bumpers, rub the bumper with a crumpled up piece of Reynolds Wrap aluminum foil dipped in Coca Cola

5) To clean corrosion from car battery terminals; pour a can of Coca Cola over the terminals to bubble away the corrosion

6) To loosen a rusted bold, apply a cloth soaked in Coca Cola to the rusted bolt for several minutes

7) To bake a moist ham, empty a can of Coca Cola into the baking pan, wrap the ham in aluminum foil and bake. Thirty minutes before the ham is finished, remove the foil, allowing the drippings to mix with the Coke for sumptuous brown gravy

8) To remove grease from clothes, empty a can of Coke into a load of greasy clothes, add detergent, and run through a regular cycle. The Coca Cola will help loosen grease stains.

FOR YOUR INFORMATION—

1) The active ingredient in Coke is phosphoric acid. Its Ph is 2.8. It will dissolve a nail in about 4 days. Phosphoric acid also leaches calcium from bones and is a major contributor to the rising increase in osteoporosis

2) To carry Coca Cola syrup (the concentrate) the commercial truck must use the Hazardous material placards reserved for highly corrosive materials.

3) The distributors of Coke have been using it to clean the engines of their trucks for about 20 years.

Now the question is, would you like a Coke or a glass of water? Have a great day, and share it with others.

Lost in the Prairie
True Story

In the 1800s, a party of surveyors had just finished their day's work in the northwestern part of the state of IL, when a violent snow storm came on. They started for their camp, which was in a grove of about 80 acres, in a large prairie, nearly 20 miles distance from any other timberland.

The wind was blowing very hard, and the snow falling so fast that they could scarcely see each other. When they thought they had nearly reached their camp, they suddenly came across some tracks in the snow. These they looked at with great care, and found, to their dismay, that they were their own tracks.

It was now plain that they were lost on the great prairie; and that if they had to pass the night there in the cold, drifting snow, the chances were that they would all perish before morning. While they were shivering with the cold, the chief man of the party caught sight of one of their horses, known as "Old Jack."

Then the chief said, "If anyone can show us our way to the camp, out of this blinding snow, 'Old Jack' can do it. I will take off his bridle and let him loose, and we will follow him. I think he will show us the way to our camp."

As soon as the horse found himself free, he threw up his head and tail, as if proud of the trust that had been placed in him. Then he snuffed the breeze, and gave a loud snort, which seemed to say, "Come on boys! Follow me. I will show you the way to your camp."

The horse turned in a new direction, and trotted along, but not so fast that the men could not follow him. They had not gone more than a mile or two, when they saw the cheerful blaze of the campfires. They all gave a loud huzza at the cheering sight.

They felt grateful to God for their safety, and threw their arms around Old Jack's neck, and caressed him for what he had done. "I know that this is a true story," says the writer, "for my father was the chief of the party on that occasion."

Ein Lauter Ruff
Yonie Esh, April 2010
Georgetown, PA

Greetings in the name of our Lord. Although we still can hardly grasp the enormity of what happened last week, I will try to put it into words. Last Friday, Amos's wife, Linda, came with the sad news that my brother Johnny and most of his family were on their way up to Iowa to a wedding. As they were going up I-65, a semi crossed the median strip and hit their van head on. They do not know if he fell asleep or had a heart attack or what but there were no skid marks on the road. Everyone in the van was killed except Leroy and Naomi's two adopted sons, age three and five. The truck driver also was killed. A passing truck driver saw it happen and stopped and got the boys out. They were hardly hurt. The trucker put them in his truck until help arrived and the boys fell asleep. Later when they woke up, one of the boys asked for their Mommy and Daddy, and they were told that they went to Heaven and they were satisfied. But later the youngest one cried for his mother.

We heard later that the truck driver had decided to get another job. He said, "This is my last trip." We also heard that he became a Christian last year.

Johns lived near Burkesville, KY, which is about a fourteen hour drive. Brother-in-law Manny Fisher got an MDS bus and two drivers and we met at the Bird-in-Hand restaurant early Monday morning, along with the Roy Stoltzfus family, John's wife, Sadie, was one of Roy's daughters. We got down before dark and got a motel then went to the viewing. It was held at the same place where the funeral was held the next day. It was a huge building. They wanted us to eat supper first, which was also in the same building. They said Joel Gingerich's father had just bought this building about a week before. Joel was also killed in the same crash.

After supper, we went to the viewing. That was a scene we will not soon forget. Eight caskets all in a row. Nine bodies. The baby was in a casket with its mother. But we still could hardly fathom that it really happened. I had to think of the Nickel Mine happening. These are things we read about in the paper but they usually happen in other states or other countries but then sometimes, the Lord has other plans. And we do not want to question His plans. We do know that His ways are not our ways, and we want to accept His will.

Johnnies had a lot of friends. There were about eight thousand people at the viewing. People from Maine to Florida and many states through the west.

The managers really did a good job. The ushers really had a big job on hand and they really dug in. One of the biggest jobs was to keep the people moving. And no wonder, if each viewer would vist with each one of the family for ½ a minute, how long would it take for eight thousand people? The cooks also did a tremendous job. There were over three thousand people at the funeral. Although a lot of the food was brought in, it still was a lot of work to cook for that many

people. They even gave us a food pack to eat on the way home on the bus. It was very much appreciated.

The preachers at the funeral were John Miller, Urie Kanagy and Leroy Kauffman. They used eight hearses to take the caskets to the church from the funeral. Then they carried them out to the graveyard and left hem down one at a time. It took a lot of time.

We then went back to where the funeral was and they gave us another meal then we headed home. We got to Bird-in-Hand the next morning about eight o'clock.

Here are the ones who died and their ages:

My brother Johnny Esh, age 64,
His wife, Sadie, age 62,
Their daughter, Rosanne, age 40,
Daughter Anna Lynn Esh, age 33,
A daughter Rachel Marie, age 20,
Joel Gingerich, age 22.
Joel and Rachel were engaged to be married.
A son Leroy Esh,
His wife Naomi Esh.
Jalen Bradley Esh, adopted son of Leroy and Naomi Esh.
A friend Ashley Kramer also died in the crash.

Until now, Johnnie's son Johnny Jr. was the only one buried in the new graveyard. He died about six years ago in Ukraine. Now he is in the middle of most of his family.

Let us pray for each other that we can all hold fast until He comes.

"A Motor Home"

The two brothers shown in the picture had come to the state of Washington from the East Coast. Their friends and relatives from the East did not believe them when they told of the huge trees of Washington.

To prove it, they felled a huge tree on their property and hollowed it out, cutting three windows and a door in it. Inside they made two narrow bunks, a counter, and shelves for holding water, dishes, pans, a camp stove, a small ice box, and space for cooking.

They mounted the big log on what was a Chevrolet truck. They drove this truck to the East Coast and back. Along the way, they stopped at the Chevrolet dealer in each city, where they sold postcards, and were paid to park their unusual truck in the Dealer's window to show the strength and durability of a Chevrolet. They paid for their trip on what they made. Could this have been the first motor home?!

"Quite Right"
Submitted by Vernon Yoder, MO 65243

The cottages of Andrew Sneck and Jacob Thorn stood exactly opposite each other on a little street in Durrenstein village. Their fields however, lay back to back on Jacob's side of the road. Jacob's field was next to the road, but Andrew's field lay behind Jacob's. This meant that Andrew could not reach his field without crossing Jacob's property. This should not have been a problem. In fact, the two neighbors could have helped each other in many ways. However, this was not the case. Instead, they seemed to try to vex and annoy each other.

For example, Andrew could have brought manure to spread on his fields in the winter, when the ground was frozen. At that time of year the wheels on his cart would have run smoothly over the ground and done no damage. But no! He waited until April's showers had turned the fields to mud. Then he harnessed up his horses, loaded his cart, and drove back and forth across Jacob's field. The heavy cartloads made deep ruts in Jacob's field.

Of course Andrew injured his own field too, but it was worth it to him as long as he did a good deal of damage on his neighbor's plot. He had a legal right to pass through his neighbor's field and it gave him great pleasure to use that right to the utmost. He acted even more pleased when Jacob, flushed and angry, pointed out the deep ruts Andrew's cart had made. In fact, the longer Jacob ranted and raved, the more Andrew smiled. He didn't say a word until Jacob had finished. Then he touched the brim of his hat with exaggerated politeness, "Just so!" he mocked. "Quite right!"

If the truth must be known, Andrew looked for every possible way to irritate his neighbor. When the time to mow the hay drew near, Andrew kept careful watch of the fields. Just before Jacob's hay was ready, Andrew began mowing his own field. This meant he must drive his loads of hay through Jacob's uncut meadow. Naturally, he damaged a good share of Jacob's hay. When Jacob objected, Andrew appeared to be astonished. "Quite right," he agreed. "Just as you say." Then he turned and drove his wagon over yet another section of Jacob's field.

At last Jacob could take no more. One night he and his two sons attacked one of Andrew's carts with their axes and reduced it to firewood. Andrew caught them at it and he was delighted, for now he had a good excuse to take his neighbor to court. Of course, the judge ordered poor Jacob to pay for the cart. As Jacob laid the money on the table he said, with a side look at Andrew, "I consider this the price of blood."

"So it is," Andrew replied coldly. "Quite right."

Jacob was furious when he returned from the trial. "Pack up everything" he growled at his wife and sons. "There is nothing but sorrow and injustice here. We will leave this wretched village and sail to America." His sons objected. "If you leave, Andrew will have the victory," they reasoned. "Why don't you go back to court and challenge Andrew's right to cross your field? When the judge hears what you have to put up with, he will surely give you justice."

The very next day Jacob went to the county seat and hired a lawyer. Of course, Andrew immediately did the same. The lawyers carefully examined the deeds and titles to the two properties and then argued the case to the judge. Alas! After much time and expense, the judge ruled in favor of Andrew. He even ordered Jacob to pay Andrew's expenses in the lawsuit.

"This injustice cries to heaven!" Jacob exclaimed, as he counted out the money he must pay.

The following day, Jacob put his land up for sale. His field was rich and fertile, but not one person made even an offer. Instead, many villagers said they would not take it even if he gave it to them. Finally Jacob hired a man to auction his property off, but no one bid on it. Of course, Jacob still had to pay the auctioneer for his time and trouble. He sighed as he laid the money in the man's hand. "I think I am the most unlucky man in the world."

Andrew was standing by. He had come out to the auction just to irritate his neighbor. Now, just loud enough for Jacob to hear, he muttered, "Quite right."

Jacob's many unexpected expenses left him bankrupt. However, he still had one valuable asset: a loving wife who stood by his side and helped him every way she could. She encouraged him to keep working and soon they were back on their feet. At the same time, she persuaded Jacob to study the Bible and pray with her. As they studied together, Jacob's malice and bitterness began to melt away. "I can't hate Andrew when I see what Jesus did for me," Jacob confessed. "We must pray for him. Perhaps God can even reach his stubborn, spiteful heart."

Andrew didn't know what was going on in his neighbor's cottage. He did notice that Jacob seemed much happier than usual. This grieved his heart. He couldn't do much damage to Jacob's fields because it was after the harvest. And so Andrew hired a man to paint QUITE RIGHT in large letters on the outside of his house. He chuckled every time he thought of his neighbors across the road seeing this message each time they looked out their front window or stepped out onto their porch.

But things did not continue quite right for Andrew. First, his three best horses came down with glanders. Andrew was forced to have them shot. Then, to stop the infection from contaminating the rest of the animals, he had to hire a man to pull down and replace the new stalls and mangers he had just installed. Every time Andrew went past his barn he could hear the carpenter inside murmuring, "Quite right! Quite right!" as if in mockery.

Things went from bad to worse. Andrew's servant girl climbed up into the hay loft one day to throw down some barley for the threshing floor. She lost her balance and fell, hitting her head against a beam. Andrew rushed to help her but it was too late—she was dead. There was not a sound to be heard, but Andrew felt as if his ears were ringing with the words, "Quite right!"

Then Andrew himself became ill. Pain racked his whole body and nothing seemed to help. Whatever he ate made him sicker; the doctor's medicines turned his stomach; visits from townfolk irritated him. Nights were even worse. Instead of sleeping, he tossed and turned while his former slogan, "Quite right!" echoed and re-echoed through his mind.

At about this time, a new pastor moved to Durrenstein. Everyone told him that Andrew disliked ministers. Still, the pastor paid him a visit. "Good morning, my friend," he greeted, shaking Andrew's hand, "How are you doing?"

"Don't trouble yourself about me," Andrew growled. "There is no help for me. Just say, like everyone else, 'Quite right! Quite right!'"

"Certainly not," the pastor shook his head. "I would say 'Quite wrong!' I also would have to disagree when you say there's no help for you. As a matter of fact, I am sure that if you would do just three things, you would be cured."

Andrew looked up, interested in spite of himself.

"I will tell you the first part right now," the pastor continued. "It is simple: Paint out those words on the front of your house."

"And what next?" Andrew frowned.

"I cannot tell you the second step until you have taken the first. But I will be back. In the meantime, I will pray for you. Good day." The pastor smiled, picked up his hat, and walked out of the house.

Andrew glared at the pastor's retreating figure. "Meddling, interfering, preacher! What business is this of yours?" Spasms of pain shot through Andrew's left side. He leaned forward, clutching his rib cage and groaning softly. Finally as the pain softened, his thoughts turned back to the morning's unwelcome visitor. "Nellie!" he shouted. "Tess!" His wife and daughter ran to his side. "Fine wife and daughter you are," Andrew scolded. "How dare you let that—that meddler in here?"

His wife held her hands out in silent apology. "Everyone says he is a good, kind man. We thought he might bring you some cheer."

"Cheer indeed," Andrew sputtered. "Why, he wanted me to . . ."

"To do what, Father?" Tessie urged.

"Oh, never mind." Suddenly Andrew didn't want to talk about it. He should his head and looked out the window until the two women shrugged and went back to their work. That night as Andrew lay moaning and tossing on his bed he couldn't get the pastor's words out of his mind. The next morning he hired a man to paint over the words on the front of his house. When the man was finished, not even the outline of the letters was visible.

Second visit. Andrew frowned only a little when the pastor stepped into his cottage a few days later. "Good evening my friend," the pastor greeted him. "I am happy to see that you have removed those offensive words."

"I—" Andrew began.

The pastor went on. "Yes, that was a good first step. Now you are ready for step two. You can be certain that those words are imprinted in your neighbor's memory. If you want to be cured you must remove them from his mind."

Andrew bristled. "Impossible. It's one thing to paint over words on a wall, but quite another matter to wipe out another man's thoughts." He felt the veins on his neck tighten. "I hoped for a moment that you might be able to help me. Now I see you have been taking advantage of a sick man." Trembling with rage, he pushed himself to his feet, "Good day, sir!"

The pastor held up his hand. "Peace, friend. You are absolutely right—you can't wipe away Jacob's memory with a paintbrush. Neither can a hired man or even your wife do anything to remove those words. But you might succeed if you tried yourself. You could do it tomorrow. You can go over to Jacob's house—you are not too weak to walk that far. It will be hard to begin, so just make a remark about the weather. Then, while you are there, add, "Neighbor, I am deeply sorry for what has passed between you and me. I have painted over the unkind words on my house. Now I beg you to put them out of your heart and your memory." The pastor hurried off without waiting for a reply. His bitter prescription must be left to work its own effect.

Andrew snatched his cap from his head and threw it on the floor. "I won't do it, I won't do it!" A stabbing pain cut across his heart. "Oh," he cried. He fell onto his bed, his breath coming in short, agonizing gasps. 'Will you go to your grave with this offense against your neighbor still standing?' For hours the thought pounded through Andrew's mind. Finally, he fell into a troubled sleep.

Before breakfast the next morning, Andrew stumbled across the road. He choked out the words the pastor had suggested and Jacob clasped his hand in forgiveness. The two parted as friends for the first time.

Step three. The pastor smiled when he once more crossed Andrew's threshold. "I can see by your face that you have taken step two." Andrew nodded and the pastor continued. "You have just one thing left to do. You have done away with the words on the wall and in you neighbor's mind, but they are still on your record in heaven. They must be washed out."

"My record in heaven?" Andrew moaned. "How can I do anything about that?"

"You can do nothing yourself," the pastor answered. "Not a thing you can do will atone for your sin against God. But you can be forgiven. Even though you do not know him, Jesus has sent his Holy Spirit to strive with you soul. He has paid for your sins and gives you peace in return. 'The blood of Jesus Christ . . . cleanseth us from all sin . . . if we confess our sins, He is faithful and just to forgive us our sins, and to cleanse us from all unrighteousness'."

As the pastor spoke, all that Andrew had ever heard or read of Christ seemed to return to his memory. Hope began to dawn on his soul. That night, he spent hours in prayer. His wife feared for his health, but the next day he seemed stronger than he had been for months. In the following days, as his soul continued to grow in grace, his health also strengthened. Soon he was fully well.

A few months later Andrew's daughter Tess married Jacob's son. The two farms were combined and given to the young people. Andrew and Jacob became the closest of friends. Often, in the evenings, they walked together through their former fields. When Andrew began to speak of the bitter days of the past, Jacob would not permit it. "No," he insisted, "God promised, their sins and their iniquities will I remember no more. This is the mind of Christ. Let us seek after the same mind."

Andrew nodded.

"We are both pardoned sinners, now let us press toward the mark for the prize of the high calling of God in Christ Jesus."

A Moonless Month . . .

The month of February, 1866 was in one respect the most remarkable in the world's history. It had no full moon. January had two full moons and so did March, but February had none. Do you realize what a rare thing in nature it was? It had not occurred since the creation of the world, and it will not occur again, according to the computation of astronomers for 2,500,000 years.

A Mule Story

Now how about a mule story. I have heard some pretty nice horse and mule arguments over the years but my conscience tells me not to start one in my *Botschaft* letter. But how many of you heard how much attention a hee-hawing mule got yesterday morning about 40 miles east of here. According to the report I got, a trucker stopped at a rest stop off Interstate 80 with a lone mule in the enclosed horse trailer. The weird bellowing of this long-eared thing prompted someone to call 911. The state troopers didn't waste much time. The news showed six or seven pale-faced, wide-eyed cops slowly approaching the trailer with guns drawn, not having any idea what kind of imported illegal creature could be making that unearthly noise. Your guess is as good as mine, who knows, possibly they figured here is a load of Islamic terrorists, calling in their own native language. I don't have the full details of the episode, but I understood these city cops had never before heard the mule's song and this was one show that I wouldn't have minded seeing. I guess it takes all kinds of people to make this world go round!

-Jacob F. Stoltzfus, 2015
Danville, PA

Daniels Gott.

Gott hat in der Löwengrube
Einen Daniel bewahrt;
Das ihm von den wilden Tieren
Nicht ein Haar geifrümmet ward,
Der den ichredlichen Gewalten
Ihre Rachen zugehalten;
Urmes Herze, glaub es doch,
Daniels Gott lebt heute noch.

Liebite Jugend, du bift heute
Hier in dieser falichen Welt
In den größten Gefahren,
Bon Berfuchungen umftellt,
Du fannit ohne Gott nicht ftehen,
Wirft in Sünden untergehen;
Liebe Jugend, glaub as doch,
Daniels Gott lebt heute noch.

Rutter, ift dir angft und bange
Grämft dich um dein teures Kind,
Das vom böfen Feind geblendet,
Sich auf breitem Weg befind't
Bift vielleicht fchon am Berzagen,
Kannft die Laft nicht länger tragen,
Arme Mutter, glaub es doch,
Daniels Gott lebt heute noch.

Und du, vielgeprüfter Bruder,
Einfam, traurig, müd und matt:
Bift von all den Weh und Jammer
Und von Sorgen überfatt.
Gott fann diene Tränen ftillen,
Dich mit füßem Troft erfullen,
Lieber Bruder, glaub es doch,
Daniels Gott lebt heute noch.

The Preacher's Problem Solved

Millersburg

A young preacher was called to be the pastor to a church in the valley. It was a lovely church in a beautiful scenic area and was attended by a congregation of people who were not poor by any sense of the word. They could pay their pastor handsomely but, in spite of all that, the church never seemed to be able to keep a preacher very long. The preacher was excited about the opportunity to minister to the people but he was also quite concerned about whatever it was that caused the preachers before him to leave.

The day came for he and his young family to move to the valley and the whole church came to help him get settled. It blessed his heart tremendously that they would be so receptive and friendly. The day was full of greetings and fellowship, eating and meeting. It was a wonderful welcome for the preacher and his family. He could not imagine what had gone so wrong that the other preachers would not stay at the church. On this first impression, the people seemed warm and kind, friendly and loving.

When Sunday came, the new preacher was preparing to deliver his first message when one of the deacons passed him a note that read, "Dear Preacher, We thank God for bringing you to us and we pray that God will use you to bring blessing to our church. Signed, Deacon Smith." The preacher was greatly impressed and comforted that he was wanted and needed. He had worried about what to say to the people and how to say it so as to not offend them. So without much hesitation he began his first message at the church. As he preached he could tell they were listening, they were nodding in agreement and he felt more comfortable than he had ever felt.

About ten minutes into the message he was really starting to make his point. He heard a stir so he looked up from his Bible and what he saw astonished him, everyone was walking out! He tried to act as though he did not notice and when he finished his message there were only a few people left sitting with his family. He was confused, he was worried, "What had I said, what had I done?" He went back over every word in his message time after time but could not find anything that could've been a problem. Many times throughout the week he would see people from the church and they were very friendly. This really confused the young preacher because they all acted as though nothing had happened.

Week after week the same thing would happen, the people would leave halfway through the sermon as though they did not believe what he was saying was for them. He tried fiery sermons and he tried funny sermons. He tried deep doctrinal sermons and he tried simple, practical sermons. Nothing seemed to keep the people in the church long enough for the preacher to make his point and give the people a chance to respond by repentance. The discouraged young preacher started to realize why all the other preachers before him had left; the people had always walked out after half the sermon.

He decided that he should go and ask his deacons about the situation. The deacons were very kind and told the preacher that except for a few sinners, all of the people of that church were Christians. They continued to explain that when the preacher would get to the part about sinners, it was not necessary for the good people to stay and hear it, since it is so negative and all.

This really perplexed the young preacher. He spent nearly the whole week trying to figure out how to keep the people in church for the whole message. Then it struck him. He figured it out. He planned a week how he would try to change the habits of the people. Then, when it was time to preach, he stood up in front of the good folks and firmly declared, "This morning I will be preaching two messages, the first message will be to the sinners. When it is over you sinners may get up and leave. Then I will preach to the saints."

Nobody wanted to declare himself a sinner in front of everyone, so, no one left until the messages were concluded. From that day on, the congregation was listening to the whole message and many lives were changed because of what they heard. God's blessing did come to that little church in the valley because the people started to listen to the whole message of God and not just what they wanted to hear.

. . . Now therefore are we all here present before God, to hear all things that are commanded thee of God.

THE MODERN FARMER

I was in bed trying to sleep the other night, when I was awakened by the sound of a modern farmer still out chopping corn. He was at it almost the whole night. He only stopped because it was milking time. I thought to myself, what a wonderful thing it is to have labor saving machinery. That modern farmer can work all day and all night out there. You just couldn't do that with horses. Why, it would take several days with regular sleeping at night to do as many acres as that modern farmer has to do.

Well, he must be done milking in his double-umpteen raised parlor, where it takes him over six hours a milking to milk his cows. (He put in the new parlor to save time and labor; then he got a whole lot more cows to milk to help pay for the parlor. He's going to increase his herd again, soon, to help pay for all the new time and labor saving equipment he bought to work all the extra ground he's rented to feed all the cows from the herd increase.) I can see him out scraping manure into the lagoon. He put that in so that he could save time and labor on spreading by only having to spread day and night once a year, instead of periodically on fallow fields. He doesn't bother with fallow fields anyway, or crop rotation either. All that time wasted trying to figure out how to change your crops around and plowing old stuff under and so on. He knows exactly where it all goes already and he takes his 16-row no-till planter out and it's done in hardly any days and nights at all. Small farmers really don't know what they're missing.

The best part of all of this is that by the time he's in his mid-50's (or sooner, if he's a really good modern farmer) he'll have saved up so much time by working day and night that he can die from a heart attack or stroke. It's sad how much time the rest of us will waste by having to live to be 80 or 90 to get the same amount of work done. There's a lot we can learn from the modern farmer.

-by Hans W. Kranhenbuhl

GROSS SAM (BIG SAM)

Memories of Fisher's Stone Quarries on Bachmantown Rd., Ronks, and the Fisher home farm and family.

Many of these stories were told to me by my grandfather Christ M. Fisher. The quarry was started by his grandfather Samuel B. Fisher, who was usually called *"Gross Sam"* (Big Sam). Evidently he was a big strong man but had some bouts with mental problems. It was said if he felt it coming he would try to work it off and worked so that it was completely out of the ordinary, so that he overworked himself day and night, contributing to an early death in his 50's.

His son Christ L. Fisher is said was the only person that could handle him and married in 1892 between Christmas and New Year's Day and moved on the home farm. His father Sam died in Jan. the following month and his widow Barbara moved onto the next farm to the East that they had just divided in 188_. In a diary he wrote in 1888 he was already dressing stones and marking tombstones to sell. The stories of his strength are almost unbelievable. At that time it was a practice of putting a young married man over a fence as a symbol of another side of life. After he married in 1892 no one was able to put him across as nobody could force him to it. My granddad Christ M. said that in his prime he weighed 260 lbs. which was all muscle and he was easily able to lift more than twice his own weight. When he became a minister in 1901 he finally allowed them to put him over the fence. Evidently they were still trying all these years and never could so he finally left it be done as it did not become a minister to be tussling with the young folks. The unmarried men would usually push them over the fence and the married men tried to prevent it resulting in some real tussles.

My uncle John Lapp gave this story. Down in Phila. they had to carry the wheat up a stairway and dump it in a bin. He carried a 120-lb. bag under each arm. But there was a naughty boy there, every time he walked up the steps with his load, the boy reached out and pulled his beard. So one time he prepared himself and grabbed the boy and took him along also and threw him in the bin along with the wheat. I guess that took care of that problem.

-LF

A MIRACLE OF GOD

On December 5, someone stopped at the shop and said the day before something happened that amazed him. Eleven-year-old twin girls attended Bible school in Tennessee somewhere and the last day of Bible school all the students were given helium balloons and they put in a request that they would like to be adopted by Christian parents. They were foster girls. Then this fall, a childless couple in northern Maryland were out raking leaves and they saw this balloon in top of their tree. So the man got a ladder and got it down and here was the request or prayer of the 11-year-old twin girls. So on December 4, the judge granted the adoption of these girls to the childless couple, stating on TV, it was a miracle of God.

-Delbert R. Schmucker, 2013

Senior Man Lost

Leola, PA
Millcreek, 2001

We had something happen in the neighborhood that probably never happened before, not that I can recollect anyway. Dave Glick, out here on Creek Hill Rd., got disoriented and lost his way going to their son's place. Joe lives in the Denver area, a good two hour's drive. Other members of the family, including his wife, had a van lined up to take them, but at the last moment Dave informed them that he would rather drive his horse. This was for dinner. What they didn't realize was that they wouldn't see him for nearly 24 hours. When he didn't show up for dinner they became a little uneasy. In the PM they got a neighbor with a car and went out to hunt Dad, but they weren't successful. Police had not been able to turn up any leads. Night fall came and still no Dave, he had disappeared. Eli, one of the sons, told me this is one experience he will never forget. At home they couldn't sleep. Sometime after midnight they decided to call the neighbors together and form several search parties, to start out at the crack of dawn. It was now Sunday morning and around 6 or 7 he was spotted going past Eli Lant's. It appears man and horse had no food or drink in that time, also a thunderstorm went through Sat. night. Dave doesn't really know where all he was, but he thinks he got lost in Reinholds area. Dave is in his eighties.

-Henry Beiler

Die Mutter Sprache

1. Wir lieben doch die Mutterfprache
Die wir lernten auf ihren ſchoße,
So tut dom eure Eltern ehren,
Rit der Sprache wie ſie es begehren.

2. Wo kommt daß her daß unſre knaben,
Ein Undre Sprache im gebrauch haben,
Wenn ſie alfo zuſammen kommen,
Haben wir dies ſchon war gnommen?

3. Was möcht dann der treiber ſein,
Undre Sprache zu gebrauchen in der Gemein?
Welcher Geiſt tut zu biefen führen,
Daß die Mutter Sprache ſte tuhn verlieren?

4. Wenn an der Gemein man daß muß hören,
Wündch ich wir würden alle wehren,
Daß nicht eine Sprach kommt herein!
Daß uns nicht ziemt in der Gemein.

5. Wir wollen daß doch recht betrachten,
Und daß doch nicht fo gar leicht achten,
Daß wir daß nur walten laſſen,
Daß rechte dann zu viel bergeſſen.

6. Der Hochmuts Geiſt, der liebt daß ſehr,
Wer Demuth liebt, dem fällt es ſchwer,
Und nimmt doch folches tief zu Herzen,
Wie daß in zeit uns macht zu ſtürzen.

7. Ich will uns alle hier noch recht warnen,
Daß wir die Kinder recht Deutſch lernen,
Daß ſie recht können leſen und ſingen,
Für dem herren ein, Dankopfer bringen.

8. Wo möchte daß uns dann hinführen,
Wenn wir unfere Sprache verlieren?
O warnet ſie doch recht in zeit,
Und nehmet es wahr, ihr liebe Leut!

So Why Isn't a Nice Girl Like You Married?

-Nancy Kauffman

Have you ever heard that question asked? Maybe it was directed to you, or maybe toward someone else. Perhaps you've even asked it yourself. I don't think I've ever been asked in those exact words, but the implications have come quite close! So . . . why *aren't* some nice girls married? Let's give that question some thought, both for our own sakes as singles and for anyone else who might be wondering about our status!

To help us come to some conclusions, let's look first at some misconceptions or "myths" that some singles (and even some married folks!) have about singleness. The first myth that comes to mind is that singleness equals rejection. Along with this myth can come a rather large variety of related problems. We're duped into believing that we're not needed, nobody wants us, or that we've been "passed over" because of some serious flaw that we have. I've met girls who actually believed they weren't married because they thought they weren't pretty enough or didn't have the right personality. Grant it, some of us are less blessed with good looks than some of our married counterparts, but let's be reasonable. Are we saying that all married people are beautiful and all single people are ugly? I think you can see how ridiculous that idea is. Personality is the same way. We may believe we're too shy or too talkative, but again the percentages indicate that both timid and loquacious people get married, not just women with nice even-keel personalities. As to not being needed: if we really believe that idea, then our focus is definitely in the wrong place. For someone who lives on an island all by herself this may be something to deal with, but I don't think it applies to very

many of us. What I'm getting at is that there are people all around us every day that have needs. We may be meeting a different set of needs than what married people do, but that should only make us seem *more* important and needed, not less.

Another myth is that singleness is a very undesirable state to be in and one that we need to be delivered from as soon as possible in order to insure fulfillment and happiness in our lives. When we believe this myth, we also believe the one that says, "Marriage equals happiness." Let's remember that happiness has nothing to do with marital status. Chances are that if you cannot be happy and fulfilled as a single, you won't be happy and fulfilled as a married person either. Colossians 2:10 says, "And ye are complete in him (Christ)." Our completeness or wholeness comes from Christ, and not from a marriage partner.

Probably about the most serious myth that some of us get tangled up in is the idea that God "punishes" us or enjoys watching us be miserable by purposely withholding something that we really want, which in this case would be marriage. Nothing could be farther from the truth. If singleness to you is "punishment," that's definitely *your* idea and not God's! Rather, God desires the very best for us, and sometimes that is the "gift" of singleness. If we fail to embrace that fact, then it's *us* cheating ourselves, and not God.

So now we've evaluated some of the *wrong* answers to our original question, but we haven't actually answered it. Or have we? Hopefully our evaluation has caused us to think about what the answer might be. I would like to suggest that there may be more than one answer, and that the answers may not be the same for all of us. Some women have actually chosen to remain single (for a short time or for a lifetime) because of commitments to missions or elderly family members or because of other circumstances.

Ultimately, though, I believe the larger, more complete answer for the truly committed Christian single lies simply within the will of God. For some reason (and you can be *sure* that He has one!), God has chosen for some of us to remain single, and it's as simple as that. The interesting thing is that when we can accept that fact in simple faith and rest in His promises, grappling for an answer to the "Why-aren't-you-married" question becomes somewhat immaterial. Certainly, our human tendencies will continue to ponder His will in our remaining unmarried, but it will not disturb us. Jeremiah 29:11 says: "For I know the thoughts that I think toward you, saith the Lord, thoughts of peace and not of evil, to give you an expected end."

So the next time someone asks you why you're not married, I hope you have a ready answer. Tell them simply that you believe it's part of God's plan for you. If they need more details than that, they'll need to check with God—He has the plans, and that's really all that matters.

Original Noah's Ark Believed to Have Been Found in Turkey

Los Angeles—Plans for a $1-million expedition to recover timbers believed to be the remains of Noah's Ark from frozen lake at Mt. Ararat in Turkey were announced recently by a team of scientists and explorers.

Ralph E. Crawford, president of Search Foundation Inc., Washington, D.C., told a news conference several pieces of hand-tooled wood more than 4,000 years old had been found in an ice pack near the 14,000 foot level on the 17,000-foot mountain in northeast Turkey near the Soviet Border.

The expedition is scheduled to set up a base camp this spring and begin studying ways to melt a 100 x 450 foot glacier covering the find in the summer of 1971. Crawford said there are no trees on the mountain. He added that the timbers found by an expedition last summer appear to be white oak and that there are no white oak trees within several hundred miles of the mountain.

Fernand Navara, French explorer who found the timbers in a deep crevasse, said he is confident they are from the original Noah's Ark of biblical history.

Navarra, who has been exploring the mountain since 1952 said he first saw an estimated 50 tons of timbers embedded in a frozen lake in 1955 and chopped out a 5-foot long piece as proof. He returned with a larger expedition in 1969 and recovered several other pieces.

Reports of the presence of a large vessel high on Mr. Ararat have persisted for centuries. The prow of a ship was seen jutting from an ice pack by avalanche work teams in 1840, and commercial pilots have reported seeing a ship-like shadow in the ice near the top of the mountain.

Crawford said the timbers recovered by Navarra have been dated at 4,500 to 5,000 years old by a method measuring the rate of decay of radioactive carbon in the wood.

INSOMNIA

There was nothing quite so dreary
As to lie awake at night.
Insomnia, they called it;
How I'd wish for morning light!

    But no! The clock upon the mantle
    Struck three, three-thirty, four . . .
    I'd turn and toss and tumble,
    Wider awake then before.

I'd worry—to myself I'd grumble,
Of course, I needed the rest,
With tomorrow's tasks before me
I could never be at my best.

    The minutes passed into hours,
    My mind tossed back and fro
    With cares and problems and worries;
    Oh, how they seemed to grow!

But, ah, I've found the secret
My insomnia to cure;
It's now a time of blessing
Instead of misery to endure.

    Now when I awaken at night
    I say, "Thank you, blessed Lord,
    For a little time of fellowship
    And thinking of Thy Word."

There are so many lonely folks
Who must their burdens bear
Because I've been too busy
To uphold them with my prayers.

    I'll now take time to name each one
    The sick and suffering too,
    The ministers and their needs—
    Just to mention a few.

Suddenly, to my surprise!
Arising time has come;
I must have fallen sound asleep
Soon after I'd begun.

VAS ISCH GNADE

I remember Amos Y. tell this story when he was overseer in our church probably late seventies.

Once a little boy asked his dad, "*Vas isch Gnade?*" This boy heard the ministers preach about *Gnade* so he asked his dad what it is. His dad had a good answer he said, "Now if I tell you to do some things like throw down hay and sweep forebay and some chores like this, and if you get these done till I am ready to leave you may go along." The boy went to work but did just not quite get everything done that he was asked to do but was told he can still go along—*des is Gnade.*

    -LF

VON DER EHEMAN GEGEN SEIN WEIBE

Alle zeit Friedlichkeit
und Freundlichkeit beweisen gegen sie
    Sie hertzlich lieben und ehren
Nach vermogen sie versorgen
    Vertheidigen und beschutzen
Nicht unzeitig gegen sie eifern
    Sondern mit vernunf regieren
und mit ihr schwacheit gedult haben
    Doch sie freundlich strafen
und Für sie beten
    Auch wohl in billigen dingen
seinem weibe Folgen
    Aber sie die Herrschaft nicht lassen

O Gott Vater, wir loben dich

O Gott Vater, wir loben Dich,
Und Deine Güte preisen,
Daß Du Dich, o Herr, gnädiglich,
An uns neu hast bewiesen,
Und hast uns, Herr, zusammen g'führt,
Uns zu ermahnen durch Dein Wort,
Gieb uns Genad zu diesem.

2. Oeffne den Mund, Herr, Deiner Knech'
Gieb ihn'n Weisheit darneben,
Daß sie Dein Wort mög'n sprechen recht,
Was dient zum frommen Leben
Und nützlich ist zu Deinem Preis,
Gieb uns Hunger nach solcher Speis,
Das ist unser Begehren.

3. Gieb unserm Herzen auch Verstand,
Erleuchtung hie auf Erden,
Daß Dein Wort in uns werd bekannt,
Daß wir fromm mögen werden
Und leben in Gerechtigkeit,
Achten auf Dein Wort allezeit,
So bleibt man unbetrogen.

4. Dein, o Herr! ist das Reich allein
Und auch die Macht zusammen;
Wir loben Dich in der Gemein
Und danken Deinem Namen,
Und bitten Dich aus Herzensgrund,
Wollst bei uns sein zu dieser Stund,
Durch Jesum Christum. Amen.

O God Father, We Do Praise Thee

1. O God, Father we do praise Thee,
And glorify Thy goodness,
That thou, O Lord, so graciously
Revealed Thyself 'new to us,
Hast led us thus together, Lord,
To admonish us through Thy Word
So grant us Thy grace to do this.

2. Open mouths of Thy servants, Lord,
Be of Thy wisdom giving,
That they may rightly speak Thy Word,
Which serves to devout living.
May it profit to Thy glory!
Make us for this food hungry;
This desire, we are requesting.

3. Give our hearts Thy wisdom also,
On this earth, enlight'nment give
That Thy Word in us may be known,
That we be truly devout;
And live our life in righteousness,
Heeding Thy Word in steadfastness,
Abiding from deception free.

4. Lord, only Thine the kingdom is,
Thine, the Power, the same;
The congregation does praise Thee,
Giving thanks unto Thy Name.
We plead from the depths of our heart
That Thou this hour with us art,
Through Jesus Christ, Amen, be.

DAS EHEWEIBS ZIERDE SOLL SEIN

Frommichkeit und Gottes Furcht
Liebe gegen ihr man und untertanigkeit
Hauslichkeit und Fleisichkeit
Schamhaftigkeit und Zucht
Freundlichkeit und verschwiegenheit
Keuschheit und Ehrbarkeit
Allen weibern die diese Herrlichen
Tugenden Nach yagten verdient die
Herrlich Namen welche einem
Tugendsamen Weibe in die schrift
beigelegt wird

THE TWILIGHT YEARS

The white-haired Deacon held the big German Bible in one hand as he looked over the congregation. He felt led to speak a few words before he read the chapter. This is what he said.

When I was younger I thought old age would be time to relax spiritually, a period of rest from life's battles, surely the temptations would be few, and one would have gained the wisdom to know what is best to do. But brethren and sisters, I have not found it so.

The deacon's voice trembled as he thought back over the 75 years of his life. He went on, it is true that many of the temptations of youth have left me. And I no longer worry about mortgages and bills and getting the hay in before it rains. The children are all married and the home is quiet with just my wife and myself. Many of the cares of life have been placed on younger shoulders, and we do not have so much to do. But fewer

temptations? No, not at all. If anything they are more troublesome than ever.

We have more leisure time. Satan comes with evil thoughts to tempt us, trying to get us to mistrust people, to think too much about ourselves and our aches and pains, to doubt and worry about tomorrow.

I sat in the audience, a young man myself at the time, I was startled by the deacon's words surely life was a series of spiritual hills to climb that broke away to level land as one grew older. The more I thought of what the deacon had said, the surer I became that young people often envied older retired people, when instead they should be encouraging them in their continuing spiritual battles.

The twilight of life, it seems to me, should be a glorious perserving in the faith, using the time and talents God gives from day-to-day in a manner that brings honor to God and happiness to others. This in itself can be a challenge to younger generations to serve Christ sincerely.

Old age should not be a longing for youth to return. Instead, the twilight years should be a resigned-to-God experience of expectant waiting, busy in His service while He still gives strength. Paul in his letter to Titus had a word of advice for senior citizens, that the aged men be sober, grave, temperate, sound in faith, in charity, in patience. The aged women likewise, that they be in behavior as becometh holiness.

When late autumn strips the leaves from the trees round about us, we can see the distant regions that were hidden from us all summer. In the same way old age may rob men and women of earlier enjoyments, but it is only to enlarge the prospect of eternity. Old-age is a threshold. (From, *Family Life*, August 1968).

The Boy Without a Name

by W. Bardsley Brash
January 1, 1931

Long, long ago there was a boy who worked at an inn. We know not his name; but we will tell you a story about him. He was the boy-of-all-work. It was his task to look after the cattle, and to do odd jobs at the inn. There came a time when there was a great stir at this inn, for the little town was full of pilgrims, and the inn was overcrowded. A number of folk wanted lodgings, and they sought for them, and found them not. Amongst these was a tired woman and a man with a troubled look. The stable boy heard them pleading with the landlord. The landlord was kind but firm, and said, "I should like to take you into the inn, but it is quite impossible. I have already turned many away." The man and the woman pleaded, but to no avail. The lad of the inn heard the eager request and the firm refusal, and his heart was strangely stirred. He slipped away from them and said to himself, "They will find their way to the stable. I will make it sweet and clean for them." So he ran speedily and made everything as tidy as possible, and put clean, fresh, sweet-smelling hay in the manger, and then went back to the inn, for there was much work for him to do there.

Some time after he slipped out of the inn and beheld a strange light in the wind-swept shed. There he saw the two tired pilgrims, and, O wonder of wonders, a babe—lying in a manger in the warm, fresh, sweet-smelling hay. All was clean, tidy and homely, and the man and woman and the child looked so happy. The boy was so merry and said, "I put the hay there on which the baby sleeps. No one knows; it is better

when nobody knows." Back again he ran to his work, and whistled for sheer joy as he bustled about, answering the quick calls of the many people at the inn. Night fell—a clear night, full of stars. The boy slipped out of the inn and ran to the stable. He said, "I should just like one more peep before I go to sleep." Amazement fell upon him. There were, O wonder of wonders, shepherds kneeling, and they were all gazing with joyous astonishment at the babe lying in the manger. They spoke of the heavenly light, of the song of angels, of tidings of great joy to all people. No one noticed the boy of the inn, for he hid himself in the darkness. But he saw all, and as he lay down to rest he said, "I placed the hay there for the wonderful child. No one knows; it is better when nobody knows."

Kindness to Beast

A man of kindness to his beast is kind. Brutal actions show a brutal mind.

Remember . . . He who made the beast, He who gave thee speech of mind, formed him mute.

He can't complain, but God's knowing eye beholds thy cruelty. He hears his cry, he was destined thy servant and thy drudge. But know ye this, his creator is thy judge.

This writing hung in bro. Elam's fore-bay all weather beaten, the writing was hard to make out.

-Sallie Stoltzfus

The next day the boy of the inn was busy—all the world seemed calling for him, for the inn was crowded, and the pilgrims needed so many things. He had no time during the day to go to the manger, but as he ran to and fro on his errands he saw the vision of a babe, lying on clean, fresh, sweet-smelling hay. He was so glad that he had brought the hay, that he had placed it in the manger, and that the child slept sweetly in this soft bed. He longed to see the babe again, but not until night was he able. Then swiftly he ran, and, O wonder of wonders, he saw kingly pilgrims, swarthy of face, kneeling in lowly adoration before the manger. They talked of a star they had seen in the East, of long journeys over burning sands, and of the wondrous joy which was theirs in worshipping the babe. They brought forth beautiful gifts—gold, frankincense and myrrh—and these, they said, were gifts for the babe. The strange light in the stable made the precious jewels flash with heavenly splendour. The little boy kneeled in the shadows, and worshiped and rejoiced, and said, "What beautiful gifts! . . . my mine was *first*, for I came before the shepherds and the distant travelers, and tidied the stable, and brought the present of clean, fresh, sweet-smelling hay. I am glad that I was the first to bring a gift, and that love led me to make a warm bed for the kingly babe. No one knows; it is better when nobody knows." And no man or woman or child would ever have known had not an angel told me this Christmastide the story; but even he did not mention the name of the dear boy, but always called him "the boy without a name."

LONESOME BLUE'S

1

Today I was having one of those days
And I felt kinda lonesome and blue
Then suddenly I was thinking of you
And wondered if you got them too

2

So I thought just in case you'd be feeling this way
And were wondering if anyone cared
I'll write you a line to say that they do
And that all our troubles are shared

3

So if nobody came to visit today
And the mailman no letters have brought
Don't think that your friends have forgotten you
No don't ever cherish this thought

4

Twas only that each one was busy today
Life demands us to each do our share
But they thought of you often as they hurried
along
And for you they whispered a prayer

5

For probably each one is remembering now
A time when you lended a hand
You always were helping another along
How you did it I don't understand

6

So if you're not feeling quite like you should
And there is work that you think you should do
Just think of the friends who remember and care
Who are glad they can do it for you

Forty-eight Hours in Hell

One of the most interesting cases of resuscitation that ever came to my knowledge was that of George Lennox, a notorious horse-thief of Jefferson County. He was serving his second term. Sedgwick County sent him to the prison the first time for a similar offense—stealing horses.

During the winter of 1887 and 1888, he worked in the coal mines. The place where he was working seemed dangerous to him. He reported the fact to the officer in charge, who made an examination, and deciding that the room was safe, ordered Lennox back to his work. The convict obeying, had not continued his work more than an hour, when the roof fell in and completely buried him. He remained in this condition fully two hours. Missing at dinner time a search was instituted for the absent convict, and he was found under this heap of rubbish. Life was extinct.

He was taken to the top, and on examination by the prison physician was pronounced dead. His remains were carried to the hospital where he was washed and dressed preparatory for interment. His coffin was made and brought into the hospital. The chaplain had arrived to perform the last rites prior to burial. A couple of prisoners were ordered by the stewart to lift the corpse from the boards and carry it across the room and place it in the coffin. They obeyed, one at the head and the other at the feet, and were about halfway across the room when the one who was at the head accidently stumbled over a cuspidor, lost his balance and dropped the corpse. The head of the man struck the floor, and to the utter surprise of all present, a deep groan was heard. Soon the eyes opened, and other appearances of life were manifested.

The physician was immediately sent for, and by the time he arrived, some thirty minutes later, the dead man had called for a cup of water, and was in the act of drinking when the physician arrived. The coffin was at once removed, and later on was used to bury another convict in. His burial robes were also taken from him, and the prison garb substituted.

On examination he was found to have one of his legs broken in two places, and was otherwise bruised. He remained in the hospital some six months, and again went back to work. I learned of his experience while apparently dead soon after from a fellow miner. Prompted by curiosity, I longed for an acquaintance with Lennox to get his experience from his own lips. This opportunity was not offered for several months. At last it came.

After being removed from the mines I was detailed to one of the prison offices to make out some annual reports. The subject of this man's return to life was being discussed one day when he happened to pass by the office door and was pointed out to me. It was not long until I had a note in his hand and asked him to come where I was at work. He did so and here I got well acquainted with him, and from his own lips received his wonderful story. He is a young man, probably not over thirty years of age. He is not a hardened criminal; is possessed of a very good education, and naturally very bright.

The most wonderful part of his history was that during the time he was dead. Being a short hand reporter I took his story from his dictation. He said: "I had a presentiment all the morning that something terrible was going to happen. I was so uneasy on account of my feelings that I went to my mining boss, Mr. Grason, and told him how I felt, and asked him if he would come and examine my 'coal room,' the place where I was digging coal. He came and seemed to make a thorough examination, and ordered me back to work, saying there was no danger, and that he thought I was going 'cranky.'

"I returned to my work and had been digging away for something like an hour, when all of a sudden it grew dark. Then it seemed as if a great iron door swung open and I passed through it.

"The thought then came to my mind that I was dead and in another world. I could see no one nor hear a sound of any kind. From some cause unknown to myself I started to move away from the doorway and had traveled some distance when I came to the banks of a broad river. There was about as much light as on a bright starlit night.

"I had not remained on the bank of this river very long until I could hear the sound of oars in the water, and soon a person in a boat rowed up to where I was standing. I was speechless. He looked at me for a moment, and then said he had come for me, and told me to get into the boat and row across to the other side. I obeyed. Not a word was spoken. I longed to ask him who he was and where I was. My tongue seemed to cling to the roof of my mouth. I could not say a word. Finally we reached the opposite shore. I got out of the boat, and the boatman vanished out of sight.

"Thus left alone, I knew not what to do. Looking out before me, I saw two roads which led through a dark valley. One of these was a broad road and seemed to be well traveled. The other was a narrow path that led off in another direction. I instinctively followed the well beaten road. I had not gone far when it seemed to grow darker. Ever and anon, however, a light would flash up from the distance and in this manner I was lighted on my journey.

"Presently I was met by a being that it is utterly impossible for me to describe. I can only give you a faint idea of his dreadful appearance. He resembled a man somewhat, but much larger than any human being I ever saw. He must have been at least ten feet high. He had great wings on his back. He was as black as the coal I had been digging, and in perfectly nude condition.

"He had a large spear in his hand, the handle of which must have been fully fifteen feet in length. His eyes shone like balls of fire. His teeth, white as pearl, seemed fully an inch long. His nose, if you could call it a nose, was very large, broad and flat. His hair was very coarse, heavy and long. It hung down on his massive shoulders. His voice sounded more like the growls of a lion in a menagerie than anything I can recall.

"It was during one of these flashes of light that I first saw him. I trembled like an aspen leaf at the sight. He had his spear raised as if to send it flying through me. I suddenly stopped. With that terrible voice I seem to hear yet, he bade me follow him; that he had been sent to guide me on my journey. I followed him. What else could I do?

"After we had gone some distance, a huge mountain seemed to rise up before us. The part facing us seemed perpendicular, just as if a mountain had been cut in two and one part of it had been taken away. On this perpendicular wall I could read distinctly the words, 'This is hell.' My

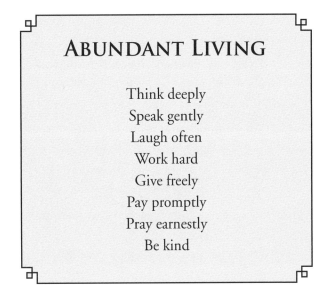

ABUNDANT LIVING

Think deeply

Speak gently

Laugh often

Work hard

Give freely

Pay promptly

Pray earnestly

Be kind

guide approached this perpendicular wall and with his spear handle gave three loud raps. A large massive door swung back and we passed in. I was then conducted on through what appeared to be a passage through this mountain.

"For some time we traveled in Egyptian darkness. I could hear the heavy footfalls of my guide, and thus could follow him. All the way I could hear deep groans, as of someone dying. Further on these groans increased, and I could distinctly hear the cry for water! water! water! Coming down to another gateway, and passing through, I could hear, it seemed, a million voices in the distance and the cry was for water! water!

"Presently another door opened at the knock of my guide, and I found that we had passed through the mountain and now a broad plain lay out before me.

"At this place my guide left me to direct other lost spirits to the same destination.

"I remained in this open plain for a time, when a being similar to the first one came to me; but instead of a spear he had a large sword. He came to tell me of my future doom. He spoke with a voice that struck terror to my soul. 'Thou art in hell,' he said; 'for thee all hope is fled. As thou passed through the mountain on thy journey hither, thou didst hear the groans and shrieks of the lost as they called for water to cool their parched tongues. Along that passage there is a door that opens into a lake of fire. This is soon to be thy doom. Before thou art conducted to this place of torment never more to emerge—there is not hope for those who enter there—thou shall be permitted to remain in this open plain, where it is granted to all the lost to behold what they might have enjoyed, instead of what they must suffer.'

"With this I was left alone. Whether the result of the terrible fright through which I had

passed I know not, but now I became stupefied. A dull languor took full possession of my frame. My strength departed from me. My limbs refused to support my body. Overcome, I now sank down a helpless mass. Drowsiness now took control of me. Half awake, half asleep, I seemed to dream.

"Far above me and in the distance, I saw the beautiful city of which we read in the Bible. How wonderfully beautiful were its walls of jasper. Stretching out and away in the distance, I saw vast plains covered with beautiful flowers. I, too, beheld the river of life and the sea of glass. Vast multitudes of angels would pass in and out through the gates of the city, singing, oh such beautiful songs. Among the number I saw my dear old mother, who had died a few years ago of a broken heart because of my wickedness. She looked toward me and seemed to becken me to her, but I could not move.

"There appeared to be a great weight on me that held me down. Now a gentle breeze wafted the fragrance of those flowers to me, and I could now, more plainly than ever, hear the sweet melody of angel voices, and I said, oh, that I might have been one of them.

"As I was drinking of this cup of bliss it was suddenly dashed from my lips. I was aroused from my slumbers. I was brought back from my happy dreamland by an inmate of my dark abode, who said to me that it was now time to enter upon my future career. He bade me follow him.

"Retracing my steps I again entered the dark passageway, and followed my guide for a time, when we came to a door that opened in the side of the passage, and going along this, we finally found ourselves passing through another door, and lo, I beheld the lake of fire.

"Just before me I could see, as far as the eye could reach, that literal lake of fire and brimstone. Huge billows of fire would roll over each other, and great waves of fiery flame would dash against each other and leap high in the air like the waves of the sea during a violent storm. On the crest of the waves I could see human beings rise, but soon to be carried down again to the lowest depths of the lake of fire. When borne on the crest of these awful billows for a time their curses against a just God would be appalling, and their pitiful cries for water would be heart-rending. This vast region of fire echoed and re-echoed with the wails of these lost spirits.

"Presently, I turned my eyes to the door through which I had a few moments before entered, and I read these awful words: 'This is thy doom, eternity never ends.' Shortly I began to feel the ground give way beneath my feet, and I soon found myself sinking down into the lake of fire. An indescribable thirst for water now seized upon me. And calling for water, my eyes opened in the prison hospital.

"I have never told this experience of mine before, for fear the prison officials would get hold of it, and think me insane, and lock me up in the crank house. I passed through all this, and I am well satisfied as I am that I am alive, that there is a Heaven and there is a Hell, and a regular old-fashioned Hell, the kind the Bible tells about. But there is one thing certain, I am never going to that place any more.

"As soon as I opened my eyes in the hospital and found that I was alive and on earth once more, I immediately gave my heart to God, and I am going to live and die a Christian. While the terrible sights of Hell can never be banished from my memory, neither can the beautiful things of Heaven that I saw.

"I am going to meet my dear old mother after a while. To be permitted to sit down on the banks of that beautiful river, to wander with those angels across the plains, through the vales and over the hills carpeted with fragrant flowers, the beauty of which far surpasses anything that mortal can imagine; to listen to the songs of the saved—all this will more than compensate me for living the life of a Christian here on earth, even if I have to forego many sensual pleasures, in which I indulged before coming to the prison. I have abandoned my companions in crime, and am going to associate with good people when I am once more a free man."

After he had got through with this wonderful story, I asked him if he was gong to tell others of his experience when he got out. His reply was that people would not believe him and he would keep it to himself. Should this little book fall into his hands and he should read of his experience while in Hell for forty-eight hours, it will no doubt surprise him. We give the account to the reader just as we received it from Lennox. We don't pretend to solve the mystery.

"Therefore, hell hath enlarged herself, and opened her mouth without measure; and their glory, and their multitude and their pomp and he that rejoiceth, shall descend into it"—Isa 5:14.

"And it came to pass that the beggar died, and was carried by the angels into Abraham's bosom; the rich man died, and was buried; and in hell he lifted up his eyes, being in torments, and seeth Abraham afar off, and Lazarus in his bosom. And he cried and said: 'Father Abraham have mercy on me, and send Lazarus that he may dip the tip of his finger in water, and cool my tongue, for I am tormented in this flame."—Luke 16:23, 24.

Friend, won't YOU give your heart to GOD? Why do you turn your back to the dear SAVIOUR who died that you and I MIGHT LIVE?

-Printed by
Gordonville Print Shop

A Long Walk for Man and Beast

When Jonas and Emma, daughter of Joshua Lapp, of Gap married in 1907 my Father gave them a cow as a wedding gift. They moved to Churchtown and Bro. Sam Lapp led her the whole way from Buena Vista to Churchtown to the farm where they moved—a distance of around 12 miles. Sam would have been 18 years old at that time.

-Aunt Susie Lapp

What You Don't Know Won't Hurt You

To Ben L. Miller of Stoneboro, PA, the butter mouse story happened in Lancaster, PA, many years ago. It happened for Sue Zook, 1881-1964. She was a sister to my great-grandfather John Lapp of Buena Vista. She was a widow for 34 years. She was known to be tight. Nothing wrong with being tight. The difference in tight and stingy is, if you're tight, you will sacrifice of yourself, if you're stingy, you will take advantage of your fellow man. But a mouse, fell into the cream and drowned. She couldn't make herself waste the cream, so she made butter. The next time she went to the store she took the butter along to be exchanged, as she said to the store keeper "What you don't know won't hurt you." So he took it to the back of the store and exchanged the wrapper and gave her the same butter back. "Yes," he said, "what you don't know won't hurt you!"

-Benuel Fisher

A Warning From God

Harvey L. Miller, 2013
Centerville, MI

December 28—Greetings to all Diary readers. The end of this year is almost upon us. When will the end of the world come? We don't know. The scriptures tell us to be ready, it will come as a thief in the night. When we pass away that is the end of this world for us. Then it is eternity.

In our last issue of Northland Newlink, the editor told a story that happened recently. A female judge in the Bay City, MI, area was driving on the expressway in her local area, I understand, when she came upon a hitchhiker. She felt compelled to stop and offer a ride. He was an elderly gentleman. It sounds as though he was not in the vehicle long when he said, "The trumpets will sound soon."

Startled, she looked over to see what he might have meant, and he was not there. She felt quite shaky and pulled over on the shoulder to catch her breath. A police officer stopped behind her to see if she needed help. When she told her story, the officer gave her a strange look.

"That's the fourth report we have received today," he said. Is this a warning from God?

24-Hour Sunshine

How would you like to live in a place where the sun shines continually every day? A friend of mine who has lived in South America for some time told me of such a place in Northern Chile. The interesting fact about this place is that no one lives there. There is too much sunshine. It never rains and nothing will grow there.

-Don Jennings

Wonderful Built Body

Lately I've been reading some very interesting bits and pieces of health information that I'll share with whoever is interested. Did you know your heart pumps twenty billion blood cells throughout the body. The human body depending on size, has approximately five quarts of blood which are constantly traveling through the entire body making three thousand to five thousand round trips a day! The body can go forty plus days without food possibly four days without water but less than four minutes without air (oxygen).

Life Begins at 80

We oldsters sure do get away with a lot just because we've managed to keep breathing longer than some folks.

I've just celebrated by 80th birthday and I've got it made; if I forget something . . . one's name, or an appointment, or what you said yesterday, then I just explain that I'm 80 and I'm forgiven. If I spill soup on my lap, or forget to wash half of my face or take another person's bonnet or hat by mistake, or promise to mail a letter and carry it around in my pocket for 2 weeks I just say I'm 80 you know and nobody will say a thing. You have a perfect alibi for everything when you're 80; if you act silly you are in your second childhood. Being 80 is much better than being 70; at 70 people are mad at you for everything but if you make it to 80, you can talk back, argue, disagree and insist in having your own way because everybody thinks you are getting a little soft in your head, they say that life begins at 40, not true if you ask me, life begins at 80, you'll see!

More Remarks of By-Gone Years *by John K. Lapp,*
Born 1897, Died 1987, New Holland

Now about a few inventions that I can remember coming in my time, which came mostly since 1900. The telephone and electricity of course came before that, I read once that when Alexander Bell was working on the phone about 1885, he did not have enough money to get it through, so he tried to borrow some at the banks, etc. They made fun of him and said nobody is dumb enough to believe that you could talk a distance thru a couple wires. They blamed him for being a fake and trying to get somebody's money for nothing, even threatened to put him in jail. They said even if he would get it done of what practical use would it be to anyone. At first the phone and electric was only in the towns and cities. I remember when there were hardly any poles and wires thru the country. About 1910 the pole lines were setup thru the country, and our Amish people, at least some of them got them and it did not seem to make trouble. Then a couple of women got to talking about another woman over the phone and this woman also had a phone. She had the receiver down and heard what they said. This made quite a stink and at last came into the *gma* to get it straightened out. Then the Bishops and ministers made out if that is the way they are going to be used we would better not have them. Some were willing to put them away and others were not. That is when the King *gma* started, the phone was one of the issues but I suppose there were some more. The Valley *deiner* came to help them and Christ King and John A. Stoltzfus were ordained on the same day I think. It seemed they could not agree long so they split. John A. Stoltzfus had the Weavertown *gma* a long time, had *gma* in the homes at first then they bought the Weavertown church house from the Dunkards. The Christ King *gma* never got very far and at last went to nothing, there is one sister living yet, age about 92. She goes to the Jake Zook *gma* now.

Now about the electric which came into use in the 1870s I think. Also only in towns and cities at first and only lights, motors, etc. came later. I well remember when no electric lines were in the country. Somebody invented the Delco electric home plants, our neighbor Ed Hoover got one put in his stripping room. It had a gas engine with generator and a bunch of storage batteries, they were good for lights but nothing for power.

I remember the first car in the neighborhood, Alf Reiser lived on the adjoining farm south of us, he used to jack it up in the fall and put blocks under the frame to save the tires etc., he could not use it in winter on account of muddy roads.

I remember the first flashlights, two of Dad's Coatsville customers came a day every summer. One Sunday when they came they had a flashlight along, we had a very dark room in the cellar so we took it down there to see how it works, it was new for them, and more so for us.

I remember when Corn Flakes were first sold in the store, which was the only cereal in the store; now the shelves are loaded with different kinds.

Oh yes I remember when we took hogs to Kunzlers, the butcher in Lancaster. Nearly always two loads at a time, two horse *blutz* wagon (no springs) we used to go to the Gap and take Route 30, it was not oiled then yet. Yes I remember the first potato planter in our neighborhood, Amos U. Stoltzfus (still single then) bought one and went around to plant other people's potatoes. We always planted ours by hand. I very well remember the first hay loader. Preacher Christ Glick had broke his leg at haying time and the neighbors came together to put his hay away, then (Vise) (white) Sam Stoltzfus came with a new hay loader, rake type which were before side delivery rake and web loader. I remember Dad saying they would have got done quicker

if Sam would have left that loader at home. Dad was not so much for these new improvements. He never had a hay loader, manure spreader, etc.

FARMING IN THE 1950'S
Sarah Stoltzfus

We are not old, yet no longer young either, so we can remember . . .

When public schools educated most of Amish children even they did not need all do the same, during blizzards, etc. if you could have school, you had!

The harvest of wheat was one of the highlights of the summer and the most strenuous.

Our people had little social gatherings during the week as most lived on farms.

The hunting of the pheasants and rabbits was exciting. Few went to the mountains to hunt deer!

Our parents yet spoke of the hardships of the Great Depression, though weren't embittered by them.

When even the newlyweds drove in buggies.

President Kennedy was shot and a crying woman stopped at the school telling teacher who ran in and turned the radio on and that was on every station.

Our dad owned a few motors and farming was a quiet and peaceful way to make a living.

There were no super jets, the largest airplanes we knew of flew within visibility and were called TWA's.

Little was known of lawsuits, our people hardly had any fear of them.

Weed killers weren't used much in fields, memories of hoeing weeds with dad through cornfields we have!

Cocoa came in brown tin boxes and Jello

in colorful pasteboard ones, bulk food stores just coming.

Many homemakers kept geraniums, coleus or begonia in tin can flower pots, petunias and marigolds were bought out of flats in town. Few greenhouses were around and most people didn't afford much more than vegetables needed.

The milk all went to market in large aluminum cans, and scrubbing them twice yearly was a dreaded job!

Corn bags were heated in the kitchen range and taken along to bed on cold winter nights for warmth!

Shoes were thrown in the spring time, partly to save leather. Going barefoot in youth crowds would've been unladylike!

Getting together to sing New Year *Lieder*, as well as for Christmas and for uncles' and aunts' birthdays was enjoyable.

To have, what we called bums or tramps, come in and ask for a meal was not unusual and mother always fed them well. They ate outside and slept in the barn. Sometimes we'd meet them on our way to school and I always felt a bit afraid. But there was no need to be. They never made us trouble. Many seemed to be unfortunate victims of the depression or World War II.

Many yet strove to have their own fruit trees. The only fruit was bought (aside of citrus) was peaches.

Sleigh rides to town or elsewhere was possible and fun and quite often done. The roads not being cindred yet, nor salted. People put chains on their tires!

No stores were open on Sundays and we seldom saw anyone working outside them either.

Generally speaking Amish children were not bold in public or among ourselves. Neither (most) of the young people. More of a sense of shyness prevailed.

Mother (or ours) as a whole didn't have much going on during the week. Though going to the store and to an occasional quilting was the expected thing.

Straw frolics were held for the straw hat Grannies, who sewed the straw hats together. After the straws were prepared and a number of grandmas (etc.) had plaited them.

Corn husking was done by hand the "little children" rode along in the back of the wagon while mother would help to husk!

MOTH'S SHADOW SAVES QUEEN OF DISASTER

You probably wouldn't expect to find a dead moth holding a place of honor in a museum, but at least one does. Why? Because one night that moth saved Britain's Queen Victoria.

The queen was aboard her luxurious, private railcar on a train bound for London. The train's crew was comprised of the best railroad men in the country. Each was keenly aware of the royal passenger.

There had been several storms that day, but the night was clear. Except for occasional patches of fog, the train rushed unhampered through the English countryside.

As the train entered an unusually heavy fog bank, the engineer quickly closed the throttle and slammed the train breaks. In the fog he had seen the darkened figure of a man frantically waving his arms for the train to stop.

The train hadn't come to a complete stop when the engineer jumped from the cab of the engine and ran up the tracks to find the man. He found no one.

At the same time, the queen's bodyguards surrounded the royal railcar. When the engineer reported what he had seen, and he couldn't find the person who had flagged down the train, the bodyguards prepared for the unknown and anticipated the worst.

The engineer was equally suspicious that something was wrong. He walked slowly down the track, deeper into the fog in front of the train. He was shocked to discover the train tracks dropped off into a raging rain-swollen river less than two hundred yards ahead of the train. The bridge had washed out.

As he hurried back to the train, the engineer discovered in the engine's dimmed headlight where the "man" he had seen had disappeared. A giant moth had crashed into the head lamp, apparently just as the train entered the fog. The moth had created a shadow on the fog like a silhouette on a white screen. Its outstretched wings had fluttered like the figure of a man waving his arms.

The name of the engineer is lost in history, but the moth is on display in the London Museum.

-Richard Bauman

A Mother's Day Thank-You to My Wife
by Amos and Lizzie Yoder, 2014

I woke up from my nap this Sunday afternoon to hear my wife making popcorn for the family. Nobody had asked for some. I don't have to beg or whine to get my everyday meals made, or for snacks on Sunday afternoons.

Last night we took our Saturday night bath. Our three boys and I didn't whine about not having clean clothes to put on, or ask on which couch or chair they might be found, because of not being put away. We simply walked to our dressers and got what was needed, again totally taking it

all for granted, not even thinking of the effort Mama put in to have this all lined out.

Church morning comes around and I'm not asking her if the Sunday clothes were washed and ironed. And again, never saying, "Thanks, Mama," we grab the clothes, change, and go to church, dirtying them again for Mama to start all over next week. Do we offer to start the water heater for her on washday mornings?

When I come home in the evenings from work, I might frown and wonder what's wrong if "she" didn't feel like keeping up the house that day. Even though most days everything is done and I don't express one word of appreciation for her efforts, even when supper is waiting on me. (Shame).

A man's tendency is to speak up when things are not done and take it for granted when everything is on time and done perfectly. If things don't go good one day for our wife, we can be a great spirit lifter to her by helping her in the evening and showing understanding instead of griping.

There is so much that a woman does behind the scenes. Nobody notices unless things are not done. The list of a housewife's duties is quite long and most of us men probably couldn't take the stress. Sick children, snotty noses, filled diapers, settling arguments, fixing lunches. It takes a mother to handle these tasks day after day, week after week and year after year.

A mother's love is the greatest love besides the love that Jesus showed at the cross. A marriage should have love flowing both ways. Do we men return that amount of love towards our wives when there are jobs she needs help with? Does she have to mention something way ahead of time and still barely get help when needed? Do we consider her our lower quality half, or our slave? Yes, the woman is under the man, but also we are taught to love her like Jesus loved us. So in our hearts we should grade her as better than ourselves.

If we men are so smart and have authority over our wives, let's prove ourselves real husbands and get that garden ready in the spring on time, without forcing our down-there wife to look up and beg for days before it ever gets done. Is it her garden or "our" garden? Is it her food or "our" food that grows in the garden? Are we actually too busy for our own gardens? If so, let's start buying everything at the grocery stores and forget about the "down-there wife's" garden.

In God's order man is to be over the woman, but not to walk over and treat her like she's good for nothing.

Patience is a must in marriage. There is no place for whining, threatening, and bad feelings. Men shouldn't lose authority over the home by listening to and respecting the woman's needs. Women shouldn't gain authority over the home by sharing advice, or by asking to have necessary duties done. Trust and love are needed on both sides, going each way. Even though 50% + 50% = 100%, man and wife can't both just go 50% and expect to meet the partner there. Both sides should aim for 100% and there will be no more sides. The overlap is where the sharing and love can thrive in. The 50/50 plan has a fence between man and wife which can create a bad setting to raise a family in.

Occupations do vary: in every occupation there are people who make/have time for family duties and there are some who very seldom make/have time. It's totally a choice of how important work is over our wife and family. We can plant a few less acres of corn or cut a few less loads of logs and get to enjoy values that should be first in life anyway. Our attitudes need adjustment if we can't afford to help our wife with some of those harder duties and even worse, if we can't do it in an en-joyable way. Gaining the whole world and losing our own souls will not have a happy ending.

A note from the writers: We are enjoying married life together and have plenty of bumps in the road of life. The above letter has a lot of room in our own marriage. My wife, family, and neighbors all know that I don't nearly get to those honey-do jobs like I should. May God bless everyone's efforts

NEW AMISH COMMUNITY EVERY 3.5 WEEKS

2014, Source: Ohio State University
Submitted by: Ivan Byler,
400 Folk Rd, Fredonia, PA 16124

A new census of the Amish population in the United States estimates that a new Amish community is founded, on average, about every 3.5 weeks, and shows that more than 60 percent of all existing Amish settlements have been founded since 1990.

This pattern suggests the Amish are growing more rapidly than most other religions in the United States, researchers say. Unlike other religious groups, however, the growth is not driven by converts joining the faith, but instead can be attributed to large families and high rates of baptism.

In all, the census counts almost 251,000 Amish in the United States and Ontario, Canada, dispersed among 456 settlements, the communities in which members live and worship. The 1990 census estimated that there were 179 settlements in the United States at that time.

If the growth of the Amish population continues at its current rate, the Ohio State University researchers predict that the census could exceed 1 million Amish and 1,000 settlements shortly after 2050, and these numbers will bring economic, cultural, social and religious change to the rural areas that attract Amish settlement.

Buffalo Snowstorm

Nov. 2014

Aaron A. Hertzlers

Mom and the siblings that had gone to the funeral in Iowa ended up being stuck in the train station in Buffalo for almost twenty-four hours due to the big snowstorm they had up there. People were saying they had six to seven feet of snow. I-90 was shut down from Tuesday morning sometime to Friday afternoon when they finally got it unstuck. Our neighbor was telling us how this one news reporter was speaking on TV Tuesday morning and telling how people are stuck in all the heavy snow then after the reporter left his job he headed for home and also got stuck in the storm.

Yes, we three girls made it home safely on Friday evening. We got to Buffalo, NY, on about schedule time early Friday morning but then had to wait about five hours till they finally got the roads open enough to have an escort get the bus out of Buffalo and I'd say so 20 miles out of there the roads were good enough that the police pulled off and let us get going on our own again. I probably got to see the biggest snow piles that I ever saw. I-90 was closed between Buffalo and Erie, PA, from Monday night to Friday morning. And I would be curious to know if there were ever Amish people stuck in a bus depot longer than 83 hours? Toby E. Mast and Leah R. Yoder of here could give you full details how that is to be stuck for so long. They left from Bridge, Canada, Monday morning and reached home on Friday evening. And I wouldn't doubt home looked very nice to them.

Our Greatest Danger

What is the greatest danger facing the plain people today? This is the question which was asked in the January issue of *Family Life*. The readers were invited to send in their opinions. The response was very good. We received more than fifty answers. We will not be able to use all of them and space will not allow us to use any of the letters in full.

MATERIALISM – PROSPERITY – TOO MUCH MONEY

Judging from the letters we received, the greatest threat facing the plain people today is prosperity, too much and too easy money. We received eighteen letters listing this as the greatest danger.

"I feel the greatest danger that threatened the people of God down through the ages and still does today is prosperity.

"Moses repeatedly warned the Israelites just before they entered the Promised Land that when things go well with them, when they possess a good land and lack nothing in it, when they have eaten and are full, then they are to beware lest they forget the Lord, their God. Yet in spite of all their warnings, this is exactly what happened. Not only once but many times over. As they prospered, they gradually turned to idols and were consequently oppressed by their enemies. When they were persecuted, it brought them back to God and He once more blessed them. But as soon as they prospered again, they began to slip until they were back to idol worship.

"We can say, 'Oh, no, we're not worshiping idols. We're not that bad.' But we may be worshiping the gods of materialism.

"The downfall of the Mennonites in Russia came about because of their prosperity. Seemingly the Mennonites and Amish in America are following the same trend.

"As you look around on every side you can see that as soon as money becomes plentiful, the tendency to spend more becomes stronger. If you go shopping with a pocketful of money, you see so many things that would be 'so nice to have' or 'too pretty to resist' and end up buying them. I know for myself that if I have only a little money to spend, I buy what is necessary and find a way to do without these other things.

"One thing I have noticed is how the older children in a family usually grow up to be plainer and do without many things. When the younger ones come along, they are apt to be finer and fancier and have many things the older ones would not have been allowed to have, or even thought of asking for. When the older ones were young the parents were still struggling financially but when the younger ones were growing up, money became more plentiful and these things started creeping in."

-Pennsylvania

A Friend in Danger

One of the best friends we have in our war with insects is the toad, and civilization threatens to destroy him. A great many toads are killed on the roads by autos, and larger numbers are destroyed by burning over fields and woods. But probably the greatest danger to toad life is drainage. This dries up the ponds and sloughs that serve as nurseries where baby toads are raised.

Meal time for toads begins about sundown and continues into the still small hours. Thus they take the night shift with birds in an almost continuous attack from spring to fall, on insect pests. Cutworms, white grubs, click beetles (from whose eggs wire worms are hatched), leaf chaffers, ants and a host of other bugs and worms enter into the toad's diet. He isn't a bit particular—any crawling, creeping thing tastes good to him.

The toad's looks and habits are against our regarding him with affection, but at least we ought to view him with respect. It would be too bad if we lost so able a helper in our annual shindy with the voracious insect world.

Satan's Tool

Here is a familiar story that needs repeating in these days. It is about the announcement that the devil was going out of business and would offer all tools for sale.

On the night of the sale, these tools were attractively displayed, and a badlooking lot they were—hatred, envy, jealousy, malice, sensuality, deceit, and all the other implements of evil. Apart from the rest lay a harmless-looking wedgeshaped tool, much worn and priced higher than any of the others. Someone asked the devil what it was.

"That is discouragement," was the reply.

"Why is it priced so high?"

"Because," replied the devil, "it is more useful to me than other tools. I can pry open and get into man's conscience with that, when I could never get near him with any other, and once inside I can use him with my discouragement in any way that suits me best. It is much worn because I use it with nearly everybody, as few people yet know that it belongs to me and that I use it to achieve my ends."

The price placed on discouragement was high, but the devil owns it still.

-Selected

Love Stronger Than Chains

-Author Remains Anonymous

A Good Slavery Story of Many Years Ago

The slave looked down at his bound limbs, and a shudder passed through his frame. Misery, hate and despair shone out of his dark eyes. He had brooded and planned and plotted, but his escape had not come. Would he ever be free of these chains that bound him? The shackles that fettered his feet?

His master knew why he guarded his slave so carefully, and this last night he was guarding the slave himself. Though it was impossible for him to escape, he was taking no chances. The master's eyes gleamed. The price of this slave was bound to be high. Slaves such as this were rare. Tomorrow in the market place he would get his pay—the nights he had spent watching and guarding, it was well worth it.

By the rattle of the chains he knew the slave was not asleep and he looked in. By the light of the moon he could see the slave's eyes upon him. The master was quite fearless but he drew back and shivered slightly. The slave's eyes were burning with hate. He would not have dared to be alone with this slave, unshackled. He knew which of the two were the stronger. He had kicked and beaten him, but he knew by the fire in the slave's eyes that his spirit was not broken. The slave would bide his time. No, the master would run no risks. Better to sell him now and pocket the money and be rid of one he could not trust. His former master had been eager to sell him. He no longer had need of a slave who was strong enough to build the pyramids of Egypt.

The slave lay in the darkness and listened as the night wore on. Sleep would not come to his eyes. He longed to move himself about and turn freely. Two desires burned within his heart. One was to get even with his master, and the other was to be free. How could he get his revenge, he a slave, in chains? And he thought of his first master, a cruel, hard man. He trusted no one.

The day dawned fair and bright. The sun rose, a shining orb in the heavens. The market place was crowded. The slave was warm and thirsty. When he was led forth, a murmur went through the crowd. He was tall, powerfully built. Slaves such as this were hard to find.

The bidders started. The slave stood before them. He was thirsty. When had he last had water? How he hated that crowd before him. Suddenly he burst out, "I will not work. Beat me, kill me, but I will not work." His manner said more plainly than words, "But I will fight." He shook his shackled arm menacingly at the crowd.

The bidders hesitated. Now and then they came across a slave such as this—dangerous and desperate. What good was a slave if he must be kept in chains and guarded? Or one who would not work? True, he could be flogged, beaten until his spirit was broken, but suppose it would not break? And a slave who fought when he had the chance? This one would no doubt try anything.

A man in the crowd pushed his way closer. He saw the slave. He saw the hate in the dark eyes, but he saw more. He saw hopeless misery. He saw the desperate gleam. The slave was dangerous, but he had never had a chance. He shook his money bag. How many coins were left? If only he were sure!

"The thing is not possible," he told himself. He thought of the long journey home, through rough and lonely land. He looked at the slave again. A reckless man, filled with hate. But what a shame! What a pity! The strength and intelligence of this young man. No doubt he had been taken captive in a fight. And now his life would be as well as lost. And he had no chance!

Suddenly, without thinking, the man put in a bid. On the other side of the crowd, another buyer pushed forward. He was a hard, thickset man. He too shook his money bag. He was rich. He had handled such slaves before. Either they gave up—or else. He had his own methods of breaking them. His eyes were cold and calculating as they looked over the slave. Yes, he would take the risk.

The bidding became more brisk. The crowd strained to see who these two were who dared buy such a slave. They saw a man slight of build, put in his bid again. Then the cruel slave trader put in his. They wondered at the first man. How could he handle such a slave? Had the slave been less fierce, they would have had pity for him. Not all the men in the market place that day were as the slave's master had been. There were those there who were merciful and kind to their servants. They thought of their families at home, and shook their heads. The noon sun was beating down. The crowd was beginning to melt away. Others stayed to see the outcome of the bidding. The slave trader was hot and tired. He had not eaten since sunup. He put in another bid.

The slight man on the other side felt his money bag again. If only he were sure of his coins! He looked at the man he was bidding against. He saw the hard face, the stout stick in his hand. He knew what life would be like with such a master. He gave his bid, and he knew it had to be his last.

He did not look at the slave trader again. It would be like a challenge. He tried to act indifferent, but now his heart hammered. He longed for the slave before him. His very fierceness told him how great a need there was, and though he knew he was risking his life, he had kept on bidding.

The slave trader hesitated. He looked at the man who was bidding against him. Why, the slave would have him down in a minute. The man was gazing off at some travelers who were approaching. He started to put in another bid, and the slave's future was in the balance. But the slave trader was hot and tired. He was hungry. The whole thing was a risk. Suddenly he shook his head. Let the other man pay such a sum. Let him find out!

Thaddeus, as the new owner was called, had the slave taken to a small room. So far, the slave's strength, and his consuming hate had sustained him. But now he sank down upon the straw. Long sleepless nights and days of weary travel had worn him down.

Thaddeus brought water and the slave drank eagerly. Then he sank back in complete exhaustion and misery. His plot had failed. His former master would pocket a large sum of money. What man was this who had dared to buy him? He knew his future was darker than ever. There was no hope of escape. A man who would pay such a price for him would take no chances. The slave was too tired to think. He dozed off.

He awakened to the sound of approaching voices. He heard one say, "Can you not see that you have bought a dangerous man? He will either run off or kill you, or do both."

"He has been badly treated," he heard a second voice say. "I am not taking him home in chains."

"It is a risk I would never take! He will cut your throat."

"My God," said the other, "can do marvelous things."

By now the voices had reached the little room. The slave seemed to be asleep. Thaddeus stopped on the threshold. He studied the sleeping man. He had spoken so surely to his companion. But the slave was not sleeping. Perhaps he felt

Thaddeus' gaze upon him, for he opened his eyes and looked directly at his new master. And what Thaddeus saw in the dark brooding face did not assure him. But had he not said his God could do marvelous things?

His voice was low and firm as he removed the shackles from the ankles of the slave. He unfastened the chains that bound his hands together. He examined the slave's wounds. The chains had worn away the skin and rubbed the flesh raw. The slave lay without speaking, his eyes half closed as his new master applied a soothing oil to his sores. How it cooled the burning flesh. He was too tired to move, but in his mind now burned one thought. Incredible! He was free! It would be easy enough to escape now.

What manner of man was this who had bought him? He had paid a high price for him. Perhaps he would have spies about the city to catch him. Had he set a trap for him? No man would pay such a price for a slave only to have him escape. He watched with half closed eyes as the man moved about. What was the master plotting? Having never known kindness he could not understand why he tended his sores so carefully.

He could not make him out—this new master. He was not much older than he, slight of build. It would be an easy thing to overpower him. He must be unlearned indeed, else why was he so careless? He laughed in derision as he remembered the new master's words, "My God can do marvelous things." He had seen the idols at Corinth. He had no fear of them. What kind of a God did his master worship, that he would be able to keep him bound to his master without chains? That could keep him from escaping?

But he did not flee that night. He would be wary. He would wait until they were out of the city. He watched Thaddeus closely. Though Thaddeus spoke to him, and told him what his

name was, the slave said very little. The less the man knew about him, the better. That night Thaddeus knelt down and prayed to his God. In the morning when he arose he again kneeled down and prayed, committing all to God. And the slave wondered.

The following day Thaddeus made preparations to leave. They each had a horse to ride and the slave laughed within himself as the thought how easy his escape would be—almost too easy. How foolish his master was—this Thaddeus, as he had said his name was. The master had wanted to know what his own name was. "I am called Demas," he had answered shortly.

As the horses were led in, Thaddeus could not fail to see the slave's look of pleasure and interest at the prancing steeds. And in his heart there was a ray of hope. The slave had not responded to any warmth or kindness. He could see that he did not trust him at all. Now, as he contemplated the journey home, alone with this slave, he wondered if he had indeed been mad. And yet he knew if he had not put in his bid he would never have been able to forget. Even if this Demas ended up in killing him, he would have at least done what he could. Now, seeing his look of pleasure at the horses, he knew that some spark of feeling, other than hate, was left in him.

As Thaddeus was lifting up a bundle on the back of his horse, the horse jumped and shied suddenly at a bit of trash, and the bundle tumbled to the ground, its contents strewed about. "My horse is skittish this morning. Would you hold him for me?" he asked Demas, as the slave stood watching.

Tying his own steed, the slave came. He had expected the master to fall upon the horse and beat him. Instead, with kind, firm hands he handled the high-spirited animal. Deftly he packed his bundle again and set it upon the horse.

The slave was puzzled. He could not figure it out. His master looked out for his slave's comfort as much as his own. His masters had always been rough cruel men. What manner of man was this? He regarded him with suspicion but now when he saw that he treated his horse as kindly as he treated his slave. . . .

"We are going home," the master had said to him. Going home. It seemed to him he remembered—but so dimly, a long ago day when he had been happy, and a mother's face had smiled down upon him. Then there had come cries and terror. Huge hands had caught him up and borne him away, to a hard bitter life. Now for years and years his one thought was to be free.

They made their camp that first night in a peaceful little grove. "Tonight I will go," he told himself. He did the duties assigned him, but he kept watching Thaddeus narrowly. He had not trusted him, until this morning when he had seen how he handled his horse. He would shake himself and turn away, and yet before he knew it he was watching him again. What was there in Thaddeus that attracted him? If Thaddeus had beaten him and chained him, he could have understood, but this kindness was quite beyond his understanding. Demas lay down to sleep and the master knelt first, and prayed; then he too lay down.

Now though he seemed to be asleep, he heard Demas move quietly. He longed to cry out, to plead with him to stay. He longed to tell him of the God who helped and gave succor in time of need, who set the captive free from hate and fear. But how could he teach him to trust God when he had not yet learned to trust him, his master?

Thaddeus broke out into a cold sweat. The slave had been sullen and quiet all that day. Thaddeus had talked. He had pointed out familiar landmarks along the way. He had talked of his God who ruled heaven and earth, a God who so loved the world that He gave His only Son Jesus. All those who believed on Him would be saved.

But Thaddeus had had no idea what his slave was thinking. And the master's talk had set the slave's mind churning with many thoughts and doubts. Demas had no fear of man-made idols, but an unseen God who ruled the heaven and earth, who made the thunders roll and the lightning flash, such a God one could fear. Thaddeus had said his God could do marvelous things. What man would dare take his slave, unchained, as Thaddeus was taking him, unless he had unseen powers? Would this God strike him down if he ran away?

But a God who ruled in love? He did not know the meaning of love. He had known only hate and force. . . . He was almost as good as free. . . . How easy it would be to go. He would have his revenge on those who had wronged him . . . But this master. He must be rich. What kingdom did he possess—what untold riches? No man would have bought him at such a price if he were not wealthy. A rich master who left his slave unguarded . . . But one who trusted in a powerful God . . . who was kind to his slave and beasts. . . . No wonder the slave's eyes had darkened and gleamed that day.

Now as Thaddeus lay with his heart beating wildly, he remembered vividly the slave's face that day. He prayed, and the minutes passed. He dared not open his eyes. Why did he not hurry, if he wanted to do something, this slave.

He felt movements by his side, and when he dared to look he saw that the slave lay quietly on the ground.

Now Thaddeus was overcome. God had spared his life. He had kept Demas from leaving. Suppose he, Thaddeus had left in fear when the slave had gone from his side. If Demas had come back and found him gone, what then? Truly, God had His hand over him. His emotion was so great that the tears rolled down his cheeks.

He was filled with an intense yearning, a longing so great, a love so deep for the poor slave before him. What was it that the dark night had revealed to him? He had thought he had cared for the slave before, but his feeling this morning was far different. He had felt the closeness of God, the love and care as God had watched over him that night. He had been in a hurry to reach home. Though he was not consciously afraid of Demas, he had felt that once with the sheltering walls of home surrounding him he would be safe. Now all feeling of haste was gone. God had spared his life for a purpose. Demas might harm him or kill him yet, but he had no fear of death. He knew that God could care for him as well in the lonely wilderness as in a village.

Demas awoke with a start. The sun was already high in the sky. He saw Thaddeus checking his horse's feet. Had not the master said they would start off early this morning? Seeing that the slave was awake, Thaddeus greeted him, but he noted that Demas was tense. He kept watching him, with an expression that Thaddeus could not make out.

He noticed how painstakingly Demas took care of his horse. Thaddeus did not ask the slave to do any tasks other than what a man would ordinarily do for himself, and these, Demas did without any word from Thaddeus. The slave had said he would not work. IF and when they reached home—time would tell. . . . As for now, Thaddeus, seeing the love Demas had for horses, talked to him about them but Demas gave little response. But it did not matter. Yesterday he had felt oppressed, burdened. Today he felt light. The weight was gone. He knew he had a God who could do marvelous things.

When they stopped to camp that evening, he noticed that Demas looked ill. With a few words he had the slave lying on the ground. His forehead was hot to his touch. Thaddeus had not made provisions for any illness. He had expected to be at home by that very evening, but he knew that another Hand was guiding their journey home. He bathed the slave's forehead, and brought him fresh water from the well where they had camped. He did not lie down to sleep until the fever had dropped, midnight had passed, and the slave lay quietly. He thought back to the night before, when he had lain in fear, wondering what would happen. This night he had been privileged to care for Demas and his heart rejoiced. Over and over, the slave had passed his hand before his eyes, as if to wipe out some memory.

Demas was better the next morning, but they did not travel on until the following day. Thaddeus could see that the man was weak. He knew if the fever returned, it would be much worse the second time.

Late in the afternoon of the next day they neared Thaddeus' home. They came to the valley and before them lay the master's home. He pointed it out to Demas. The slave looked in silence. He saw no palace, no fine buildings, no great lawns and gardens, no great flocks dotting the hillsides. He saw a humble dwelling. He saw the rough land and knew the hard, hard work that would go with it. He looked back at his master, but Thaddeus was gazing at his home. They had reached it in safety. He spoke in quiet words of thanksgiving to Demas. God had seen them safely through. They had not been attacked by robbers, or beasts of prey. He had protected them from numberless dangers. Now they would thank God in praise and thanksgiving. "Tomorrow," said Thaddeus, "we will talk of certain matters."

That night the slave rose again. He stood silently for a time gazing out into the darkness. This was the night he must make his getaway. He had now seen his master's kingdom. But the master was not rich. Why had he bought him? What matters did Thaddeus want to talk over with him, his slave? Maybe he should wait until the next night to go. "Then you will never get away," whispered a voice. "Go now." He was pulled one way and then another. But finally he turned and lay down upon his bed.

The next morning the master came. His face was drawn and strained. But he smiled as he handed a paper to Demas. The slave took it. Curiously he unfolded the paper. He looked in disbelief from the paper to Thaddeus. The words seemed to leap out at him, words he had never dared to dream of seeing. He was free! Free! He would not have to live the life of the hunted, life in hiding and fear, fear of being found and put in bondage again. Free to move about, do as he pleased—free to find his old master and pay back a black debt! He gripped the paper tightly. His exultant feeling had suddenly passed.

He looked at Thaddeus, but he had turned and was looking out the window. Other thoughts now crowded his brain. He had not let himself trust this Thaddeus. He did not want to. He must escape. He must have his revenge. If Thaddeus had made one move towards him—one false move, it would have been too bad for Thaddeus. But Thaddeus had made no false moves. He had nursed him in his fever. He had shown him a way of life that the slave had not known before. He had felt it drawing him—pulling him and he had pushed it away. He had lived on hate too long. . . . Now the master had given him his freedom. There was no need to escape now. He was free. But the exultant feeling was gone.

"Why," he demanded, "why did you pay such a price for me—you a poor man, only to set me free?"

"You knew I was dangerous. You knew I would fight, and yet you brought me unchained through this wilderness, when you knew I might kill you, only to set me free?"

"Yes," answered Thaddeus, "I knew you might kill me, but God is very great. He can do marvelous things. I trusted my God. This same God who loves and watches over me loves you, oh how He loves you!" And the voice of Thaddeus broke. He turned to the window to hide his emotion. Had it all been for naught? Would Demas leave him, untouched by the love of God?

Thaddeus felt he must cry out, he must plead with him but he was silent. He had freed a dangerous man. Where would he go and what would he do? Doubt and uncertainty filled him. He thought of the night on the desert, when God had been so near. He put his head into his hands and prayed.

There was silence in the little room. The slave gazed on the bowed head of the man who had bought him and freed him from his chains. He had felt that tightening within him that night in the desert. Now it gripped him. He

---

Our daughter-in-law was telling Bible Stories to their girlies and explained the picture of the Crucifixion saying they nailed Jesus to the cross so we can go to Heaven. A few days later she found three-year-old Kathryn struggling to hold her kitty on its back to a board, with hammer in hand. When asked whatever she is trying to do, she said she wants to nail the kitty to the board "so she can go to Heaven!"

-Pete C. Yoder
Chetopa, KS

knew now what he could not believe before. The hard stone wall was crumbling away. It would not stay, it melted before the bowed figure of Thaddeus.

"I once thought to harm you," Demas said, brokenly. "But now you have bound me. You have bound me with something stronger than iron chains. And yet . . ." The slave's face lighted with a dawning joy, "And yet your chains are light, lighter than feathers. You have bound me with love. You have shown me your God and I see it now. He is a God of love."

At these unexpected words from Demas, Thaddeus was overcome. Finally he spoke, "Then you will not leave?" Was it possible, this man who had been so fierce, so full of hate? What miracle had God wrought?

The slave shook his head. He handed back the paper that stated he was a free man. Never had he felt as free as in that moment.

"I will not leave you," said Demas quietly.

In that moment Thaddeus had a glimpse of the true worth of the man he had bought and freed. He handed back the paper to Demas. "Then we will be as brothers," he said, as he gripped his hand. "Truly, our God can do marvelous things!"

FOR TIRED AND BUSY MOTHERS

Enjoy your work, even washing out messy diapers, and be thankful you have them to wash out.

Let your baby sleep outdoors on nice days, protected from the wind. Don't let the sun shine in his eyes. He will sleep better. If he cries, put him in his coach, if you have outdoor work. If he continues to cry after you have done all you could for him, let him cry. You can stand it better outdoors. Talk to him and sing.

I started this when my baby was two weeks old and the weather was not too cold, or stormy. He slept outside all winter and hardly had any colds.

Stop feeding him during the night as soon as possible for mother and baby need a night's sleep. I let one of our babies cry for one hour one night when she was 6 weeks old. I read once that crying will not cause a rupture. Since then, she never asked for a feeding during the night. At times she was wide awake and kicking. A cool, well-ventilated room helps.

Learn to relax. I try to do my work for the wellbeing of my family instead of trying to keep up with my neighbor. Spend time with the little ones; they'll soon be grown. What if the yard has a weedy borderline and dirt waits to be swept away!

Take children along when convenient, even though it takes a little longer. Teach them to do little things, such as, putting away their own toys when done playing, hanging up their clothes, making their beds, and countless other things. Let them have their own little garden.

Learn to enjoy the necessities of life instead of letting it be a drag. This can be our best medicine. Should not a Christian be cheerful, which is hardly possible when burdened with overwork. How many nasty words could be avoided if we would practice good honest labor and not so often overwork. The cause of this may often be for a bigger income and not just to make ends meet. When the income is bigger it is too often spent freely for things that could be done without. The more we have the more we want. The less we have the more we learn to be satisfied with little.

Feed babies 4 or 5 times a day. Never give feeding closer together than 3 hours unless when nursing and they weren't satisfied with the feeding before. If they are too insistent, I allow a half hour earlier. Feeding too often will upset them.

-One who has learned from experience and wishes to learn more

WHAT'S A GRANDMOTHER?
Letter from a Third Grader

A grandmother is a lady who has no children of her own. She likes other people's little girls and boys. A grandfather is a man grandmother. He goes for walks with the boys, and they talk about fishing and stuff like that.

Grandmothers don't have to do anything except to be there. They're so old that they shouldn't play hard or run. It is enough if they drive us to the market where the pretend horse is, and have lots of dimes ready. Or if they take us for walks, they should slow down past things like pretty leaves and caterpillars. They should never say "hurry up."

Usually, grandmothers are fat, but not too fat to tie your shoes. They wear glasses and funny underwear. They can take their teeth and gums off.

Grandmothers don't have to be smart, only answer questions like, "Why isn't God married?" and "How come dogs chase cats?"

Grandmothers don't talk baby talk like visitors do, because it is hard to understand. When they read to us they don't skip or mind if it is the same story over again.

Everybody should try to have a grandmother, especially if they don't have a television, because they are the only grown-ups who have time.

Tom's nephew Bill Hershberger and wife Susan told us an unusual story about their one-year-old Micah. The children were playing marbles one evening and left the game out. During the night Micah was awake for three hours and very restless. Susan finally gave him Motrin, thinking he's getting sick. The next day she changed his diaper and found six marbles. He kept passing marbles for the next 48 hours. He passed 40 marbles altogether. The next day he was their happy little boy again. We have all heard of people losing their marbles (in fun). This time the marbles were literally lost . . . and . . . found! All's well that ends well.

Editor's Note, after checking into this story this is the letter I got back from Tom Bylers:

Dear Botschaft printers, we had to chuckle when your letter came in the mail not believing this marble story.

But I can tell you this story is 100 percent true. I did not get it from hearsay. The story came straight from the boy's mom and dad. They told it to us face to face right here in our house.

So I can assure you this is a true happening. The marbles were the oval-oblong flat marbles. This little boy will be two years old in November and big for his age but it did happen in October.

-Mrs. Thomas Byler, 2014
Carlton, PA

6 Amish Barns Set on Fire in 2 Hours

BELLEVILLE, PA—Six Amish barns were set on fire by an arsonist within two hours March 14, killing 177 horses and cows, the Associated Press reported

The fires crippled the Amish farming community at the beginning of planting season. Some of the Amish had been plowing fields to prepare for planting this month. The fires took their horse teams, plows and seed.

The fires also killed dairy cows, whose milk is the only source of income for many farmers during the winter.

Twenty-four fire companies from four counties fought the fires. A concrete company was solicited to carry extra water in its cement trucks.

After putting out the fires, firefighters went from house to house warning farmers to watch their barns.

Area resident John Yoder said the community would have a busy season of barn-raisings, in which Amish neighbors build a barn in a day.

-1992

Pennsylvania Amish Raise Barns After Arson Spree

Belleville, PA—Amish from across Pennsylvania are helping the six Amish farmers whose barns were set on fire within two hours March 14 in the Big Valley of central Pennsylvania.

The losses totaled up after the Saturday night fires were more disastrous than the $1 million price tag implied, according to an article originally published in *The Baltimore Sun*.

Included in the losses were 139 cattle, the main livelihood on these dairy farms; 38 horses, among them the big Belgian draft animals that pull plows and hay wagons; the plows and wagons; seed for this year's planting; milking sheds and equipment; and four old threshing machines that are almost irreplaceable because the Amish have religious rules against using more worldly technology.

MONDAY MORNING March 16, in buggy after buggy, Amish began arriving with picks and shovels at all six farms. By late afternoon they had cleared the rubble and buried the dead animals.

On March 17 they marked and dug foundations for new barns. Scores of Amish began arriving in vans and buses from other Amish communities in the state.

More than 100 men worked at each site, neglecting the chores of their own farms to begin raising the frames of the new barns. Oak beams were sawed from the forests at the edge of this central Pennsylvania valley.

Clair DeLong, who was Mifflin County's agricultural extension agent for 30 years, said some of the Amish families are lucky to clear $3,000 a year. So dropping everything on the verge of spring planting to help a neighbor for a few weeks is to risk financial ruin.

So far there have been no arrests for the arson. Authorities say there are no suspects.

-1992

Six Torched Barns Rebuilt in 20 Days; Amish Get Donations and Media Attention

BELLEVILLE, PA—Six Amish barns, set on fire by an arsonist the night of March 14, were rebuilt in 20 working days, and people across the country gave more than $650,000 to help the families recover their losses.

As the Amish faced a major tragedy with the help of Mennonite Disaster Service and non-Amish people, the exposure they received brought them in contact with the world in new ways.

News of the Saturday night fires spread quickly over the Kishacoquillas Valley, known as the Big Valley, in central Pennsylvania. By Monday, the Associated Press had distributed the news of the tragedy across the United States. Later CNN television carried it across North America.

THE FIRES, in a 22-mile circuit, were a major loss of livelihood for the Amish families. Livestock, farm machinery, buggies and work horses needed for planting spring crops were destroyed in the fires.

Samuel Moses Yoder lost 11 Belgian work horses, one of which he had purchased a month earlier for $3,000.

The Old Gap School was also set on fire. Firemen responding to the other fires saw it and were able to save most of the structure, now used mainly for storage.

Telephone calls came to Ivan and Ruth Peachey, MDS

> *"I have about 70 telephone calls a day from people offering to help." —Ivan Peachey, MDS*

After an arson fire, a new barn was built for Crist R. Yoder, son of Bishop Sam Z. Yoder, along Coffee Run Road near Reedsville. During the fire, wind blew the heat away from the farm house, only 15 yards from the barn, and firemen were able to save it.

coordinators. The Kishacoquillas Valley National Bank collected donations. More than 20,000 letters of inquiry and sympathy were received by mid-April.

Five Amish bishops and the people who lived on the farms where the barns had burned met at the bank and distributed the donations equally among the six families.

By early May the donations surpassed $650,000. No more donations are needed.

ON MONDAY, March 16, MDS organized more than 300 volunteers with bulldozers, tractors, skid loaders and trucks. Deep pits were dug to bury dead animals, charred structures and ashes. By evening all six barns were cleaned up. At one place new footing was being poured.

In 20 working days, trees were cut, logs sawed, beams mortised and tenoned, and the outside walls and roofs rebuilt for six barns. Many Amish, Mennonites and "English" from Pennsylvania, Virginia and Ohio worked on the barns.

Work continues in the rebuilding of granaries, stalls, milk houses and silos.

The Amish have appreciated in a new way the help of the wider community and other church people. An Amish committee had expressions of thanks published in local newspapers.

-Reported by Lee H. Kenagy, 1992

FARMING IN THE 1940'S

I will start with filling silo as that is something that I can remember so well as a five year old. We were at the breakfast table then somebody said here comes Uncle Sam Lapp in the lane. He had the tractor and cutter; the field of corn was right behind the barn close to the silo. Then I saw the boys line up with each a corn chopper about 5 or 6 of them. They went out thru the field and each took a row. Then other men and boys with wagons started loading the corn up and took it to the cutter. I think there were 5 or 6 farmers that helped each other if nothing went wrong with the tractor or cutter. The 10 by 50 silo could be filled in a day.

Then about threshing—everybody farmed wheat so there was a lot of threshing to do with not so many threshing rigs around. Dad always hauled his wheat in the barn then when the peo-ple were done the ones that threshed right out of the field then they threshed for the ones that had it in the barn. Most times was beginning of August. A very dusty job as we baled ours with a stationary baler that came with the threshing rig. Some people just blew it in a mow. Also heard of some people that took a mule along and left him tramp it down.

About hay making, that was done in later part of June. That was mixed hay, Timothy and clover not much alfalfa. A five foot ground drive mower was used no crimpers then yet. A hay loader was used till the beginning of the 50's when the balers came out. Probably some of you readers do not know what a hay loader was. You towed it behind a wagon then as it went the hay went up the loader right on the wagon. Two men were on the wagon evening it out and loading it nice. Then for unloading hay once it was in the barn, there was a track in peak of barn with a trolley like thing with fork to grab the hay off of wagon and took it up and dumped it in hay mow.

Corn husking in fall of the year when the corn was ripe. Dad chopped the corn and put in shocks. Then the next job was husking corn. Shocks were tore down and the corn husked and hauled into corn crib. Corn fodder was set up again in big shocks to dry a little more. Then that was for bedding and cows also ate some which saved on hay.

Field work, walking plow is what you used then. Was a little like a garden shovel har-

row with two handles. That was the first plow I used at age 14 or 15 years of age. It was very easy if you had a nice field. About all you had to do was just keep hold of the handles and guide it a little and that wasn't much. From walking behind that plow four hours or so gave you a good appetite, also good sleeping. A farmer spent a lot of time in fields those days. Shovel harrowed corn 3 times.

Dad had around 20 or so cows milked by hand of course.

-LF

HOUSEKEEPING IN THE 1940S

Houses were plain, very little running water, no flush toilets or bathtubs. Baths were taken once a week under normal conditions. You just got a bucket of warm water, soap and wash cloth and went in a bedroom or some private room to do it. Grocery bill was not much at that time. We had a big garden. Lots of canning was done, plus milk and eggs were right there on the farm. Also butchering was also done in winter time to last for the year, you did not have to buy meat. About heat, kitchen was the only room with heat and that was only a cook stove that burned coal or wood so bedrooms upstairs were cold but that was alright you had plenty of covers. At that time, there was no propane either. I remember when it was first used around 1950 maybe. Everybody took church in their houses, no basements or shops although church was at

times in upper barns in warm summer months so we knew what it was like to move furniture around and make room for church services when the time came.

About outside work, only push mowers were used. Power mowers were not allowed. In those days you didn't have so much mowing. No big yards as of now. We only mowed the inside yard like around the house. Outside you used sheep if you had them or leave the horses out. At that time everybody had an open carriage no storm fronts. Although a few had market wagons but were not used much on Sundays. Since there was no propane in the '40s, Dad had an ice refrigerator instead of like we have upper part of refrigerator is freezer. Ice refrigerator looks much like that except that is where the ice was put. Ice man came around once a week to put a chunk of ice in but only in summer months.

-LF

STATEMENT

—

LANCASTER, PA. _8/30_ 193_9_

Levi Fisher

ACCOUNT OF _Levi Fisher Jr._

THE LANCASTER GENERAL HOSPITAL, Dr.
528 NORTH LIME STREET

ALL ACCOUNTS MUST BE FULLY
SETTLED BEFORE LEAVING HOS-
PITAL. PLEASE DO NOT ASK US
TO MAKE EXCEPTIONS TO THIS
RULE.

BILLS PAYABLE WEEKLY

M	TO			
		Ward Rate @ $ Per day for days		
8/21	8/30	Board and Room @ $ 5⁰⁰ Per day for 9 days	45	00
8/21		Use of Operating Room and Anesthesia	7	50
		Use of Delivery Room and Care of Baby		
		Use of Ambulance		
		Board of Special Nurses days @ Nights @		
		X-Ray Service		
8/21		Drugs		75
		Physiotherapy Treatments @		
8/21		Laboratory Examinations	5	00
8/21		Telephone		15
		Cots @ Trays @		.
		Receiving Ward		
		Heart Test		
			58	40

RECEIVED PAYMENT

30 1939

LANCASTER GENERAL HOSPITAL

Per _A.M.W._

Relationships That Matter

When I was a boy in the 1950s, we lived in a close-knit mountain community. We spent time helping each other with field work, with construction projects, and with butchering. In summer, it was common on a Friday or Saturday evening for neighbors to gather on each other's front porches to visit, sing, and tell stories. While the older people visited, the children would play hide-and-seek and other games in the gathering twilight.

But things began to change. One of our neighbors bought a television. His family would sometimes invite certain neighbors over on Friday or Saturday evening to watch television shows. Then others wanted to come, but that became old. Our neighbor said, "Why don't you get your own TV?" And so, in a period of about six years, the community went from having no television to almost every family owning one. Sadly, something else happened too. Those times of neighborly gatherings all but stopped. The television and the outside world became the focus. The resulting changes in our community were dramatic.

Now sixty years later, the social change continues with the Internet and social media. Neighbors and families are becoming more disconnected as people focus on the outside world. People live in a world of "friends" outside the home and community, often with devastating effects on the relationships that truly matter.

Even worse is the way that television and the cyberworld affect people's relationship with Jesus Christ. Now people have even less time for the relationship that matters most today and in eternity. Are we cultivating and building that relationship? What robbers of time are we allowing to hinder the work of Jesus in our lives?

-Roger Berry (Dayton, VA)

Points From Here and There

While somewhere in the world, ten thousand people are dying of starvation every day, Americans are spending fifty million dollars a year for reducing pills.

Thirteen times as many African as American infants die before the age of five. Meanwhile, Americans are spending over four billion dollars a year for toys.

In the United States there is one doctor for every 650 people. In Ethiopia there is one doctor for every 72,000 people.

The average Asian consumed 400 pounds of grain per year. It takes 2,000 pounds of grain a year for every American. Of this amount only 150 pounds is consumed directly in the form of bread, pastries, cereals, etc. The rest is used up to produce meat, milk and eggs.

For every $2.50 the bigger nations like the United States spend for relief in helping undeveloped countries, they spend $100 for guns and armament.

The United States uses three million tons of fertilizer each year on its lawns, golf courses and cemeteries—which would be enough to produce about thirty million tons of food and keep millions of people from starving.

-1975

One Solitary Life

He was born in an obscure village, the child of a peasant woman. He grew up in still another village where he worked in a carpenter shop until he was thirty. Then for three years he was an itinerant preacher. He never wrote a book, he never held an office. He never had a family or owned a house. He didn't go to college. He never visited a big city. He never traveled two hundred miles from the place he was born. He did none of the things that usually associates with greatness. He had no credentials but himself. He was only 33 when the tide of public opinion turned against him. His friends ran away. He was turned over to his enemies and went through the mockery of trial. He was nailed to the cross between two thieves. While he was dying, his executioners gambled for his clothing, the only property he had on earth. When he was dead he was laid in a borrowed grave through pity of a friend. Nineteen centuries have come and gone, and today he is the central figure of the human race and the leader of mankind's progress. All the armies ever marched, all the navies ever sailed, all the Parliaments ever sat, all the kings that ever reigned, put together, have not affected the life of man on earth as much as that.

THEODORE ROOSEVELT

When Theodore Roosevelt St. and his wife, Martha Bulloch Roosevelt, welcomed their second child on October 27, 1858, they had high hopes for their son. Beginning at age three, however, the boy was plagued by severe asthma and he remained small and weak. In 1870, a concerned Theodore Roosevelt Sr. approached his twelve-year-old son and told the boy that through hard work he must make his body as strong as his mind.

At that moment, the young boy resolved to overcome his challenges and prove himself to both his father and the world. Surely his parents could not have guessed that their once-sickly child would plunge into life with an unstoppable spirit and become the powerful and well-loved Theodore Roosevelt.

Raised with a large, loving family and the privileges of the aristocratic class, young Teddy Roosevelt did nothing halfway. Each day he improved himself by lifting weights, boxing, hunting, and indulging his passion for reading and nature. When he left for Harvard in 1876, his family expected him to become a naturalist. But after graduation, Roosevelt became involved in the world of local Republican politics. There the bespectacled Roosevelt, with his boundless energy, toothy grin, and unapologetic manner, found his calling. He was elected as governor of New York in 1898 and became vice president of the United States just two years later. Though he had aspirations of becoming president, his time came sooner than expected. In September 1901, President William McKinley was assassinated, and Theodore Roosevelt suddenly had a monumental new responsibility.

As age forty-two, Roosevelt was the youngest president in history, but years of fighting personal and public battles had prepared him for his responsibilities.

BORN: October 27, 1858
DIED: January 6, 1919
ACCOMPLISHMENTS: Vice President and President of the United States

Die Kinder Zucht

In Kinder Zucht ein groffer gewinn,
So Kommts mir vor in meinem finn;
Wo Die geiftliche liebe geht voran,
Da ift dann fhom gar viel getan.

Die Kinder Zucht geht viel verloren,
Es beweiß fich in den letzten yahren;
Weil wolluft, Ghregeiz und bofheit,
Möcht fpäter kriegen herzeleid.

Die Kinder Zucht geht oft vergeffen,
Weil wir unf viel auf geld verlauffen,
Und ganz zu viel thun nach dem ftreben,
Wo uns nicht hilft ins ewige leben.

Wanns mit der zucht dann geht verfehlt,
So kommt die zeit das es uns noch quält,
Weil die nature foll zuerft gebrochen fein,
Sonnft bringts noch ftreit in die gemein.

Da nocht fein arbeit aufhand,
Berhüten unliebe, widerftreben und fhand;
Rartfpielen, Tanzen und Hurerei
Wird öfters erfunuen noch babei.

Die Kinder, die keine ftraf thun kreigen,
Tun oft die eltern noch fehr betrüben;
Wann die liebe dann ift nach rechter art,
So treibt die ftraft doch nicht fort.

Wer die vechte liebe zu ihnen hat,
Der hilft ihnen nicht in hochmuth fort;
Mmit kleider prawt und über muth,
Bis unliebe dann auf fteigen thut.

Un Kinder Zucht ift iel gelegen,
Tut eir pflicht fo folgt Gottes Segen.

Wo nicht, fo fteht ihr in gefahr,
Nicht zu kommen zu der Heifigen Shaar.

Die rechte Zucht gibt das fundament,
Von der gemein, fofht bis aus end,
Wann das zu viel verloren geht,
Dann wirds falz dumm, menn das gefhieht.

Wenn ihr als auf dem wege geht,
Denkt doch daran, was euch zufteht,
Und lehrt fie recht von Jefus Chrift,
Wie Er uns doch fo gnädig in.

Und wann ihr nieder fitzt zu effen,
Eut das wieder nicht vergeffen;
Auch wann der abend kommt herbei
Denk doch baran was dein pflicht fei.

Und Gott auch bittne, wann Er will,
Sie doch balten Reufch und ftill;
Vor Lafter, Sünd, recht Ubfchei haben;
Röftlich find doch folche Gottes gaben.

Hochmuth follten fie nicht lieben,
Vilemehr fich an Demuth üben,
Und fich Dünken klein und fchlecht,
Die liebe üben gut und recht.

Was due fie erft gewöhneft baren,
Das ift hernach gar leicht getan;
Gewohnheit=hat gar grofze kraft,
Viel gutes und viel Vofes fhaft.

Wir haben kinder grofs und klein,
Ein gefhenk von Gott, fo fie gehorfen fein.
Haben deheim noch viel arbeit,
Dann eur fürbitt vonnöten alle zeit.

MADALYN O'HARA'S REMAINS FOUND

She is the woman who worked hard to get the Bible and Prayer out of the schools and public places. She was robbed and murdered in Texas. She was born on Palm Sunday, 1919. Her parents were very devout Christians in a Presbyterian Church in Pittsburgh. She was baptized and attended church regularly. Then as a teenager she announced, "I don't believe in that stuff anymore," and became a very wicked woman.

She was known as the most hated woman in America and loved to be called that.

PRAYER REMOVED FROM SCHOOLS

Some of you recall in 1963 a Madalyn Murry O'Hara directed a campaign to remove prayer from public schools. And was successful in early fall 1963. Later on she disappeared, along with 2 of her family associates.

Just last week her dismembered body was found near Camp Wood, TX, was identified by the Serial No. on a hip replacement part (she had this surgery).

Recall the Lord's Prayer was taken out of the public schools about Sept. Then in late Nov. President Kennedy was shot. Then the whole country prayed.

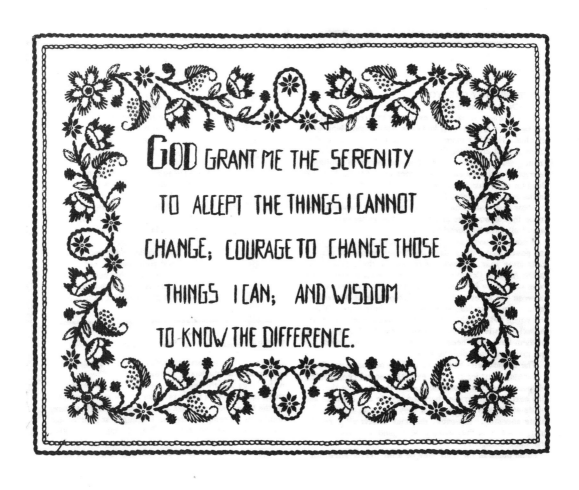

GOD GRANT ME THE SERENITY TO ACCEPT THE THINGS I CANNOT CHANGE; COURAGE TO CHANGE THOSE THINGS I CAN; AND WISDOM TO KNOW THE DIFFERENCE.

Meditations of Psalm Twenty-Three

by E.L.

THE LORD IS my shepherd. . . . We are His lambs. As a shepherd takes care of his lambs, so will He take care of us. He will never leave us nor forsake us (Hebrew 13:5 altered).

I shall not want. . . . The Lord supplies all our needs. If we love Him, what more do we need? Material things are of little importance if our focus is on God. Sometimes it is hard for us to trust Him. We are afraid to leave everything in His hands. Oh, what a blessing if we can simply trust and find sweet rest in Him, our Shepherd.

He maketh me to lie down in green pastures. . . . Just as a shepherd knows his sheep cannot travel on and on, so the Lord "makes us to lie down in green pastures" to refresh us. Time spent reading the Bible, visiting shut-ins, or other lonely people, or writing letters can refresh and inspire us spiritually.

He leadeth me beside still waters. . . . A shepherd can lead his sheep to water, but he cannot make them drink. Likewise, through conviction, the Lord can lead us to read the Bible and to go to church, but if we do not truly meditate on and listen to what the ministers are saying, we are refusing the water our Shepherd is offering us. Let us drink and be satisfied.

He restoreth my soul. . . . Even when we make mistakes the Lord is there ready to help us if we ask Him. He wants to restore peace to our soul and help us get up and go on. But if we are not ready to confess and repent, He will not force us. We need to humble ourselves, then He can work in our hearts.

He leadeth me in the paths of righteousness. . . . It is the Lord's will that all should walk in paths of righteousness, yet it is our free choosing. He gave us each the ability to make our own choices. What a blessing it would be if we always kept our focus on Him and trusted Him to lead us through whatever comes. If we feel we can't go on or that life is too hard, then we are not trusting in Him.

For His name's sake. . . . Our Lord is perfect. His life was perfect. Therefore He leads us in paths of righteousness, so we can be perfect in Him. When we sin, we bring disgrace to His name. But if we dwell in Him, we can be made perfect through grace. He commanded, "Be ye therefore perfect, even as your Father which is in heaven is perfect" (Matthew 5:48).

Yea, though I walk through the valley of the shadow of death. . . . Sometimes life may seem so dark we can hardly see our way through. It is then

DECISION LEFT TO THE HORSE

In the 1876 Amish Church split two young couples were good friends and didn't know which church they wanted to go. On Saturday evening before church the one couple went to see where the other couple is going to church the next day. At midnight neither of them had decided which church they were going to. The next morning both couples let their horses go the way they wanted to go. Both horses took them to the Old Order Amish Church. Later both of these men were ordained ministers in the Amish Church, and the one was also ordained Bishop in the Amish Church.

we need to trust and let the Lord help us. We cannot of ourselves "climb out of the valley," but will only go in deeper if we refuse to ask the Lord for help.

I will fear no evil for thou art with me. . . . What a special thought! We need fear no evil. The Lord will be with us even if we don't realize it. If we love Him, we can say like David, "I will fear no evil, for thou art with me."

Thy rod and Thy staff they comfort me. . . . With the Lord's help there is no obstacle too large for us to conquer. What was the purpose of the rod and staff? The rod was used to drive wild animals away, the staff for the shepherd to pull his sheep to him. God's power can keep Satan away from us. When God in His love allows things into our life to draw us to Him, let us not struggle against Him.

Thou preparest a table before me in the presence of mine enemies. . . . The Bible is like a table on which spiritual food is spread. Even if we are surrounded by earthly cares, troubles, sorrows, and Satan's snares, we can face each day by partaking of the food the Lord has provided to keep our soul strong.

Thou anointest my head with oil. . . . If the Lord's pure oil of love and joy is poured upon us, how can we help from being loving and happy? If we truly live for Jesus, He will bless us with the anointing of His love.

My cup runneth over. . . . Daily living for Jesus makes our cup of true joy, happiness, and contentment full and running over. Living for others, not for self, going the second mile, and accepting the circumstances, then making the best of them, will bring true joy.

Surely goodness and mercy shall follow me all the days of my life. . . . As long as we live, the Lord will be with us. He is always merciful and ready to forgive us when we do wrong. We can never live a perfect life, but if we ask God to help us, we can withstand temptation and receive forgiveness through the blood of Jesus Christ.

And I will dwell in the house of the Lord forever. May this be our ultimate goal. There is nothing more joyous than to think of living in the house of the Lord forever. "When at last the battle's won, May we hear the Lord's Well-Done."

BUENA VISTA'S MISS HERSHEY
by Esther Eby Glass

"Only memories turn back the calendar to the one-room schoolhouse of 100 years ago."

Autumn, 1968. The first day of school in the country. Orange school buses flash red lights as they stop to pick up pupils waiting beside the mailboxes at the end of lanes. Presently these buses will stop to unload their noisy passengers at some large elementary or high school.

Some of the teachers awaiting these pupils will be teaching for the first time. They come to their schoolrooms equipped with college degrees and periods of practice teaching. And still some of these teachers admit to "butterflies" on that first day of school.

Turn back the calendar 100 years to autumn, 1918. There are no school buses, few grade schools or high schools. Miss Grace Hershey, age

18, begins her first day of teaching at the Buena Vista School, near Gap, Pennsylvania, without "butterflies." Her credentials for teaching include a high school diploma and a temporary teaching permit which she acquired by passing an examination that qualified her to teach for two years. If, at the end of two years, she wished to continue teaching, she would be asked to begin attending Normal School during summer vacations, to prepare for a teacher's certificate.

One reason she wasn't afraid, she told me, was that the books she would be using were the same ones she had studied only a few years before. She had eight years' acquaintance with each book, since all eight years of her elementary school life were spent in one room. She felt quite competent to teach anything she had studied, and the previous teacher had left her a lesson schedule.

"Also," she told me with a smile, "I knew I was at least a few years older than any of my pupils."

Instead of attending a faculty meeting the day before school opened. Miss Hershey, who was also the one-woman maintenance department, cleaned the schoolhouse.

THE THREE R'S

When 42 pupils made their appearance the following morning she discovered that children were enrolled in each of the eight grades. Among her five beginners she had several Amish children whose knowledge of English was limited. Added to her other teaching duties was the responsibility to help them to learn English.

These were the days of the three R's, Reading, 'Riting, and 'Rithmetic. She taught these

At 18, Grace Hershey owned a high school diploma and a temporary teaching permit.

three subjects, plus spelling and drawing, to all eight grades, and grammar, history, and geography to the higher grades.

Pupils took writing seriously 100 years ago. They practiced arm movement, push and pull, filling pages with ovals and up-and-down lines. Beautiful penmanship was considered an accomplishment.

To be at the top of the spelling class was a place of honor, sought after and guarded jealously. The spelling bee was a popular form of evening entertainment for young people and a diversion for the children during rainy-day recess periods.

"We had geography bees too," Mrs. Hershey said. "We would have two sides, and I'd call questions. For instance, I would name states and they would name the capital cities. There was keen competition between the two sides."

And poetry was for memorization. "I remember that I had them learn 'The Children's Hour.' Somewhere along the way I myself memorized lines from 'Thanatopsis' which I can still recite word for word," she said. "Memorizing had its good points. Some of the poetry stays in your memory, and like "Thanatopsis" means more as one grows older.

"I taught drawing, too. The children liked to draw. We hadn't heard about contemporary art. They drew flowers and animals and landscapes. The pictures were supposed to look like something! The more natural, the better.

"We didn't have a music teacher 100 years ago. I sang with the children. There was a reed organ in the school. I played it for opening exercises, pumping up and down as I played and sang. 'Twilight Is Stealing,' was a favorite, and 'How Gentle God's Commands.'"

"Some of my children were from Mennonite homes, some from the Old Order Amish, and some from other Protestant families. All of them knew and liked to sing hymns. I read a portion from the Bible and we repeated the Lord's Prayer together each morning after we sang together."

She added, "Three of the boys I taught that year are now ministers, and three girls are wives of ministers. Most of them are active church workers."

CLASSROOM CLEANUP

Besides trying to instill into her pupils a love for music, poetry, and literature, she also enlisted their help in some very mundane tasks. Her maintenance job was not confined to cleaning the schoolhouse before the opening day. She swept the bare board floor of the schoolhouse each evening after school was dismissed and dusted with a cloth called a dustrag!

And there was a heating system for her to control in the form of a pot-bellied coal stove. Since Buena Vista School did not boast a basement, wood for kindling, an ax, and coal were kept in a shed in the schoolyard. The teacher either split her own kindling or asked an older boy to do the job. She needed to know how to kindle a fire, how to add coal to keep it burning properly, and how to bank the fire so it would not go out at night in the bitter cold weather of midwinter. She always arrived a half hour early to get the fire going and the schoolhouse warmed for the children. "The stove created some problems," she said. "It was very warm near the stove, and very cool in corners farthest from the stove. You had to move your pupils from one place to another to keep them all warm.

"Another problem was the lack of indoor plumbing. Water had to be carried from a neighboring farmhouse. Each morning I sent two of the older pupils to bring the water which was put into a crockery cooler with a spigot at the bottom. We had progressed beyond the pail and dipper days. But to use the toilet facilities meant a trip outside. In the winter helping small children put on and take off boots and coats and mittens was a time-consuming job for the teacher.

"Mowing the lawn was no problem, however. In the summer the cows were turned into the schoolyard and in the spring and fall the children kept the grass tramped down.

"Hot lunches were unknown 100 years ago. The cafeteria was a row of tin lunch boxes on a shelf. Of course, there were no Thermos bottles then. But country children had good lunches, sandwiches and apples and cookies."

"Did you direct games at recess time?" I asked.

She said that wasn't necessary. Children who worked hard at home, as country children

Grace Hershey welcomed first-graders on Buena Vista's front porch in 1918. Throughout the years, only the extra windows have been added to the original Gap, Pa., schoolhouse.

did 100 years ago, were glad for a chance to play. They didn't need supervision. They played running games and ball games. There were never enough boys for two regular baseball teams, but they had their own system of batting and catching and were resourceful enough to adapt it to the players they had. Shortage of numbers or lack of equipment didn't spoil the fun for them. The older girls sat in groups and crocheted lace or did other fancywork as they talked. On rainy days she kept them occupied with games like "Upset the Fruit Basket," which might seem tame to children today, but was hilarious to her pupils.

"100 years ago was 1918 not a normal year," Mrs. Hershey said. "I will always remember hearing the whistles blow and blow over the hills at Gap on the eleventh of November. But we didn't know for sure why they were blowing, until the mailman came by, tooted his automobile horn, and shouted to the children in the schoolyard: 'The war is over.' Everyone was happy."

They were not through with the aftermath of the war because the flu epidemic hit the area after the armistice came. "Our school was closed for four weeks over Christmas and New Year's," she said. "This meant that the Christmas program, a high point in the school calendar, was not held that year.

"One of my first-graders died. His mother asked the teacher and some of his schoolmates to sing at his funeral. The song she selected for them to sing was his favorite, 'When the Roll is Called Up Yonder.' We got off tune, but a neighbor who was a good singer tiptoed down the aisle and helped us. A small school is a closeknit group, and this death saddened all of us."

EDUCATION, A PRIVILEGE

"How about discipline?" I asked.

"I can't remember any serious discipline problems," she said. "Children were disciplined at home and taught to respect authority. Going to school was a privilege, not a punishment. A few went on to high school, but most students knew that what they learned in these eight years would constitute all their formal education. They wanted to learn, and I wanted to teach them all that I could."

"Did you go on to get your teacher's certificate?" I asked.

"No," she admitted. She met Rine Hershey that year. And he changed her mind about continuing to teach. She decided to begin filling her hope chest instead. But her husband had been on the school board for many of their married years, so she keeps in touch with the schools.

"Buena Vista School is still in use as a school," she said. "When the township sold it at auction, the local Amish people bought it for a parochial school. My husband was at the sale and bought a souvenir for me—something I had used."

"The organ?" I asked.

"No. The ax I used to cut kindlings!" She chuckled. "But I bought that organ at a sale soon after I taught at Buena Vista and moved it into our farm home after I was married."

"I suppose you saved some of your teaching salary to buy things for that hope chest, not to mention the organ," I said.

"My salary was $50 a month, and I paid three dollars a week for board and room near the school. Each Monday morning my sister brought me four miles from home by horse and buggy, and each Friday evening she came for me. But $50 was a lot of money then."

As we were finishing our interview, Mrs. Hershey's husband was leaving for a meeting of the school board.

"The Teachers' Association is asking for a salary increase," he said. "We are discussing the matter tonight."

"They've come a long way from $50 a month," I said, as he went out the door.

"Yes. We have better schools in many ways. Better buildings and equipment, better trained teachers, wider choice of courses," Mrs. Hershey said. "But we have lost something, too. The small country school brought the neighbors together. At the annual Christmas programs parents met and talked across church and cultural lines. All of our children played together. We understood our differences and we respected each other's beliefs and customs. Now we don't know many of our neighbors. And my grandchildren can't even name all the other members of their own graduating classes. I can still name every child I taught 100 years ago."

I said good-bye. A school bus with flashing red lights was stopping at the end of a lane down the road.

Only in memory can we turn back the calendar 100 years.

THE EXTRAS

This is probably an old story, but it was new to us and may be new to you. One of our readers sent it in to us and we would like to share it with you.

It is about a farmer who bought a new car and was surprised by the cost of the "extras." Later, the car dealer wanted to buy a cow from the farmer, and the farmer quoted him this price list:

Basic cow	$100
Two-tone finish	$45
Four-barrel stomach	$75
Genuine cowhide upholstery	$125
Product storage & dispensing device	$60
Four spigots @ $10 each	$40
Dual horn	$15
Automatic fly swatter	$35
Field fertilizing device	$45
Total price	$540

Hope you enjoy this as much as we did.

A DREAM—2014

Dear Readers,

I want to share a dream that I had. I don't mean to offend or judge anyone.

I dreamed I was looking into Hell, yes I know it was, a large dark cavern, a boiling lake of fire and lava, a throne, yes Satan also sits on a throne; the king of evil. There he sat, vile, wicked, and inhuman. Above the boiling lake of fire was a walkway and ledge, a line of people moved slowly, all holding cell phones. As they got close to the ledge, they threw their cell phones into a huge pile, then fell into the boiling lake. The pile of cell phones got bigger and bigger and glowed red hot. All kinds of vile language, pictures, and sins screamed out of the pile, as these people fell, they cried, "We've thrown our cell phones away, please take us out of here, please!" But Satan laughed, I can't even describe how it sounded, he said, "It's too late, I have you. It was so easy." Laughter, moans, and cries went on and on as the pile got larger and larger, as more people fell in. Yes there were all kinds of people from the world, but there were many Amish too.

Please let's not make it easy for Satan. Let's pray for each other. If reading this helps even one person it will be worth it.

An Amish girl dreamed this.

TRAGHERT
Phares Z. Stoltzfus, Sr., 2008

Hello from Conoco Lane.

That was a cold and windy week with a low of seventeen degrees on December 31st. I extend my sympathy to the sick and sorrowing. Uncle Mike's Miriam parted with her husband. I never forget what the minister said at Ben Blank sie Annie's funeral. We can't tell a person how it is that has not parted with his companion, and those of us who have we don't have to. However there are a lot of different situations in people's deaths that we can't tell someone else just how it is. The lesson we have of the ten virgins that Jesus tells us about is for all of us, it doesn't matter what the cause of our death. One evening after I was finished with the evening prayer, Amos asked, "What does *traghert* mean?" I looked it up in a German dictionary, it said, *"fal longesom und un be kimmert."* In English it means, "slow, lazy, and unconcerned." That brings our thoughts to the five foolish virgins, Jesus does not say that they were guilty of big time wrong doing, they just didn't get ready for the bride groom. The thing is we can miss out on judgment day if we don't get ready now.

WHERE'S THE FIRE?
by Catherine Denman
Morongo Valley, California

When the alarm bell ran back in 1919,
this old fire horse was ready to "mow 'em down."

When I think about it now, "Jumbo" was a strange name for a horse. It was okay for an elephant, maybe…but a horse? Not that he wasn't nearly as big as an elephant!

Back in the earliest years of this century, Jumbo was the lead horse for the Newton, Massachusetts Fire Department. He could race like the wind and seemed to have an unreasoning dislike for anything being in front of him on the road, including the few automobiles around then.

When the fire department retired Jumbo back in 1919, my dad "adopted" him. A golf course greenskeeper, Dad used horse-drawn equipment for cutting fairways.

Dad figured Jumbo had great spirit and plenty of power left in that huge body. He certainly filled up the stall in the barn—I remember being overwhelmed by his size when I was a little girl of 4.

Jumbo proved ideal for Dad's work, but he had one fault—whenever he heard the fire alarm ring, he took off at full speed.

Dad had all he could do to stay astride the little metal seat on the mower. He could barely hold the reins. Jumbo just *had* to get to that fire, and when he reached the street, he'd put on a burst of speed that had the bouncing mowers chattering on the pavement. No wonder Dad spent so many hours sharpening damaged blades.

Nowhere to Hide
When they finally reached the scene, Dad could only sit there red-faced with embarrassment for having arrived on a grass cutter.

"By Faith"

We are born wanting our destination to be up in heaven,
There are examples on how to get there in Hebrews eleven.
It tells us of people that had strong faith with a zeal,
And what it can do for us if our faith is also that real.

Faith is the key that will fit to open up heaven's door,
And faith is the substance of things we hope for.
By faith Abel offered God a more excellent sacrifice,
And Enoch was allowed to bypass death in this life.

Without faith it is impossible to please God and win,
We must believe he is a rewarder of those seeking him.
By faith Noah built an ark to save his own house,
Including all three of his sons and each one's spouse.

By faith, when God spoke to Abraham he fully obeyed,
Knowing when God makes a promise it will be paid.
By faith Sarah was also given strength to conceive,
And delivered a child past her age because she believed.

By faith Abraham embraced the promises of God as right,
His descendants became as many as the stars at night.
By faith Abraham became willing to sacrifice his son,
Because he believed God had a plan for the outcome.

By faith Isaac blessed Jacob and Esau about future things,
And Jacob blessed both sons of Joseph when still worshiping.
By faith Joseph gave commandments concerning his bones,
And spoke of the children of Israel yet before he was gone.

By faith Moses was hid for three months from his birth,
When his parents saw they had a child with special worth.
By faith Moses decided as a man to suffer affliction,
With God's people rather than the pleasures of sin's addiction.

By faith Moses left Egypt not fearing the wrath of the king,
By faith he kept the Passover and many other things.
By faith they passed through the Red Sea like dry land,
By faith the walls of Jericho fell as if they were sand.

By faith the harlot Rahab received spies and did not perish,
And there are many more works of faith we can cherish.
Time is short and what more would there be left to say,
So we can have faith in God regardless of come what may.

By faith, Barab, Samson, David, Samuel, the list is long,
Of people who out of weakness were made strong.
Subduing kingdoms, obtained promise, waxed valiant in fight,
And turned the armies of the aliens into their flight.

By faith others endured whippings as they were mocked,
And some were stoned or put behind doors that were locked.
Still others were tormented, afflicted, and slain with sword,
Through this they obtained a good report for eternal reward.

By faith Jesus Christ still has the world's greatest name,
Choosing death on a cross while despising all of its shame.
And he is now sitting at the right hand of God's throne,
Waiting till God sends him to bring all his faithful home.

~ *Orva Hochstetler*

*Now faith is the substance of things
hoped for, the evidence of things
not seen. For by it the elders
obtained a good report.
Hebrews 11:1-2*

History of Valentine's Day

Ida Miller

Ever wonder the reason for Valentine's Day? It all started in the third century. The Roman emperor Claudius decreed all Romans to worship twelve gods, but Valentinus was dedicated to the ideals of Christ. Not even the threat of death could keep him from practicing his beliefs.

He was arrested and imprisoned. During the last weeks of Valentinus' life, a remarkable thing happened. Seeing that he was a man of learning, the jailor brought his daughter Julia to Valentinus for lessons. She had been blind since birth. Valentinus read of Rome's history to her. He taught her arithmetic and told her about God. She saw the world through his eyes and trusted his wisdom and found comfort in his quiet strength.

"Valentinus, does God really hear prayer?" Julia asked one day.

"Yes, my child. He hears each one," he replied.

"Do you know I pray each morning and night? I pray each morning and night. I pray that I may see. I want so much to see everything you told me about."

"God does what's best for us if only you believe in Him," Valentinus said.

"Oh, Valentinus, I do believe," Julia said fervently.

She knelt and grasped his hand. They sat quietly together, each praying. Suddenly, there was brilliant light in the prison cell. Radiant, Julia cried, "Valentinus, I can see! I can see! Praise to God!"

On the evening of his death, Valentinus wrote one last note to Julia urging her to stay close to God. He signed it from your Valentine. He was executed that day February 14, 270 AD

and buried in what is now the Church of Praxedar in Rome. It is said that Julia planted a pink blossom almond tree near his grave.

Today, the almond tree remains a symbol of abiding love and friendship and messages of love and affection are exchanged around the world on February 14th, St. Valentine's Day.

The Crippled Beggar

Well, a long time ago in our PA a farmer was busy a diggin' away, his drain was clogged up and the water wouldn't run, so he dug a deep hole and it wasn't any fun. A beggar came a walking up the road, it seemed as if he carried a load. Held his hand out front for all to see, won't you please have pity on a cripple like me. He was a big fellow and so forlorn, his hand was crippled since the day he's born. Said not a thing that I can do, cause I don't have good hands like you. Oh won't you share some money with me, cause I don't have good hands like thee. Then the beggar grew still and looked not the same as if he choked on a pill and his face red with shame. The farmer got his wallet tucked it under his arm, fished out some money with a generous charm. Handed it over as though to say, it must be awful to be crippled that way. This little tale I'm telling to you happened long ago and all of it's true, the beggar then left with one more look, at the farmer with a shovel, a hand and a hook.

This "farmer" Morris Zook, Honey Brook, PA.

The Quaker Girl's Dream

I dreamed I was on my way to school when suddenly I noticed a great crowd upon the lawn. People were hurrying to and fro, and when I asked what all this commotion was about, a girl said, "Why, don't you know? It's Measuring Day, and the Lord's angel has come to see how much our souls have grown since the last Measuring Day."

"Measuring Day," said I. "Measuring souls?" I never heard of such a thing, and I began to ask questions, but the girl hurried on. After a little I let myself be pressed along with the crowd upon the lawn.

There in the center, on a kind of throne under the green elm, was the most beautiful and glorious being I had ever seen. He had white wings. His clothes were of shining white, and he had the kindest, and yet most serious face I ever saw. By his side was a tall golden rod, fastened upright in the ground, with curious marks on it at regular intervals from top to bottom. Over it in a golden scroll, were the words, "The measure of a perfect man."

The instant each one touched the golden measure a wonderful thing happened. No one could escape the terrible accuracy of that rod. Each one shrank or increased to his true dimensions—his spiritual dimensions—as I soon learned, for it was the index of the soul growth which was shown in this mysterious way.

The first few who were measured after I came, I did not know. But soon the name of Elizabeth Darrow was called. She is the president of the "Aid for the Destitute Society," and she manages ever so many other societies, too. I thought, "Surely Elizabeth Darrow's measure will be very high indeed." She stood by the rod, and the instant she touched it, she seemed to grow shorter and shorter, and the angel's face grew very serious

as he said, "This would be a soul of high stature if only the zeal for outside works which can be seen of men, had not checked the lowly secret graces of humility and trust and patience under little daily trials. These, too, are needed for perfect soul growth."

I pitied Elizabeth Darrow as she moved away with such a sad and surprised face to make room for the next.

It was poor, thin, little Betsy Lyons, the seamstress. I never was more astonished in my life than when she took her stand by the rod, and immediately increased in height, till her mark was higher than any I had seen before, and her face shone so, I thought it must have caught its light from the angel's who smiled so gloriously. Suddenly I envied poor little Betsy, whom before I had rather looked down upon. As the angel wrote in the book, he said, "Blessed are the poor in spirit, for their's is the kingdom of heaven."

The next was Lillian Edgar, who dresses so beautifully that I have often wished for such nice clothes, and so much money. The angel looked sadly at her measure, for it was very low—so low that Lillian looked pale as death, and her beautiful clothes no one noticed at all for they were quite over-shadowed by the glittering robes beside her. The angel said in solemn tones, "Oh, child, why take thought for raiment? Let your adorning be not that outward adorning of putting on of apparel, but let it be the ornament of a meek and quiet spirit, which is in the sight of God of great price. Thus only canst thou grow like the Master."

Old Jerry, the cobbler, came next. Poor old clumsy Jerry. But as he hobbled up the steps, the angel's face fairly blazed with light, and he smiled on him and led him to the rod. And behold, Jerry's measure was higher than any of the others.

The angel's voice rang out so loud and clear that we all heard it, saying, "He that humbleth himself shall be exalted."

And then, oh, my name came next. I trembled so I could hardly reach the angel. But then he put his arm around me and helped me to stand by the rod. As soon as I touched it, I felt myself growing shorter and shorter, and though I stretched and stretched and strained every nerve to be as tall as possible, I could only reach Lillian's mark—Lillian's, the lowest of all, and I a member of the church for two years! I grew crimson for shame, and whispered to the angel, "Oh, give me another chance before you mark me in the book as low as this. Tell me how to grow. I will do it all gladly, only do not put this mark down."

The angel shook his head sadly, "The record must go down as it is, my child. May it be higher when I come next. This rule will help thee: 'Whatsoever thou doest, do it heartily as unto the Lord, in singleness of heart as unto Christ.'"

With that I burst into tears, and suddenly awakened to find myself crying. But, oh, I shall never forget that dream, for I was so ashamed of my mark.

-Selected from an old writing

Plain Sect Virtues Outweigh Shortcomings
2011

To the Editors:

When I read all the negative letters, written about the plain people, I am embarrassed at times to be identified with them. Shame on us that there is reason to accuse us of abusing our children and misusing our animals.

Yes, I know there are times when we are unfairly singled out, but we need to receive this criticism graciously. Some of these things should never be named among us.

Nevertheless, when I observe the moral decline in American society, and see how America is rejecting the Christian values it once embraced, I am thankful to be numbered with the 60,000 plain people in Southeastern Pennsylvania.

America, the nation that was founded on Judeo-Christian principles, the land that God so richly blessed and was the envy of the whole world, now has approximately one of every 100 adults in prison, over 100,000 children in juvenile detention centers, a 50 percent divorce rate, 30 million children not living with both biological parents, 40 percent of its babies born to single mothers and over one million aborted each year. Over 250,000 children are rejected or taken from their parents annually and placed in foster care.

One can hardly imagine the misery and insecurity that this social upheaval must be having on American children. It has been estimated that incarcerating over two million citizens and the results of broken homes cost the American taxpayers close to $200 billion each year.

When I consider these things, I realize how privileged I am to live in a community where people continue to honor the Bible as the word of God and endeavor to put it to practice; where children are desired and loved; where very few are born out of wedlock, and where divorce is practically unheard of and children are raised by both biological parents; where Christian ethics are taught, the Lord's day honored, and working with hands is still considered a virtue. It's a community where people work together and are there to help each other.

I am not trying to give the impression that the plain people are better than anyone else. But I do believe the plain community is a living example of how the application of Biblical principles can have a positive effect of an imperfect people, and how the rejection of these principles is having a negative effect on modern society.

-Benuel Lapp
New Holland

THE GIFT OF AGING

Dan A. Hochstetler

My body's older, Lord and it doesn't move as spryly as it once did, but I "Thank you for this gift of aging. As I move through life more slowly, I capture more of what is going on around me, the beauty of nature, the kind words of friends, the smiles of children eager to learn the mysteries of life, the needs of others.

There is the joy of not trying to race my way to the top. The bliss of knowing who I am, Your child. The joy of being content with whatever You give me to do. I no longer have to strive to make more money. I know from past experiences that "enough" will always come from You.

Instead of feeling that the best years are gone, I appreciate the true beauty of this time of my life. I feel such thankfulness for my children (now responsible adults); for life's renewing cycle in our grandchildren; for the love and loyalty of a spouse through years of both agony and joy; and for the surety of Your constant presence and acceptance of Your will.

Most of all, I "thank you" Lord, that I now have so much more time to spend with You and the things which last into eternity.

"Thank you" for the comfort of knowing that when this life ends, another, "more radiant" one, begins in your glorious realm.

SEEING DOUBLE 4 TIMES OVER

TROUBLE COMES IN TWOS: Teacher Michelle McGanty, center, has her hands full with four sets of identical twins enrolled in her kindergarten class at St. Cecilia School in Beaverton, Ore. The twins from left, are: Christopher and Michael McKay, Madeline and Meghan Gregg, Peter and Paul Nistler, and Alexandra and Teresa Orazio.

-Sept. 5, 1991

AMISH REACTIONS TO THE SINKING OF THE *TITANIC*

by David Luthy

Seventy years have passed since the majestic ship, *Titanic*, sank to the bottom of the ocean. It had been heralded by its builders as "unsinkable"; yet on its first Atlantic crossing it sank. While most Americans have consigned the tragedy to past history, the Amish have kept the event alive, preaching about it and even singing about it.

Since no Amish travelers were aboard the *Titanic* when it went to its watery grave, one might wonder why the story has been retained by them. The answer is simple: the catastrophe contains important moral lessons. First of all the ship carried some of America's wealthiest citizens, worth hundreds of millions of dollars. The luxurious ship was designed to cater to their pleasures—dancing, card playing, drinking. Thus, the *Titanic* symbolizes the fashionable and corrupt world of which the Amish want no part and which they warn their children to avoid. The world, like the *Titanic*, will some day pass away.

A second object lesson which the Amish take from the tragedy is that Man placed himself higher than God. Hadn't some people stated that the ship was so well built that "God Himself could not sink it?" Even the ancient Greeks living before the time of Christ had considered this a sin, calling it "hubris." Hadn't this also been the sin committed at the building of the Tower of Babel? Is it, then, any wonder that the Amish continue to be impressed by the fact that the "unsinkable" *Titanic* went down on its maiden voyage?

While the content of Amish sermons is generally very Biblically based, other valuable lessons are sometimes drawn from modern events. The tale of the *Titanic* is occasionally mentioned. If this is true today, then what must have been Amish people's re-action to the event when it occurred on April 14, 1912? The place to look for this would be the periodicals published by the Amish at that time.

In the very year that the *Titanic* sank, an Amish magazine, *Herold der Wahrheit*, had begun publication. Its publisher was Samuel D. Guengerich of Johnson County, Iowa, and its editor was Bishop Eli J. Bontreger. This latter Amishman had been raised in Lagrange County, Indiana, moved to North Dakota and then to Wisconsin where he was living at the time the *Titanic* sank. Later he moved back to his former home at Shipshewana, Indiana, and was well known throughout the Amish settlements. In the May 15, 1912, issue, Bontreger wrote an editorial about the sinking. He said it was a thought-provoking happening because of the sheer number of people, nearly 1,600, who had perished at the same time. He pointed out that for the unrepentant aboard the ship, "Death for them is the door to hell." He reminded the readers that while the loss of nearly 1,600 lives at one moment was remarkable, each day saw more people than that dying across the world from less dramatic causes. He concluded his German editorial, saying:

> At our homes and in our daily work we live with the possibility of death, and many die even so quickly, even so unexpectedly, and even so unprepared in his house as those on the ocean. "O Man, consider your end."

In the following issue, June 1st, of this same periodical, a German article *"Fehlt noch Eins"* appeared in which reference was made to the *Titanic*. The author was Jonas B. Miller, a bishop in the Conservative Amish Church. He commented as follows:

> The large steamboat *Titanic* was perhaps an offering of avarice *("Opfer des*

Geizes")—both honor and money—grandeur and carnal amusements. It appears according to reports that much effort and preparation was expended to make it jolly and amusing; yes, perhaps one may say that the "Queen of the Ocean" was prepared for revelry, and was not prudently readied for rescue should it suffer shipwreck; and when the great distress came upon them in the quickness of the disaster, there was no rescue for the greater percent and their portion was—death. Traveling through the disaster, they brought their trip to a sudden end and went quickly into eternity.

While the story of the *Titanic* has often been used by Amish ministers to bring out valuable lessons, a few instances are known where the event has been used against the Amish Church itself. One day a few years ago a woman in her thirties visited the Amish Historical Library. I realized that she and her husband were not members of any church and that her father, once an Amish minister, was no longer Amish. I had to wonder what in the library would interest her.

As we passed the center desk I spied the full-page newspaper account of the *Titanic* displayed there and thought, "Here is something that will interest her." I pointed it out to her.

"Yes, I know the story of the *Titanic*," she commented. "Dad preached about it in his last sermon in _____ County, saying the Amish Church is the *Titanic* and people should get off, for it is sinking."

I was shocked speechless by the remark. I had heard many references to the *Titanic* before but never in this vein. Later as I thought about this incident, the truth dawned on me. Here was a minister who had been overly critical of the imperfections in the church. Forty years have now passed since he compared the Amish Church with the *Titanic*. The sad truth is that his family is like the *Titanic* and has sunk. Among his children are churchless couples, atheists, and divorcees living out in the world.

Triple Screw Steamer Titanic *was the largest and finest vessel in the world: 882.5 feet long, 45,000 tons register, 92.5 feet wide.*

Harvesting in 1800

The combines are thrashing thousands of acres of wheat. They started the last week of May which is very, very rare. An old neighbor of ours said he didn't see that since the 60's. Today at Aaron and Katie Beilers at church in pm, two combines cut a big field across the road from Aarons. Made me think back about 30 years ago when we lived in Kirkwood when my Grandfather's youngest cousin, Mose Fisher, told me a man invented the cradle to harvest wheat. Before that they cut with a scythe, then the women came on behind and gathered it in bundles and tied it with wheat strands. The men and boys shocked it and hauled it in later to thrash. It was trampled by oxen or flailed to separate; the same as for thousands of years. Now, to get back to the newly invented cradle. The cradle was a scythe with a rack attached to hold an arm full of wheat as it was cut. That arm full was thrown on the ground, eliminating the need for the women to gather a bundle. It was a time saver and a great success. Mose Fisher told me this young inventor told his father to come see what he made. When his father saw how it works, he told his son to take that thing to the wood pile and demolish it. "These modern inventions will bring the end of the world." If that man would come out of his grave and see these big combines coming toward him, don't you think he would quickly jump back in? The cradle was invented around 1800 because by 1831 Cyrus McCormick invented the reaper, which was the first horse drawn apparatus to cut wheat. It had a cutter bar and a revolving rack to dispense the cut wheat in piles to be tied by a crew on behind. This was a big improvement in saving man hours. The next improvement was the knotter to automatically bind the cut wheat. That was called the binder of which we use in these days. Not many are used here, but a lot of Amish and Mennonites in other areas use

them today yet. We read in the history books when the reaper came into use the work force stuck steel rods into the wheat fields to discourage the farmers to use the reapers because they were afraid it will put them out of work. I still have a longing to farm a 20-acre field of speltz, but majority would vote that out the window faster than it came in. When I get enough of power, we will be on the market for a binder and thrash machine and our mules will eat speltz happily after.

Teaching Children to Obey

Young mothers, do you need help to make your child obey? A lady asked me one time, "How do you plain people get your children to obey?" And this is what I told her to do. She had a girl several years old and she did this with wonderful results. Years later she told me she had 2 younger children and said I did this to them when they were younger and they never were self-willed like her oldest one was. They were so easy trained with this method.

Try this—sit down and ask your child to come, whatever he may be doing. And if he doesn't come, get up, go over to him, get a hold of the lower part of his ear and bring him back to where you were sitting and say, "This is where I told you to come to." (No harm will be done by pinching his ear.) And it doesn't look near as bad as hitting him. Do this several times a day and keep it up 'til he obeys promptly when asked to come. He will soon obey you in everything. (Taken out of *Botschaft* years ago.)

-Emma Weaver

First to Be Killed by a Car

On 17 August 1896, 44-year-old Bridget Driscoll became the first person to be killed by a motor car. Mrs. Driscoll and her teenage daughter were visiting London to watch a dancing display. On a terrace in the grounds of Crystal Palace, she was hit by a car which was offering demonstration rides to the public. The car was traveling at four miles per hour when it hit Mrs. Driscoll, and the impact proved fatal. As he delivered his verdict of accidental death, the coroner said, "This must never happen again."

But it has. Since then, some 25 million people have been killed in road traffic accidents. If current rates continue, an estimated 1.17 million more will die each year—two people every minute of every day—and a further 10 million people will be injured or crippled. It's a problem of such magnitude that it's led many to speculate whether the inventors of the motor car had any idea what they were unleashing on the world.

In the 20th century, death by road accident had become an epidemic in the Western world. In 1930, there were just over a million cars in Britain, and 7,300 people died on the roads—more than twice the number of deaths in 1999, when there were 27 million cars. By 1960, President John F. Kennedy identified traffic accidents as "one of the greatest, perhaps the greatest of the nation's public health problems." By then, nearly 40,000 people were dying on the roads each year in the U.S.; today, that figure is pretty well unchanged, despite there being three and half times as many vehicles. Now, the people most affected by road accidents are the world's poor.

The statistics paint a somber picture. Seventy percent of road deaths every year occur in developing countries. Sixty-five percent of those killed are pedestrians. The majority of people hurt or killed in road accidents in the developing world are not the vehicle occupants; they're walking, they're on motorbikes, they're on bicycles or other non-motorized vehicles.

Life of Widowhood

Marriage is an ordination from God, therefore it is human nature for man and wife to live together. It is accepted by governments of all civilized countries on the face of the globe. Scripture teaches us that marriage is a free choice for those who wish to accept the responsibilities of married life.

We all know that life has a sealed span. Sooner or later all human beings, young or old, single or married, will face death. We have no specified time as to when death will occur. Records show that people have lived in matrimony for as long as seventy years. It is estimated that more than 40% of married couples will experience widowhood, and in some instances two or more times. Parting by death among Christian married people is always a shock for the remaining spouse. It is a condition that is almost impossible to be prepared for to its full extent. We try to imagine how life would be if our life companion should be suddenly called away. If a married partner were in failing health or seriously ill and living in great misery between life and death where restoring to health is impossible, out of love and respect people may come to the point where they pray to the Lord in His mercy to send eternal rest and peace to a married companion. In all conditions the parting makes such a great change in the manner of living that it creates a shock. It effects the body emotionally and physically.

A young person who never had such an experience may feel that older people could adjust better to the condition of parting than a younger person can. In other words, we may feel that old people would more or less expect it, those who had lived together to a ripe old age, and rocked the boat of life through times of progress as well as hardship, times of pleasure and times of sorrow, good health and sickness, and reared a family through times of spiritual enlightenment as well as trials and tribulations. That keen step and alert mind had changed to a slower walk and feeble memories. But still the nature of human beings has proven that spiritual love does not grow old. The longer that married people live together the greater the tie. Because people have lived together to old age gives no assurance that parting by death is an easy matter to make adjustments to.

Death is very uncertain, and there are many ways in which this life on earth will end. How heart touching it is when a young couple is separated by death, the one leaving this world and the other spouse left to rear a family of small children who (in our opinion) would need the love and prayers of both parents. Or where there are young adults in the family who are seeking their life's pathway, taking examples from others for their pattern of life, leaving a mother or father alone to teach respect for Christianity.

Some people experience widowhood for a much longer period than their married life extended, rearing a family where the children grow to adulthood without the love of a father or mother. And there is the matter of earning a living, paying off debts, or the remaining mortgages. In a few cases orphan children are left behind where trustees or guardians are required by the state to give them their rights to the estate.

When the Lord makes a call for one or the other married partner, the change goes much deeper than a person can realize without the experience. In other words, human nature cannot grasp the depth and sincerity of the parting in Christian marriages, because of the deeply rooted love in by-gone years.

Following the shock of adjusting to conditions in giving up a life companion, homesick usually follows *(zeit lang)*. This kind of homesick is different from that when a person is away from home for a period of time, and has the privilege of returning to their loved ones in due time. Homesick after the death of a loved one is sometimes expressed as pressing or painful homesick. It usually brings back long forgotten memories, which are renewed as dreams. Days of overcast shadows and sleepless nights are spent in thinking of the past. And without the spirit of comfort from Jesus Christ our Saviour, the future can look like mountains without boundaries. But with the spiritual influence that is promised to Christians, the future can again have rejoicing days. This can come in many different ways.

Our fore-fathers started many life patterns which we keep as traditions, and we more-or-less take them for granted. We were taught out of respect to share our sympathy with widows, widowers, and sick or unfortunate friends and relatives. Visiting, sending cards of comfort, writing letters with a spirit of sympathy, or small gifts are much appreciated. Sharing our thoughts and remembrances often make a deep influence on unfortunate people.

The value of such kind deeds can't be expressed in words. Being respectful to one another is the master of friendship. We hope that these traditions can be kept in practice from generation to generation.

After the remaining spouse has spent a period of time in a state of widowhood, they may have a desire to renew marriage. This is a rather touchy subject to write or talk about, because the family conditions are all different, where there are children involved, the age, holding a job, etc. A long list of items could be mentioned that enter plans of second marriage. It is quite often a serious decision to make because of conditions. People without the experience cannot imagine how a person may feel, with a burning heart of sadness trying to make adjustments and still having pressing homesick from past experiences. Then being watched for any move that is made when conversing with a person of the opposite sex. Quite often such people are kept from visiting a person with the same experience because of the ideas it may form in someone's opinion. On a certain occasion a widower left for home in mid-afternoon, after attending a neighboring wedding, because of continually being teased about a certain lady.

Among the Amish society there are more widows than widowers. We may wonder why this is. There could be a few reasons for it. Records show that in the first half of the 20th century there were more female births than male among the Amish in Pennsylvania. This showed up in later years. For that reason there were a certain percent of those left over blessings (old maids). Then when a widower wishes to remarry, very often a maid is his choice instead of a widow. Government records also show that females have a longer life span than males. These two factors have proven that there are more widows than widowers. Even though a widow needs the help of a husband as well as the widower does from a wife, we must admit and believe that our Lord has control over such conditions.

It appears that in the last twenty years the cycle has changed to more male than female births. What the outcome will be remains to be seen.

-Gideon Fisher

Fredericksburg, Ohio–1927

I remember when I was a young lad; the people lived quite different than they do now. I heard say of one boy (of age) worked at a farm, I can't recall what his wages were for the summer, but when fall came and the fall work was finished, the boss said he is now free. He had no work elsewhere, so he asked the boss if he could stay for the winter and work for room and board. The boss let him stay.

I heard of one family where they didn't all have Sunday clothes, so they changed off to go to church.

I was raised in a big family of thirteen and our dear parents always managed to have enough food to eat. To think back, we had many good times together. I think people were happier than they are today.

-Ammon J. Miller

Gordonville, PA–1914

I had a brother that was fourteen years older than I. He had Diphtheria and there was no cure. His throat filled up with mucus and he could not get it out and died in a few days. They were quarantined for thirty days, no one to enter, and no funeral. Only two preachers on the outside porch with the window open a little for the parents with the casket inside. One sister had it in the stomach that survived. Also one sister three years old that they took to their sister who had no children for thirty days so she wouldn't get it. A sad time for the parents, no company for thirty days. There were only three teams to go to the graveyard. Sometimes two died in one family.

-Amos C. Fisher

The Missing Son

In the year 1955 in Lower Pequea an 18-year-old boy disappeared—his loving parents having no clue as to where he was. He seemed to be in good standing with young folks and so on, he would have been with the young folks two years and was said in those years he never once missed Church services. He was always right there. Many tears were shed; also some sleepless nights. The mother, when serving meals for the family, always put an extra plate on the table for her son hoping and praying some day her son would come home and also every evening when going to bed they had a kerosene light burn in the kitchen as a welcome sign if he would return. This went on for 2 long weeks before they found out where he was. He came back to Lancaster Co. but sad to say no longer Amish.

I'D RATHER BE TIRED THAN LONELY

A few years ago when my children were small
And I had so much to do,
I'd often wonder at the close of day
If my work would ever be through.

There was washing and ironing and mending,
And work of every kind,
Till sometimes I grew tired and weary,
Both in body and mind.

There were little hands and faces to be washed;
Little hungry mouths to be fed;
And other duties kept me busy
Till it was time to go to bed.

Sometimes my footsteps were heavy,
And I wished I could slip away,
And rest my weary self
For just a single day.

Now the years have passed so quickly,
And my little ones are grown;
Not a single one is with me—
They all have homes of their own.

My house is quiet and empty;
It seems that it can't be true,
For there is plenty of time for resting;
And there's not much work to do.

But gladly would I toil again,
From morning until night;
For I'd rather be tired than lonely,
With never a child in sight.

-Selected

A TEENAGER'S PRAYER

God in heaven, I am young and don't understand what it is like to be a parent, but it must be very hard because so many people are failing at it these days.

I pray for Mom and Dad, God, that you will help them be good parents—strong in the ways you want them to be, so I can look up to them with admiration and feel confident that their instruction is right.

Help me, dear Lord, to understand my parents. Remind me that when I don't get my way it is because they love me and not because they want to be mean or deprive me of a good time.

Help me, God, when I become stubborn and refuse to listen, to accept the fact that they have wisdom and experience because they were once teenagers, but I have never been a parent.

Put in my heart the respect and consideration they deserve for their years of hard work and sacrifice. They raised me as best they could. Let me not repay them with grief or shame. Rather help me to give them obedience, respect, forgiveness, and love. Most of all, God, while I still have my parents here on earth, help me to appreciate them and let them know that I do.

LANCASTER COUNTY TORNADO

August 23, 1982

It was a sunny day with high humidity. Weather forecasts called for possible thunder showers by evening. As the sun sank below the horizon, thunder heads appeared in the west, with a gentle breeze from the southwest, which indicated a good night's sleep. No storm warnings were given by the weather bureau.

By 9 o'clock daylight savings time, light showers with occasional thunder and lightning were among the rolling clouds. After about ¾ of an inch of rain had dampened the top soil, the thundering ceased. Most of the folks in the residential area of Intercourse had probably thought about retiring from the day's work. Some had gone on visits, others had planned to spend a quiet evening at home. By 10 p.m. a powerful tornado hit the ground about one half mile north of Gordonville. It plowed a path of about eight miles, from 50 to 100 feet wide through corn and tobacco fields, as well as over the southern part of the town of Intercourse on its way to the Welsh Mountains where it died out. It crippled everything that was in its path. Buildings were torn apart making heaps of kindlings. House roofs were torn off, timber and sheets of tin went flying through the air as though they were made of cardboard. Slate and tin were stripped from roof decks like sheets of paper, windmill towers were bent and twisted as though made of match sticks. Trees from 10 to 34 inches in diameter were twisted off or torn off or completely out of the ground and carried away, leaving behind a splintered stump. Farm machinery was picked up and carried away. A few animals were picked up by the funnel, carried a short distance and dropped, left to die from the impact. A man was

determined to see what the outcome from the storm would be. He was standing about 500 feet from the main funnel, picked up by high winds and carried a short distance not knowing how far in the air he was. He was not injured. In a cemetery large tombstones estimated at 500 pounds were pulled from the ground and laid on their side. About 800 customers had power failure, as well as telephone lines tangled.

The first residence and farm buildings that this violent wind storm struck was John E. Esh's along Clearview Road. Johns had plans made to go away that evening and were not at home when the tornado hit. Only minutes later they returned home to approach the ruins of their farm buildings. The children had already retired for the night, except two of the boys were still in the barn attending to a sick cow.

The 32'x60' tobacco shed was demolished. It had housed a number of pieces of farm equipment, it was swept off at floor level. Most of the structure was piled about 39 feet from the foundation like a heap of kindling. Heavy pieces of timber were broken or twisted into small bits. Very little could be salvaged. The tin roof was scattered out over the countryside for a quarter of a mile or more. A part of a rafter 10 feet long 3"x5" went through an 8"x10" window pane in the second story of the house into one of the children's bedrooms, only scratching the paint along the side without further damage to the window sash. The pieces of timber lost its force after penetrating through two panel doors, and stayed resting on the bed. Only minutes before a young girl had been in this room with the intention of sleeping in this particular bed, but because of fear from the storm she stayed in an adjoining room with two of her sisters. If anyone had been in that particular bed at the time of impact, severe injuries or even death could have been possible. Other parts of timber from the tobacco shed ripped siding from the house, or punched holes through the roof. This mighty wind came from the southwest, but the 10-foot pieces of rafters came in from the east, indicating that it was a tornado-like storm. Window panes were broken in every room of the house, either from the suction of the funnel, or from pieces of flying timber, or from bricks from the three damaged chimneys.

A windmill stood a short distance from the house. Its steel tower was twisted about twelve feet from the ground to the extent that the main wheel with gear box was left lying partly on the roof of the nearby tool shed. A maple tree in the yard about 20 feet off was twisted off about 10 feet from the ground and shredded to pieces and scattered over a nearby cornfield. Two good sized apple trees were pulled out of the ground and left lying about 20 feet away. A total of nine fair-sized trees were taken.

Part of a hog-fattening building was lifted three blocks from the top and let down again without much damage. A smaller brooder house 12 by 16 feet was totally demolished. The main barn which was 90 by 100 feet with attached straw shed was twisted three feet out of line at some places. A lot of tenets and mortises were pulled apart. All the barn doors were completely torn off. The tin roof on the west side had the least damage, but the east side was practically all sucked off from tornado impact. It was necessary to replace about 75% of the barn roof. The question was: "Could this large building be straightened out without dismantling it totally and starting to build from the bottom?" Or was it possible to pull the structure back to its original position with cranes and winches? To make this a substantial building again was left to the carpenters and contractors to decide. After some consideration, figuring time and labor, it was decided to try to

straighten it out with a number of cranes and equipment, including a lot of manpower.

Four cows that were injured were sent to the slaughterhouse the morning after the storm. Four other cows had some injuries but were kept for some time. One of these was partly paralyzed and never fully recovered. A number of the cows gave bloody milk their first few milkings. It appeared to effect their nervous system due to the suction of the tornado depriving oxygen from the air.

The two boys that were in the barn treating a sick cow when the tornado passed were at a loss as to what was taking place. They reached a handhold at whatever was in reach so they would not be sucked off their feet. They also could not get their breath for a short period.

Farm machinery that was standing out in the opening had some damage from flying timber. But the equipment that was left standing on the remaining floor of the tobacco shed had very little damage.

John's top carriage was parked in the barn with the doors open. After the storm it was partly over the fence across the road. Apparently it was sucked out of the barn, got into the main funnel of the tornado and was dropped over the meadow fence about 50 feet away. It appeared that the wagon was lifted up in the air then dropped, almost totally demolished.

After the disaster it was decided that three carpenter crews would rebuild the damaged buildings. One crew was given the responsibility of building the tobacco shed, one to repair the house, and one, the main barn. Besides these three carpenter gangs, hundreds of volunteers arrived to clean up and help rebuild. Lumber companies were very lenient in furnishing lumber and giving good service. After two weeks the buildings were again pretty well repaired and rebuilt with a total of thousands of man-hours of donated labor.

Daniel Esh's farm, Harvest Drive, R. 1, Gordonville, an adjoining farm to John Esh, was right in the path of that vicious tornado. It totally destroyed a three-story block and frame building 42 x 80 feet which was formerly built for a chicken house.

The first floor housed 21 heifers of different sizes and ages. Nine were killed, three were injured and later slaughtered. On the second floor were stored 1,100 bales of hay and 150 used window panes and 20 window sashes. The third floor was used for storage.

It so happened that Daniel had worked in the building and was about to leave when he heard the roaring sound of the wind storm. All of a sudden the building collapsed. He was left standing at a corner where no falling timber or concrete blocks were piled up, the only spot in the whole building where he could escape serious injury and only a short distance from where the heifers were fatally wounded from flying pieces of the building structure. Daniel Esh escaped without a scratch, but was badly shaken up from the close call.

Approximately 50 feet away a 280 x 44 foot cage pullet house where there were 54,500 four-week-old chicks, was three-fourths demolished. Fortunately the chicks were in cages; only about 600 were lost. The young birds were transferred to a vacant chicken house in the Mt. Joy area which happened to be empty at the time.

The Esh house was a truss rafter building surrounded by four foot block, with windows and aluminum siding. The part that was not totally destroyed was shifted about four feet from the foundation. About two-thirds of the building material was salvaged. The roof had to be replaced. Parts of the tin roof insulation were scattered over the town of Intercourse as far as a mile and a half. The north side of the house was damaged from flying lumber penetrating through the structure.

Also a ten foot section of the roof—rafters and all—was found lying out in the field. This allowed the driving rain to do some damage to the house. It was necessary to replace more than one half of the house roof.

The main barn and cow stable was not damaged. It was located about 100 feet from the chicken house and heifer pen. A large tree that was standing close by the farm building was twisted off at the top and carried off to a neighboring field. After a month the young pullets were again housed in the new building.

Yes, after a busy day making corn silage for the dairy herd, Benuel K. Stoltzfus, Old Philadelphia Pike, Gordonville, and Joel King were working late trying to finish the job before retiring. They noticed the dark, rolling clouds coming in from the west. They were coming closer at a fast rate. Benuel headed for the house and warned Joel that he should also go for shelter. By the time Benuel reached the house he heard a roaring sound that he could not describe. He ordered the family to go to the basement when the house started to quiver. Before they got to the cellar the wind storm had passed. It was followed by a hard rain. After the storm Benuel checked the building but could not see any major damage.

The next morning one of his better cows failed to come in with the other cows. Upon investigating he found her dead with her head under her body. The vet claimed she was picked up in the air by the powerful tornado and dropped to the ground in such a manner that she suffocated. A farm wagon fully loaded with corn bundles as they come from the corn binder, which was standing close by the farm building, was picked up and carried about 200 feet without losing a bundle of corn. A P.T.O. corn binder with engine and loader attached was carried about 50 feet and dropped on a wire fence. It is believed that this equipment was also in the air then dropped, because part of it was on both sides of the fence. Fortunately no major damage was done to the binder.

Two trees of about 20 inches in diameter were twisted off, with tree limbs shredded into small pieces and spread over the countryside. After the storm more than two wagonloads of tin, parts of building material, road signs, furniture, and—you name it—were gathered up from his pasture land, corn and grass field.

Benuels live on the first farm east of Intercourse. The items that were scattered over his land were partly from the town folks.

Benuel felt very fortunate that they left their place of work when they did, for in less than a minute the storm passed that very spot where they were working.

Jacob Zook Jr. and his son Samuel Zook give us their experience of damage from the tornado. Samuels had just come home about 15 minutes before the eye of the tornado passed over their residence. A shingle barn roof almost new was torn off with some rafters being 300 to 400 feet from the barn. The frame barn structure was crippled and twisted. It is believed that the barn well filled with hay and straw is what kept it from being a total disaster. And ¼ portion of the weather stripping was ripped off from the 20 x 40 foot straw shed. A 10 x 40 foot wooden stave silo was twisted off at 10 feet from the ground, and scattered in the driveway where Samuels had parked their team only a few minutes before the storm hit. The roof of the silo was carried about 200 feet into the meadow where 5 mares with colts were pasturing. They were not injured. A 14 x 40 foot chicken house was ripped to pieces and scattered for a few miles. A 50 ft. windmill tower was twisted, breaking the gear box when it hit the ground.

The greater part of the slate house roof was torn off. 35 window panes were broken without damaging a lot of the window frames. However, a lot of window blinds were damaged. A tree standing not far from the house with a 34 inch trunk was twisted off four feet from the ground and taken over the remains of the windmill tower.

Fire companies with rescue trucks and neighbors worked all night covering the house with plastic to keep the rain from entering and doing more damage to the structure and household goods.

The next week carpenters and people donating their time worked from early morning till late at night to restore the damaged structure of the building. The families expressed their thankfulness to all who helped to restore their building, and whatever was needed, including the abundance of food that was used to feed the working folks.

At the farm of Emanuel K. Esh, Kinzer, R. 1, the tornado passed through his corn and tobacco field, causing extensive damage. It picked up a round wire corn crib, carrying it a 100 yards and slamming it to the ground as though it were made of cardboard. The roof of another crib that was still full of corn was found about 300 yards away. A frame building, 20 x 50 feet two stories high that was used to stable cows and heifers was totally destroyed. One cow was killed from falling timber, another was trapped and was crippled but recovered. Part of the tin roof was ripped off the barn. A number of trees different sizes were either twisted off or up-rooted.

Emanuels had retired early that evening and had no knowledge of the storm until the next morning.

Henry S. Esh, Queen St., Gordonville, operates a bulk tank milk cooling and diesel engine business for the Amish farmers. He gives us a description of his experience. His land joins that of Daniel Esh. The powerful tornado passed through his lot causing thousands of dollars of damage to used stainless steel bulk tanks.

A 1000 gallon tank, weighing about 2000 lbs. was loaded on a trailer ready for delivery to a farmer. It was picked off the trailer and carried about 30 feet and slammed into the ground, damaging it to the extent that it wasn't usable and was sold for junk. The lid of the tank, about 100 lbs. was slammed against his house at the second story about 300 feet away, leaving an imprint on the brick wall that was noticeable on the room inside.

The inside refrigeration part of another tank was carried about 1000 ft. to a neighbor's lot across the street causing a lot of damage to the coils. A stainless steel sheet 4 x 8 feet was found resting on the main electric line causing a short circuit. The electric was off for a few hours for about 800 residents around Intercourse.

About one-half of the aluminum siding was ripped off the east side of the shop and scattered for a mile around. A number of window panes were shattered at the shop, house, and barn. Two trees 30 inches in diameter were up-rooted. A smaller maple tree was twisted in the ground about one-fourth turn but did not fall over and kept on growing. The family was shook up and was about to descend to the cellar when the storm passed on its way.

Henry had planted about 1 ½ acres of tobacco in his lot. The tornado funnel passed through it, shredding it to pieces. The tobacco would have been ready to be harvested in a few days.

Mrs. Warren Denlinger of Intercourse gives us a description of the damage to their house and garage. Fortunately they were not at home when the tornado passed. They had spent the weekend in the vicinity of Mt. Gretna. Their son was the only one at home. He went to the cellar when he felt the danger of the powerful wind storm.

A two car garage about 20 x 20 feet was lifted from the foundation. A fair sized tree standing about 100 feet from the building was twisted off and landed on a car in the garage, causing damage of $2000.

The north side of the house roof was torn off and scattered over town. There was not a great deal of water damage. There appear to be some miracles in every tornado. A hat was left undisturbed in the attic of the remaining part of the house roof, while a rafter from the house was carried about 500 feet. A piece of lumber 4 feet long was sticking in the ceiling.

It is rather unusual for a tornado to strike this part of Pennsylvania. People in Lancaster County are not aware of such a powerful wind storm, except once in a great while we do get after effects of a hurricane, so this was a hair raising experience for a lot of folks.

Imagine how a tornado funnel whips its tail as it travels along, totally demolishing parts of buildings, while other parts are left untouched. Twisting off trees of 30 inches in diameter and only a short distance away trees were left standing with no damage. Also the way they go up over some buildings for a distance, then come down again, sucking up anything that is in its path.

In the eight or nine mile stretch as this tornado passed through Lancaster County, we may feel fortunate that no human being was in the direct path of the funnel. In interviewing I have not learned of one person that was injured, but many a close call. We must believe that our Lord had control over that powerful wind storm. But what is the Lord trying to teach us?

Practically everyone in these days carries some kind of insurance, which is set up as a helping hand to replace the damage when some disaster strikes. Sometimes large sums of money are donated to the unfortunate one in expressions of sympathy. This is well and good, but money alone will not build a barn, or repair a battered up house. It also requires manual labor. What is more heart touching than to see people coming from far and wide, bringing food and working tools along to clean up and repair the damaged buildings. Women help prepare meals for the hungry working men. In such cases we would all rather be at the giving end than at the receiving end. But we never know how soon we ourselves will be at the receiving end. The writer feels that such occasions are what keeps our society together. It is not only for the ones directly involved, but for all of us.

In making the survey almost everyone expressed their thankfulness for the generous folks that come to help clean up and offered their help for whatever was to be done.

Intercourse is in the heart of a well known tourist attraction. When this tornado struck the community in the midst of the tourist season in Lancaster County, many of these people were amazed by what took place when the buildings were again restored. A farmer from Utah stopped at one of the places where the building project was going on. He asked to see the owner of the place. After a short conversation he handed the owner a nice sum of money. The man was shocked and hesitated to take the money. It was heart touching, here was a total stranger from a far away state. He had traveled this area and seen with his own eyes the great financial loss from the tornado. He wanted to share his sympathy by giving the money. The owner felt it would be a reward to the tourist if he accepted his offer, which he then did.

Now the questions remains, how do we respect other people who are total strangers? Are we willing to help those who are stricken with hardships?

People from the mid-western states would probably class this tornado as a twister or an ordinary wind storm. This is probably true compared to the tornado that swept through three states in 1965. Indiana then had the most damage. Or the one that struck Alabama on April 3, 1974. That one went on history as the most destructive tornado for a single day, hopping along through 13 states claiming 75 deaths and 838 injuries, with hundreds of millions of dollars of property destroyed.

-Gideon L. Fisher

Noah's Ark Would Cost $21 Million Today!

If Noah built his biblical ark today, he'd be up to his beard in debt.

The job would cost a whopping $21 million—about half the price of Exxon's largest supertanker.

"The cost would be unbelievable," says Melbourne Smith, a ship designer who has overseen the construction of many historic replicas.

"You have to remember the ark would be the size of a Great Lakes freighter—absolutely enormous. The amount of wood required to build the ark is staggering."

According to the Bible, Noah's ark was "300 cubits long, 50 cubits wide and 30 cubits high," which translates into a colossal 550 by 91 by 55 feet!

And that translates into a total cost of $20,642,562, based on a cost of $750 per cubic foot. The total includes paying 150 workers $31,200 apiece for a year's work!

THE BLACK BONNET

When I was 18 years old in 1931, I was working in Millersburg, Ohio, for the John Elders. He was a dentist and his wife Mary was an optometrist. I did the house work, cleaning, washing, and cooking. Everything was handy and I enjoyed being there alone through the day while they were in the office from 8:00 to 5:00. On Saturday PM I'd be free to walk uptown, two streets and if by chance I'd see a Mennonite neighbor I could go home with them, if not the Elders would take me home after office hours. Most home people around Berlin knew me and offered me a ride before I'd ask.

Back to the Elder home, the dentist and his wife went on a two week vacation, out of state. That meant two weeks vacation for me at home. "Those were a happy two weeks." All were glad to have me home as "absence makes the heart grow fonder!" It was over all too soon and it was Tuesday morning again. I was to go back to work and unlock the lonely house and have it all cleaned and dusted by the time they arrive home that evening.

I dreaded all the more to go back to town life, but never dared to complain to my mother as she had all she could carry with the younger children and all, without the older ones burdening her blessed heart.

That morning she called me early so I could ride with a neighbor who also had a job there. I was slow getting ready and of course missed my ride.

Well I thought I can walk the mile to the main road, a U.S. highway and catch a Slate Co. truck going from Berlin, to Millersburg. They always slowed down whenever they saw me walking to give me a ride and I was not really worried. My mind was somewhere else, after the two weeks at home, away from the different environment of the city.

I swung my coat over my shoulder and put my black bonnet on, with my small suitcase in hand, I was on my way walking down the small country road. My heart was merry and my steps light as thoughts flashed through my mind of the pleasant weeks I'd had with my parents, brothers, and sister. Having had even one extra day, as this was Tuesday. Yes my parents were not rich, but always had enough and never too much. We were taught from the Bible that if you have food and raiment to be thankful for it.

I was now the oldest in the family (with my sister married), and earning just enough for the family's grocery bill. Since my father's misfortune of losing his arm in a shotgun accident and being a hemophilic (bleeder) he had not gotten back to earning anything for his now quite large family of ten.

As I was approaching the main highway, I was wondering what the day was going to be like. Yes the Elders had gone on a trip to PA, I had worked in this house for a year, and I would have it spic and span by the time they returned. I'd be alone all day. "Did I have the keys?" I thought. "Yes they're here in my pocket."

Just then the sound of wheels behind me interrupted my thoughts. Yes, here comes a Slate Co. truck, I reckoned, with a chance to ride. It would be six more miles. "Have a ride?" "Hop on," he said. Scarcely had it stopped at the curb, till I was on the running board and into the cab, thinking it was a local truck. Yes they had often picked me up before. Hardly any other trucks went at that hour. (7 A.M.)

I had not noticed the unfamiliar driver, (who now tightly gripped my arm) or his cargo, and was on his way. "Where are you going?" "To Millersburg," was my answer. "Where is that?" he asked. "Six miles ahead." My lips quivered at that, him not knowing where Millersburg was. He must be a total stranger!

"How did you risk driving with someone you don't know?" was his next question. "Did you ever ride with a stranger?" "No," but shakingly and truthfully, I told him I took him for a Slate Co. truck, but saw too late it was not. We had always been warned not to ride with strangers.

"Didn't you see what was on behind?" he next asked. "No," I answered. "Well look out the back window," he replied. Looking back I saw a big red boat, a yacht, of some kind. "That is nothing but the devil's trap," the man said. "I'm from Ontario, driving to Louisiana. There is a large bay out there with an island and a house of recreation. There they do everything but what is right. They go out partying on yachts like this one I'm delivering. Yes, from which the girls never return."

My heart beat fast, offering up a prayer, "Lord help me."

"What have you in your suitcase?" he inquired. "Only a few extra clothes for the week," I said. "Why do you have that black bonnet on your head?" he wanted to know. "It's our way of dressing to represent our church, our belief," I replied. "Do you always wear a black dress?" he then asked. "No it just happened today, usually I wear other colors," I said.

"What do you do with the money you earn?" he asked. I told him of my father's misfortune and I told him I was earning the bread for the family of ten. "Do you always take all the money home?" he asked. "Yes," was my reply.

The man was becoming a bit uneasy. "What's your nationality?" he wondered. Not knowing exactly what nationality meant, I said, "Well we believe in God and the Holy Spirit. I am presently taking instruction for baptism in Jesus Christ."

The driver who was seemingly around 60 years of age, was still clasping my arm tightly. What would happen in one more mile?, I won-

dered. I was praying in childlike faith, "Lord help me." The blinker lights stopping traffic would not be on till 8:00 in Millersburg. There was no reason he would have to stop in town. It was only 7:30 A.M. Would he stop when he got to the square?

Silence went on for a few moments, then the man spoke, "My intentions were not to let you off. I travel all over this country and I'm afraid of no one, but I am afraid of God and I will let you off. I don't know much about God, but I'm afraid of him." Even the devils believe and tremble, I thought. If I ever prayed in earnest I did then, "Lord save me."

"Where do you want off?" he asked. "At the courthouse," I said. It was a block before my actual destination, but I thought this would give me a chance to try and escape if he didn't stop. "I will let you off, but if it were not for that black bonnet and the clothes you are wearing, you would never have seen your family or friends again!"

The air brakes slowed the truck and he soberly said, "Good-by little girlie, I will never see you again, not on this side, and not on the other." He let go of my arm and I jumped out. He waved his hand, pulled his air horn and headed south.

Like a dream I didn't feel the sidewalk as I walked to the Elder house. But I felt the presence of a living God. As soon as I got inside, I locked the doors. I went to the telephone and called some neighbor close to home to tell my folks I got there alright, though they knew nothing about my experience and neither did I tell them then. I was too shaken.

(P.S. Mother said she often prayed for this man until she knew he was too old to be living anymore, that God would touch his heart, so he would come to know Him and perhaps his soul could still be saved.)

(Sent in by her oldest daughter)

New Drivers Needed More Than "Horse Sense"

IT MAY HAVE been 60 years ago, but I still remember my dad's first solo drive in our Model T! He'd only had a few lessons in starting the car, but decided he was capable of handling it alone.

After Dad started the car, he headed down the driveway for his first spin in his Model T. The car began picking up momentum, and he quickly realized he wasn't going to be able to make the turn onto the street.

Dad was used to driving old "Jerry," our horse, so he began yelling, "Whoa, *whoa*, WHOA!" and pulling on the steering wheel the way you'd pull on reins.

Of course, four-wheeled Lizzie didn't respond the way four-legged Jerry did, and the car flew across the street and up an embankment and bounced into a stone wall. Luckily, Dad wasn't hurt; amazingly, neither was the car!

-Mrs. Preston Townsley, Ashfield, Massachusetts

John Maxwell, of California, says that in a lifetime the average person directly or indirectly influences ten thousand other people, and those in leadership positions influence many, many more. It is incredible the responsibility that rests on the heads of the home and church. And also, the influence of youth, how they influence others to do good or evil.

Bible Used

When I was a young boy my dad got a man to dehorn some cows. Sylvan Douctric was his name, I think. After dehorning an older cow with large horns they just bled and bled. So he sent my brother in the house to read Ezekiel Chapter 16 verse 6. It did stop then.

-LF

Unruh in the Sixties

In the fall of 1962 in Lower Pequea, due to growth a Church district was divided with a line having the bishop and two *mit deiner* in one dale and only one *diener* in other dale. Some people did not think that was right three in one district and only one in other dale. After a few years of *unlieve* and also not having communion a few years, in 1965 other bishops were called in and the *Gmay* line was changed which put one minister over in the dale that only had one minister. So now it was two and two but that did not last long as our ways are not always God's ways. In Oct. of the same year (1965) the minister that was put in other dale which only had one minister was suddenly called away. He was found laying peacefully on top of a low brooder house roof where he had been working that day, his hat was laying by his side. Life was gone. He did not have any sickness or heart problems that was known of. He was 63 years old at the time.

-LF

"World's Strongest Man" Dead at 61

VIDALIA, Ga. (AP)—Paul Anderson, once recognized as the strongest man in the world, died Monday at a Vidalia hospital after a long struggle with kidney failure and arthritis. He was 61.

Anderson, a native of Toccoa, set nine world records and 18 American records in weightlifting in the 1950s.

He won a gold medal in the 1956 Olympics at Melbourne, Australia, and set three Olympic records. He is the last American heavyweight to win an Olympic gold medal.

He is still listed in the Guinness Book of World Records for having lifted the most weight with his back in 1957—6,270 pounds.

Anderson's other feats included lifting a table with a half-dozen people on top, the back end of a pickup truck with horses onboard and a carousel with children sitting on ponies.

His health problems started in 1983 and he received a kidney from his sister, Dorothy Johnson of Toccoa. Anderson almost died when his colon ruptured a year later and he was in a coma for 10 days.

Anderson left amateur weightlifting in the late 1950s and began performing and speaking around the country up to 500 times a year to raise money to open youth homes for troubled and homeless young men.

-Aug. 16, 1994

About the Good Old Days
...1790...

By an old lady who likely lived in those days. She said there were no carpets or oil cloths, on the floor, or locks or hinges and keys for the doors. Father made nails as past time in the winter. No alarm clocks, but had six foot Grandfather clocks. We had no matches, coal, kerosene, and no cookstove. The fire was held on the hearth, buried by ashes. If it went out, we had to borrow from the neighbors, or the flint and steel or sun glass to help strike fire.

There were not rubbers for the feet. Fruit cans and jars were not in use, the foods were dried. There was no granulated sugar to can with and only rarely used. Coarse rye bread was generally eaten, wheat or white on rare occasions, only like harvest time. We had no caustic soda, baking powder or soda. We had no sweet potatoes, or tomatoes, no patent medicines. Ironing was not in style, nor wash machines, nor wash boards or sewing machines.

There were no seed catalogs, department stores, illustrated magazines, lead pencils, photographs (maybe in tin type pictures), no telegraphs, bicycles, autos, telephones or no railroads. No newspapers, our nearest store was six miles away.

The post office was 14 miles away, and the medical doctor 12 miles away. There were no public school systems, no school superintendent to come around. The teacher of private schools had to make their own quill pens.

There were no steel pens, they had to rule their own paper. School lasted for four months. They got a bit of reading and writing, less arithmetic.

Das Gericht.

Zum Schriftgelehter und zu uns
Sprichts Jesus in sein'm Wort:
Bon Jerusalem zu Jericho,
Da ging ein Jünger fort.

Und da er wandebt auf dem Weg,
Unter die Mörder fällt,
Die schlugen ihn gar haber todt
Und nahmen ihm sein Geld.

Ein Briehter aber ging hinab,
In Kleider schon und neu,
Und sah ihn liegen in der Grube,
Doch ging er an borbei.

Desselben gleichen ein Levit,
Der gudte hin und her;
Und da er meint daß niemand seh
Lies er ihn liegen leer.

Ein Samariter aber komm
Mit einrm wahren Herz,
Und sah ihn liegen an den Weg,
Begehrte seinen Schmerz.

Goßz Ol und Wein in seine Wehe,
Berband ihm seine Wund;
Er nahm sein Aovi in seine Hand
Und fühlte seinen Mund.

Er hobihn auf sein laitbar Tier;
Berbenge fand so gar;
Den Noften nahm er auf sich tebft;
Mitleidigbeit das war.

Nun will ich meiter sagen hier
Zu euch von dies Geichicht;
Denn diese Menschen sterbten auch.
Und kommen vor's Gericht.

Da kommt der Briester dann vor Gott;
Barmhergigkeit begehrt,
Er sagt wie er in dieser Welt
Sein Wort oft hat gelahrt.

Er sagt wie er so viele Leut
Bermahnt an vielen Ort,
Mit Tränen wies sie auf das Recht
Nach seinem heiligen Wort.

„Ja," spricht der Herr zu diesem Briest,
„Dies ift mir wohl bekannt:
Haft mohl gelehct doch nicht belebt.
Steh him zur linden hand.

„Nahmft meinen Hund in deinen Mund
Und raubeft mich die Ehr;
Dein Leben sagt mir was du bift;
Was hilft dir dein Gelehr.

„Zum Zeugnis teht es nun vor dir;
Dein Leben war ein Schein:
Durch engen Lur kommit nicht zu mir;
Geh hin zur Höllen Bein.

Da nun der Lebit ftand vor Gott
Ein Lämmlein war er gleich;
Die Tranen fliezen wohl und sein,
In Demut war er Reich.

Er sagt wie froh dafz er nun ift
Dafz er sein Lebenlang
Sich g'ubet hat zu loben Gott,
Im Wort und im Gesang.

„Biel Guteshab ich nun getan.
Biel Freundlichkeit bewies;
Gilf jedem der in Nöten war,
So er sich helfen lies.

Mufrichtig lebt ich auf der End
Und heilt ein mancher Schmerz:"
Doch weil er redet, in sein Bruft
Berdammte ihn sein Herz.

Da spricht der herre Gott zu ihm,
„Dein Leben ist mir fund,
Wie jagst du solche Soch zu mir
Aus deinem eigen Mund;

„Und weiß't du ectrogen haft
Mit deinen stolzen Herz,
Ubst deine Luft in deine Bruft
Und machst ein mancher Schmerz.

„In Sunden hait du jert geblebt
Und Mein'st ich weis es nicht;
Dein Heuchelei ist mir besannt;
Bei mir ist alles Licht.

„Du jagst im Wort und im Gesang
Haft du gelobet Gott;
Dies iag ich Dir, dein G'fang zu mir
War nur ein bloizer Spott.

„Die Ehr von Leut du begehrt,
Ein groben Nain' geliebt.
Und war'st auch von veil betrübt.

„Barmbergigfeit haft nicht getan;
Schäm'ft dich von meinem Rind,
Doch lag ich bei ihm auf dem Weg;
Nun bleibte deine Sünd."

Nun jeh ich liegen vor dem Her
Auf jeinem Anglesicht
Ein Menfch, es üt der Samarit,
Des bin ich wahl bericht.

„D Herre Gott," Spricht er zu ihm,
„Woll'ft dich erbarmen mein,
Ich weis daß ich verdienet hab
Berdammnis, Höll und Bein.

„In eignem Willen hab ich, Herr,
Mein Leben zugebracht:
Ich hab dich, Herr, und meinen Bruder
Ganz zu viel veracht.

„Zu viel gelebt für mich allein,
Die Liebe nicht geübt:
Ich jeb vor mir die Sünden mein
Ich hab dich viel betrübt.

„Nun lieg ich vor dir, Herre Gott.
Univert das ich fann jein;
Muf deine Gnad ferlies ich mich;
Wollft dich erbarmen mein?"

Nun büdte einen Engel fich,
Wahl zu derielben Stund,
Und nahm jein Nopf in jeine Hand
Und fühlte jeinen Mund.

Und fprach, „Du jollft dich jürchten nicht."
Und fürder hat gemeldt
Wie ihrer Serzen verlangt nach ihm
Da er war in der Welt.

Nun fommen viele Engln bei
In wundenlichen Zier,
Und fprachen. Daß der Bimmel rang,
„Der Samarit ift hier."

Und jangen auch ein neue Lied
Weil Fejus auf fein Throne
Sich büdt und legte auf fein Script
Ein güldone LebensDrone.

Und fprach, „Aomm her, mein lieber Sohn.
Bon Sünden bift du frei;
Bei mir jollfst vonen ervigich;
Dein Trubial ift vorbei."
                                    —Ein Bilger

A Handful of Nuts

MARIE'S STOMACH did some flips as she anticipated her first bus trip to the city alone. She had been to the city many times in the past with her mother, but today she was going by herself.

Later, entering the huge plaza in which her dentist had his office, she decided to browse through several stores before her appointment. Ambling up and down the aisles of the Fresh-Mart, her mouth began watering. Surely being in the city all day would justify buying something to eat, even if she had a packed lunch along from home.

Then she noticed them—nuts. They seldom had nuts at home, because her parents considered them a luxury. But today she was her own boss. She could buy what she wanted. Taking a bag from the roll, Marie deftly scooped some nuts into it. She walked on and without thinking, reached into the bag and popped a handful into her mouth. As she walked she noticed more things that would taste good and she began having second thoughts about the nuts. As her parents had taught her, there were other things less expensive which were just as good for her. Replacing the nuts, she picked up a bunch of bananas and a bag of cookies and headed for the cash register.

That night, as she returned home on the bus, she reflected over the day and felt good about how things had gone. All except for those nuts. Had she actually stolen a handful of nuts from a big city store? Should she go back tomorrow and admit what had happened? Surely not. It was such a small thing. So Marie put those nuts out of her mind and life went on as before.

With rapt attention, Marie listened as the minister spoke of the things that would keep one out of heaven. When he mentioned stealing, immediately a handful of nuts popped into her mind. "You are a thief. You will be condemned." She shivered. What if it really was so? Oh, surely she would not go to hell because of such a small handful of nuts. She tried to still her conscience as the minister went on talking.

Several times in the next number of years the scene of guilt would rise before her, but always she battled it down as insignificant.

Now ten years later the time had come for another dentist appointment. Marie had been to the dentist several times in between, but always she shook off the nagging feeling and returned home without making things right.

Descending the steps of the bus, her determination almost failed her again. What if the store had closed since that long ago day? But no. There was the sign big as ever, Fresh-Mart.

With quaking knees and trembling heart she entered the store. Where should she go? How should she do it? She had been so ashamed of her actions that she had never admitted to anyone what she had done. So here she stood, alone, unsure what to do.

Finally, mustering courage she did not feel, she approached the cashier and asked if she could speak to the manager. With a strange look on her face, the cashier admitted it would be possible. She turned and called him over the speaker system.

"You may step aside and he will be with you shortly." The words rang loudly in Marie's ears. Now everyone would wonder what was up. If only she could drop through the floor. But here came the manager toward her with businesslike strides. Kindly enough he inquired what he could do for her. Cheeks hot and hands cold, she stood there. Finally, with trembling lips she confessed her crime.

The manager looked incredulously at Marie. "You say you have felt guilty for ten years over a handful of nuts?"

"Yes."

"I have never heard of such a small thing making trouble with a conscience for such a long time, but thanks for making it right. I will gladly forgive you." He shook her hand firmly.

Marie felt as if she were floating on clouds as she left the store and made her way to the dentist. If admitting wrong brought such peace, why had she not done it sooner?

MARRIAGE IN AMISH BISHOP'S BLACKSMITH SHOP

To have taken place around the turn of the century in Holmes County, Ohio. A widower named Beiler, from Geauga County, Ohio, had been published to a Holmes County Miller girl in her late thirties.

As is often the case with the marriage of older people the ceremony was to be performed at the end of a regular Sunday worship service, without festivities or special meal. As the service was coming to an end and the presiding Bishop *"glay Daufit"* Miller was about to ask the couple to come forward for marriage, he was informed that the Miller girl had slipped out during the service and had not returned. Without further ado the service was dismissed.

Some days later the disappointed Mr. Beiler who was staying with his sister's family a half mile north of Bunkerhill (the recent Dan J. Miller farm)

became deeply depressed over the situation and realized it was time he spoke to someone about it. Walking across the fields to Bishop Miller's place (the recent Eli Raber farm) he found him at work in his blacksmith shop and began to pour out his troubles to him.

At about the same time the Miller girl, by now also deeply distressed at her actions, had came to Mrs. Miller for help. Mrs. Miller suggested they go out to the blacksmith shop to seek council of her husband. To their surprise Beiler and the Miller girl met each other for the first time since Sunday morning.

Miss Miller expressed her deep regret for what she had done and explained that her action was not due to any dislike or distrust of Beiler, but that during the service she had suddenly been struck with the overwhelming realization of leaving her home of over thirty years. Unable to cope with the thought, she had walked out.

Bishop Miller then explained to her the ancient marital law of "leave and cleave" (Mark 10:7) and reminded her of the Biblical account of Rebecca leaving her home for Isaac. Upon this she was comforted and gathered the courage to express her willingness to go with her commitment. After some further council with the couple the Bishop suggested that since they had been duly published and he had already preached their wedding sermon he could see no reason why they could not be married right there if they both desired. And so it was, with Mrs. Miller as witness to the occasion, that the Miller girl became Mrs. Beiler in Bishop David Miller's blacksmith shop.

Indiana Tornadoes

In April 1965, Palm Sunday Eve., the Elkhart Lagrange area of Indiana passed through an ordeal that will long be remembered. Tornadoes strong and mighty passed through.

BEDENKLICH HAPPENINGS

There were instances where buildings were lifted in the air and were seen floating in the sky. William McIntosh (29) lived with his wife Pat and their 15 month son Chris. The McIntosh's new automobile which had been bought only two days before was never found.

On the Bishop David Bontrager home it came fast. They hurried to the cellar. A moment later there was a roaring sound and crashing of timbers. Then the house was gone. They just stood there and looked around. We were in the clear and the house was gone. The Bontragers lost nearly everything. He was to preach at a funeral the next day, and had to borrow clothes and a hat to go.

Evan Lambright lost one leg several years ago so he could not move fast. They saw they could not make it to the basement as the black cloud enveloped the house. They embraced each other and were carried away with the house. If I lived to be 400 years old I would never forget it. When I opened my eyes we were in the middle of the road 35 ft. from where the house had stood.

Mahlon Eash watching from his home ¾ mile east said he saw the barn carried in the air. It was holding together and rolling over and over broadways in the air.

The license plate from the Rheinheimer tractor was found near, Jonesville, Michigan a distance of 80 miles. A Bible belonging to their son Ralph was blown away but later found not damaged at all. Loose papers which were in the Bible were still there.

It was supper at Dan Miller's along Road 5. This elderly couple lived alone, and Dan operated a harness shop. His wife Salome felt there was something in the air. Then she saw a sight she will never forget. With tears in her eyes she related how she saw the rolling black clouds bearing down on them. "Why Dan," she gasped, "those black clouds are right behind the shed." And they were, before they got to the cellar the windows in the rooms above them were falling in, all their buildings were wrecked but they were not hurt. Dan had purchased $300 worth of collar pads the week before, and they were scattered from Road 20 to Howe ten miles away. His harness shop was picked up and carried away.

West of the Vernon Mullet home was the residence of Harvey Millers. The Millers were away visiting her sister two miles south. When they tried to get to their home they found the road blocked. When they finally did get home their house was a shambles. The next morning their son Gerald was walking over the scene of the destruction where only the day before their home had stood. He noticed a book among the other debris. It lay open. A picture of a tornado caught his eye. He picked up the book. It was entitled *You and Science*. At the place it lay opened there was an article on tornadoes with a picture of one approaching. Beneath the picture was the advice "Take cover fast if you ever see a funnel like this one for a tornado is near." The book contained 594 pages and is considered no less than a miracle that it should have opened on the one page containing the article and picture of a tornado.

5 Children in One Year

Centreville, MI – Harvey L. Miller

Our son Owen and Ann Miller had a daughter Judith Lynn, born to them on June 10. Also a trio of triplets were born to Ezra and Martha Bontrager on June 22. They were born in Fort Wayne, IN Hospital and came home two days after they were born. One boy, Loren, 5 lb. 11 oz. and two girls, Lori and Leanne, each 4 lb. 9 oz. They are all three healthy and doing well.

When I told this news to my son-in-law from OH he said there is a non-Amish couple in OH who are van drivers now for the Amish. When their fifth child was born, all five of them were under 1 year old. The first two children were twins then 11 months later they had triplets. One month out of the year they are all five the same age.

Hard Times in Past

Was told of years ago when times were hard. The teacher had the children make rules and say what their punishment would be. The first offense was a poor boy stealing a big boy's lunch. He needed to take his punishment, which was a paddling across his back. The boy came to school the next day with only baler strings for a shirt. His only shirt was at home so his mother could wash it. He had a coat on but had to be removed to be punished properly. When the big boy saw this and knew why he stole his lunch because he was poor and hungry he offered to take this boy's place to be whipped. This is what Jesus did for us.

-Selected

No Cars on the Sabbath

Luke Chap. 16 vs. 20-25, should we desire our good portion in this life and inherit with Lazarus the kingdom of heaven where there is fullness of pleasure at the right hand of God evermore. This is impossible as trying to put the water of the Susquehanna River in a quart bottle. Just before World War II a large number of Hussitic Jews came from Germany to the USA to escape Hitler's gas chambers. Today they own a large section of New York City. They park their cars just before their Sabbath begins so that not a single car is going on their streets on the Sabbath. They all walk where they want to go, even to their church services. When they were asked, why would they all walk to church if they have cars? Their answer was, God told Moses Exodus Chap. 35 vs. 3, that they were not allowed to kindle a fire on the Sabbath Day. They explained that cars are fire wagons, which they are not allowed to start on the Sabbath because that would be kindling a fire. If there is no fire they do not move. When a chariot and horses of fire picked up Elijah and took him to heaven in a whirlwind 2 Kings Chap. 2 vs. 11, this was a different kind of fire wagon then the car. But today there are many people taken into eternity and the grave by the fire wagon the car. There have been accidents with God's good creatures as the horse, killing a man. Being killed by a horse is being killed by God's created animal which God calls very good in Genesis Chap. 1 vs. 25.

Our memories seem to echo from our loved ones who perished in silent slumber by the intemperance of speed. To elude our conscience is like trying to drown a fish.

Until reclaimed I remain in prayerful concern for those struggling in the under current of luxury.

-Titus B. Hoover, Sr.

Bedente Mensch das Ende

Bedente, mensch! das enbe, Bedente deinen too, Der tod kommt oft behende; Der heute frisch und roth, Kann morgen und geschwinder Himweg gestorben sehn; Drum bilde dir, o fünder! Ein täglich sterben ein.

2. Bedente, mensch! das ende, bedente das gericht: Es müssen alle stände Vor Jesus angesicht: Kein mensch ist ansgenommen, Heir muß ein jeder dran, Und wird den lohn bekommen, Rachvem er hat gerban.

3. Vedente, mensch! das ende, Der höllen angst und leib, Daß dich nicht satan blende Mit seiner eitelseit: Heir ist ein furzes frenen, Dort aber ewiglich Ein fläglich schmerzens schrehen, Ach fünder! bute dich.

4. Bedente, mensch! das ende, Bedente stets die zeit, Daß dick ja nichts abwende Von jener berrlichseit, Damit vor Gottes thorne Die seele wird verpflegt; Dort ist die lebensfrone Den kommen bengelegt.

5. Herr! lehre mich bedenfen Der zeiten leßte zeit, Daß sich nach dir zu lenfen, Mein herze sen bereit; Laß mich den too betrachten, Und deinen richterfuhl: Laß mich auch nicht verachten Der höllen feuerpfuhl.

6. Hilf Gott! daß ich in zeiten Auf meinen leßten tag Mit buße mich bereiten Und täglich sterben mag: Im tov und vor gerichte Steh mir, o Jefu! ben, Daß ich ins himmels lichte Zu mohnen würdig fen.

Bro. Billy had a frolic for his shop last Friday and again Monday night to replace the one that burned down this spring, their son Joey 19, fell or jumped around 8-10 feet and hurt his ankle and foot. He was otherwise okay. Then there was this one lady who was sewing on the porch. She went in to make supper leaving her 11-month-old baby on the porch, never thinking that wouldn't be alright. A few days later in his messy diaper she found 24 buttons, 1 snap, 1 hook, and one small eraser! She had not noticed anything different in the child at all.

-Mrs. Rosie Byler, 2015

THE ARAB FARMER *still uses camel power and a wooden plow as he did in the time of Christ. Jewish farmers are rapidly going to modern methods and machinery. 1954*

A Young Wife and Mother's Struggles

THE TWITTERING OF the birds and the other forest sounds went unnoticed by Mary as she sat in the pine grove, staring moodily into space. Her thoughts were in a turmoil, which was easy to see by the unhappy look on her face. She shivered at the thought, "Bound to a husband." Just what all would it involve?

"No, I won't ever marry," Mary told herself. "I want to be free. I want to teach school and travel and do the things I want to do."

Even as she pondered these thoughts, she knew they were not true. She, nineteen-year-old Mary Miller, was going steady with twenty-four-year-old Neil Miller. He was handsome; there was no doubt about that. But looks didn't mean that much to Mary. It was his character that drew her to him. He was steady, dependable, kind, and friendly. If he weren't, she would not be going with him. She loved Neil; she was confident of it. Her love had not come suddenly, but slowly over the months. And now she had promised to become his wife.

"But no, I don't want to be tied down with a husband and family," Mary told herself. And yet, deep down in her heart she wanted God's will for her life, and she felt God was leading her to marriage. But how, with her yearning for freedom and for teaching, could she submit to a husband?

Mary had another problem. She was a quiet person by nature, and found it hard to express her feelings to someone else. How would that work out in marriage? Wasn't a wife supposed to share her innermost thoughts with her husband? Another thing, she liked to spend her spare time in reading and writing, rather than visiting. She enjoyed going away by herself, like right now. A quiet time in the woods or down by the creek always gave her a lift. Would she have time for these things after she was married? And even if she had time, what would Neil think when she went off by herself?

"No, Neil," she whispered tearfully. "I can't do it. You will have to do without me."

And then the still small voice spoke to her. "But what about My will for you. Doesn't My will mean anything to you?"

"Yes, yes, it means everything to me," Mary sobbed. "But how can our marriage be successful if I can not express myself to my husband? And what if I can not submit my will to his?"

"My child, My grace is sufficient for thee," the Voice said.

Mary trembled. Dear, kind Neil. She had been so hard on him already. He tried so much to help her, and he came twelve miles to see her, Sunday after Sunday. With her moody spells, Mary often wondered why he kept on coming to see her. Was it love that brought him? The thought cheered her, and yet the feeling of dread and uncertainty was always there.

Mary jumped as something landed at her feet. Looking up into the tree, she spotted a bushy-tailed squirrel. He had dropped the acorn at her feet. She watched as the squirrel scampered away. "Even the wild animals are free to come and go as they please," she mused.

After a while, Mary was able to put her troubled thoughts in order. "Oh, Father, have thine own way in my life," she prayed, and this time she found it easier to surrender fully to whatever God had for her in the future, even if it meant being bound to a husband.

As she headed home to help with the evening chores, she found herself humming,

"Have thine own way, Lord, Have thine own way. Thou art the potter; I am the clay. Mold me and make me After Thy will, While I am waiting, Yielded and still."

THE DATE OF THE WEDDING was fast drawing near. Mary was busy helping her mother and sisters get ready. Yes, by now it was a day she was looking forward to—at least most of the time. She still felt small and incapable of being a wife, and possibly a mother, but she trusted that God's grace would be sufficient, as He had promised it would be.

Mary still had her doubts the day they were published. Neil, sensing that something was wrong, asked her about it. Her heart beat hard. "Are—are you s-sure you want me for your wife?" she asked fearfully.

A hurt look crossed Neil's face. Mary hated herself. She knew she had hurt him again. How could she be so cruel. Surely, a kind and loving man like Neil deserved a wife that was more normal than she was. Surely, no one else had ever had doubts about their marriage like she had.

Neil did his best to reassure her, after which she felt better again. And yet, "bound to a husband…" Could she truly live up to those words?

Mary remembered something a minister had once said at a wedding. A certain man and his wife could not get along with each other. One day the man decided something had to be done about it. Getting a rope, he threw it over the roof of their house. Then he called his wife and told her to wait until he gave the signal, and then to pull on the rope as hard as she could. He went to the other side of the house, took hold of the rope, and pulled, telling his wife to do the same. Both pulled and pulled with all their might, and neither of them got anywhere. Finally he told her to stop pulling, and to come over and help him pull from his side. Of course, the rope came their way very easily. The man then explained to his wife the need for them to pull together in marriage, rather than against each other. Mary had smiled at the minister's story at the time she had heard it, but it didn't seem

amusing to her at all now. Her concern was, would she be able to submit her will to her husband's, and pull with him instead of against him?

Neil had once said that marriage partners had to be like a good team of horses. If they pulled together, they could accomplish a lot. But if they didn't pull together—well, that was not very nice to think about.

Mary thought back to the different places she had worked. Some of the couples she had lived with and worked for did not have the kind of marriage she hoped she and Neil would have. But then there were others who always seemed kind and thoughtful toward each other. She was convinced it took love and patience and work on both the man and the wife's part if the marriage was to be successful. Would she be able to do her part?

THE WEDDING DAY ARRIVED. By looking at Mary and Neil, no one would have guessed the struggles the bride had gone through. And the struggles were not over. All throughout the sermon, many bits of advice were given to the young couple. And again and again it was stressed that their lives were to be bound together, and the two were to become one.

"Please, Lord, help me," Mary prayed repeatedly.

Mary's uncle was a bishop and had the main part. When the right time came, he called Neil and Mary up to him, and asked them the questions that preceded the marriage. Then, after the usual prayer, he placed their hands together and performed the ceremony, pronouncing them man and wife. He told them they could not part until death parted them, except in a sinful way.

The chills ran up and down Mary's spine. Marriage was such a scared, blessed union. Once more her thoughts went heavenward. "Father, help me do my part," she pleaded.

A FEW DAYS AFTER the wedding, Neil and Mary moved close to Neil's parents' home. Mary missed her family as she did not get to see them often. However, she liked their new home, and found her in-laws easy to get along with. Having lived in a large house, it took some adjusting to settle down in a trailer.

At first Mary thought things were going very well. She had tried to prepare herself for the adjustments that went with the first year of married life. But just as she thought things were going smoothly, small annoyances started to bother her. Neil burped right in her presence, and didn't even excuse himself for it. When he ate, he made such loud, cracking noises that nearly drove her to distraction. He also had the habit of turning his shirts and pants and underwear inside out to pick off the small tuffs of lint that gathered on the seams. He rolled those tuffs into a ball and she would find them on the floor later. Sometimes he even threw them at her, just to tease her. She didn't mind that, because then she could at least pick them up and put them in the waste basket where they belonged.

Mary soon found out that she and Neil were exact opposite in many ways. She liked to work fast and see how much she could get done in an allotted time. Neil worked slowly and carefully. She could make up her mind and change it half a dozen times before Neil made any decision at all.

Most provoking of all was when she had a meal ready and Neil didn't come. What could be keeping him? When it happened over and over again, things got the best of Mary and she lapsed into one of her moody spells. Afterwards, she repented and felt selfish and guilty. "When and how will I ever learn to live in harmony with Neil?" she wondered.

Neil often spent time talking to Mary. He helped her whenever he could, and asked forgiveness when he had hurt her feelings. It seemed to Mary that she, too, was constantly in need of apologizing to Neil. She often felt she was not cut out to be a wife, and wondered if she had done the right thing by getting married. However, finding it hard to express these thoughts even to her husband, she kept them to herself.

Most of the time Mary felt she could not ask for a better husband. Sure, Neil had his faults, but so did everyone else. He was kind and patient and considerate—more so than she was. She knew Neil did his part, in fact, more than his part.

A FEW DAYS SHORT of eleven months after their marriage, Neil and Mary were blessed with a healthy baby boy. But as it turned out, silence seldom reigned at their house anymore, because little Neil was a colic baby. Mary now had little time to spend with her husband, and it seemed she was always tired. Many were the times when she walked the floor with the baby. Neil helped with the baby at night, but he was such a heavy sleeper he seldom awoke to hear the infant's cries.

Sitting on the rocker one night with the baby who simply would not stop crying, things sort of got the best of Mary. Tears of bitterness and self-pity rolled down her face. "I can't accept this, Lord," she wept. "I simply wasn't made for marriage."

The battle was a long and hard one. One part of herself wanted to hate her husband and baby, and everything that had changed her life from being a carefree, happy single girl. She could not help but envy her single friends and the freedom they had. But no, that was not right. When these thoughts had stilled themselves, she heard the still Voice deep within her heart. "My grace is sufficient for Thee." As Mary pondered on these thoughts, other followed. "I have sinned, Lord. I know I love my husband, and this precious baby You have given us. Give me strength to bear up under these new responsibilities I am so weak and small. I can not walk this way alone."

Again the small Voice said, "I will help you, and so will Neil, if you but ask for help."

It was in that dark hour that Mary saw the need of confiding in Neil. And even though it was not easy, she found it possible, with God's help, to do so. Neil was understanding, and blamed himself for not being a better husband and father. They promised each other that they would spend more time in prayer, each for the other as well as for themselves. Together they made a new beginning. Mary could not believe how close she felt to Neil after she had shared her innermost thoughts with him. It drew a bond of closeness Mary had never experienced before.

At four and a half months, Baby Neil turned into a sweet, quiet baby. How much more enjoyable it was to care for him now, and Mary found herself relaxing. How thankful she was that the first year of marriage was behind them, and that God had blessed her with such a loving and understanding husband.

Before Baby Neil was quite a year old, Nathan arrived. He turned out to be just what little Neil had been—a colic baby. Once again Mary went through some discouraging days. She had her hands more than full. Little Neil was at the age that he got into everything, especially when she was occupied with Nathan, which was most of the time.

Mary found that Neil could be a big help to her, but even so there were times when she wondered why this was to be her lot in life. Oh, to be free to come and go as her friends were! But she always felt guilty over such thoughts. It was wrong to covet, and she knew there were many childless couples that would have been happy to exchange places with her.

Once again Mary turned to God for help, and once again she found her husband loving and patient and willing to help. He always had a knack of seeing the bright side of life, and of making the best of things. When little Neil got into mischief, his daddy reminded Mary that he was a normal, healthy boy, full of energy. With training, which they were trying to give him, he would hopefully outgrow his naughtiness and become a well-adjusted, lovable little helper.

YEARS PASSED. Another baby arrived. Once again Mary sat up nights caring for her little one. But for some reason, she found it easier to do. One day she suddenly stopped to think. She had not had one of her moody spells for a long while. "I guess I'm too busy for them now," she mused with a smile. "And I'm a lot more contented with Neil, and find it easy to tell him about my troubles, and my joys, too."

Mary was folding diapers. She let her mind wander. What had made a difference? She knew the change hadn't come on a certain day, or through a certain incident. It had come gradually, little by little, over the months and years. By sharing their thoughts and feelings, their joys and struggles, she and Neil had become one. Their lives had blended, and they could live together in peace and love and harmony.

"Yes, our Heavenly Father has kept his promise," Mary mused thankfully. "His grace was sufficient, and now I'm bound to a husband, and happy to be his wife and the mother to his children."

No Lights

Some time ago I read a story about a strike of electrical workers in the city of Paris, France. The workers felt they were providing a valuable service to the city, but were being underpaid. "Just let them do without electrical power for a while," the workers fumed. "Then they'll realize how much our work is really worth."

The very day the strike was to begin, the child of one of the workers was stricken with a severe illness. When the doctor arrived, he examined the girl carefully. His face was very grave as at last he straightened his back and looked into the worried eyes of the mother standing near the bed.

"She will need an immediate operation," the doctor announced. "It is urgent."

The mother clasped her hands. "Oh, how I wish my husband were here to go with us to the hospital," she moaned. Anxiously she glanced out the window and down the street. "Usually he is here by this time."

"I'm sorry," said the doctor. "We don't have time to go to the hospital. We will have to operate immediately—right here. It is our only hope."

The skillful doctor, who had experience in coping with many emergencies, quickly prepared the kitchen table for the operation. He hurriedly sorted from his bag the tools and instruments he would need. The sun had gone down, and darkness was just beginning to fall. When everything was ready, the doctor flipped the switch quickly for the light. But nothing happened. The room remained dark. There was no electrical current. It was impossible to perform the operation. Just at that moment the father burst into the room, unaware of the doctor's presence and exclaimed, "Hurrah! The strike is complete. There isn't a light burning in Paris!"

How short-lived that poor man's elation turned out to be, as the life of his precious daughter slipped away, the first victim of the strike her father had helped to plan. He had planned to make others suffer—never dreaming that he would be the first to be harmed by the strike.

-1978

The Word Up

The English language is kind of mixed up in the word up! If you ever thought about "up" means up toward the sky or top of the list. But when we wake up in the morning we get up. At a meeting why does a topic come up? Why do we speak up. And we use it to brighten up a room, polish up the silver, warm up leftovers and clean up the kitchen. We fix up our buggies, people get stirred up, line up for tickets. Work up an appetite, think up excuses, a drain needs to be opened up because it's plugged up. We open up a shop in the morning then we close it up at night. Some people seem to be mixed up about up, so I guess I'll wrap it up—times up, so it's time I shut up.

-Selected

Tractors in the 1920s

In the 1920s when tractors were starting to be used, some Amish also got them. When the Bishops decided to *fersalk* them one man could not give himself up to put it away. He left the Amish church. In later years that item that he could not give up was the cause of his death in 1960. He died in a tractor accident.

THE SILENT PREACHER

Stephen and Anna King

Good morning everyone. It is a nice November morning with the wind howling from the north. On Sunday, we hitched Rosy to the carriage and headed for dad Ebersol's. It seemed empty without aunt Becky there. There were several funerals in this house in the past years. Daudy Abe died in 1974 and then my wife's mother died in 1991, her age was 50 years old. Then Alvins Emma died in 1989, age four years old, and then mommy Annie told stories of years ago. Her parents were John Zooks, east of Intercourse area. Her parents died when mommy was quite young yet. Mommy had an uncle Joe Zook who was a minister with whom she had her home with. In 1921 this uncle Joe Zook moved to Dover, Delaware. Mommy told the story as if it happened yesterday. She went with the family out to the train station and bade them farewell; which caused some tears. This Joe Zook was the first Amish minister to move out of Lancaster County. They then moved from Delaware to Tennessee. There were a lot of these *nochkomene* out west at this time. When we were out west we met up with some of them and they gave us the family tree of this Joe Zook and also the history of his life in Lancaster and his movings. This was not who they called Tennessee Joe. At the time, uncle Joe was living in Dover. There was a dispute in the church as one of the ministers were silenced and he told the church that he would never preach to them again. Well, the time came that he got his position again. He stood up to preach and the church people could see his lips going, but no voice came out. He never did preach again.

AT MILESTONE FIFTY-SEVEN

Through the rich rolling farmlands of eastern Pennsylvania winds the old Lake To The Sea Highway which is now known as Route 322. Along its many miles as it stretches from Philadelphia to Lake Erie are many landmarks and every so often is still seen an old-fashioned milestone. If these milestones could talk they would tell many stories of hundreds of horses trotting past, pulling stage coaches, Constoga wagons, loads of produce going by on their way to the markets.

They could tell of creaking wheels passing both in summer and winter, in heat and cold and all kinds of weather. They would tell of the coming of the horseless carriage, the cars, trucks, and busses, the heavy semi-trailers that make the few remaining milestones tremble as they pass by. They could tell of many lives lost along this road.

Today the traffic is very heavy on this highway both night and day. It is not very safe to travel with horse and buggy or by bicycle, in spite of the fact that it goes directly through the heart of the Old Order Mennonite Settlement around Ephrata and through the town of Ephrata. There have been many accidents on this highway and many of our people have been killed on this road including Bishop Harvey H. Nolt.

Also along this highway is located the Stauffer Mennonite Church with its adjoining cemetery. This church was built in 1845 and its horse barn is the only one in the country. The Stauffer who established this church is the same one who wrote the Stauffer booklet which is still in print today.

But our story, which is taken from the pages of history is about a stretch of this road where the milestone is inscribed with "27 to T., 57 to P." Jacob Stauffer (a relative of the man who founded the above mentioned Stauffer church) grew to manhood as a member of a prominent Mennonite family who attended meeting at Groffdale. Jacob became wealthy and owned many acres of land in the vicinity of what is now the city of Ephrata. In about the year of 1807 he married a pious Mennonite girl by the name of Mary Weaver. Jacob and Mary went to housekeeping on one of Jacob's large farms and were a happy couple for a time but this did not last.

Sad to say, Jacob had very little in common with the woman he married, for she was a pious Christian girl and he was of the earth— earthly minded. He did not care for the Mennonite meetings and gradually took to drinking and kept himself up in bad company. Mary perceived that she had not made a wise choice but she did not murmur. About this time Jacob announced he was going into the hotel business and started building a hotel along the highway. No one can tell what sorrow this must have brought to the soul of the pious Mennonite girl who was his wife for she felt that surely a curse would come over their family. Steadfastly she prayed that the Lord might stand by her and the children and not suffer any of them to wander into the paths of wickedness, even if she were no longer there to help them. Weary and broken in health she moved with her husband into the hotel he had built at Murrel which is close to Ephrata at the milestone which says, "27 to T., 57 to P."

Here the mother toiled with her nine children. Fearing that they would follow the path of their father, she prayed for them and worked with them both night and day and hoped the Lord would guide them right. While the mother's toils were bringing her closer to Heaven, the father was fast traveling the downward path. Jacob held fox-hunts, all kinds of gatherings, dances with much drinking, dragging his daughters among the drunken men. But they remembered the teachings of their mother and fought against all temptations. In later years, Solomon, one of the sons, said he could never enter a hotel without shuddering.

One evening a stranger came to the inn and asked for something to eat. When Mary went to the barn to get some eggs, she was frightened by a drunken man who got up from among the hay. Stepping backwards, she fell from the haymow and was severely hurt.

The next day as she lay on her deathbed she called her son, Solomon to her side and said, "I cannot pray for the children any longer so I want you to promise to pray for them every evening." That evening the mother passed away. Solomon kept his promise and prayed for them and tried to help them as his mother had.

After the mother's death, the children were alone and tried to do their best. Their father seemed to care less for them. Later he married a southern woman who was cruel to the children, so they were put out into other homes, all except Mary who was retarded. She was put into the alms house in Lancaster.

When the older children married they remembered their younger brothers and sisters and took them into their homes. All of them that grew to manhood were Christians, so in the end the prayers of the pious mother were answered.

STRENGTH FOR TODAY

When you are afraid, read.....................Psalm 46

When you are sick, read.........................Psalm 121

When you are lonely, read.......................Psalm 23

When you are discouraged, read.................Isaiah 40:28-31

When you are in sorrow, read....................Psalm 34

When you are in danger, read....................Psalm 91

When friends fail you, read......................Psalm 27

When you need an ideal, read....................1 Corinthians 13

When you want peace, read.........................John 14

When God seems far away, read.................Psalm 130

When you have sinned, read......................Psalm 25

When you forgot your blessings, read............Psalm 103

When your faith seems failing, read..............Hebrews 11

When the world seems too big, read...............Psalm 90

When you want Christian assurance, read.........Romans 8

When you seek happiness, read....................Colossians 3

When you want to pray, read.......................Psalm 86

When you feel misused, read......................Matt. 5:3-10

When you are tempted, read.......................James 4

When you are discontent, read....................Phillipians 4:4-13

When you are thankful, read......................Psalm 95

Has anyone else seen or heard of this wondrous thing that was seen in the sky one day in June of this year? 2013.

The sun was shining bright as was 10 or 12 noon when suddenly there was a rainbow colored face with wings like an angel and a heart shape and hands holding the heart. This was sent to us by our daughter living in the Auburndale, WI area. Their English neighbor saw it and took a picture of it and showed it to them.

Makes a person wonder what it means.

-Chris Herschberger
Bloomfield, IA

A Trick Horse

About 1950 I was in need of a driving horse and heard of a certain horse dealer who got a load in from Kentucky. I made it my business to see what kind of horses this dealer had, and whether he had any that would suit me. After showing me a number of his horses, we discussed prices. He had a nice black horse 7 years old that appealed to me. The dealer said he was trained to be a trick horse. But I was not the least bit interested in his tricks.

At this time I wanted a gentle type horse, well broke because of my family of small children. The horse was a nice sized carriage horse. The dealer asked $125 for him. I hitched him soon after I got him home, and was well pleased with him. One morning when I was currying him, he laid down right beside me in the stall, I was scared for I thought something had come over him, for he lay there and grunted as if in pain. In a few minutes he got up on his feet, and everything appeared to be alright. A few days later the same thing happened. Then I was curious to know why the horse would lie down while being curried. It came to my mind that the dealer had told me that the horse was trained to be a trick horse. I thought that I had probably touched a certain spot on him that was used to train him to lie down.

I went over his body trying to locate the spot. Sure enough I found it. So I took him out to a plot of grass, then I touched him at that certain spot and down he went, stretching out as if he was sleeping. When I talked to him he jumped on his feet again. This I did a number of times, and the horse seemed to enjoy getting so much attention. My conscience was not quite satisfied so I tried to find some more of his tricks. I discovered that by touching certain spots he would shake his head "Yes" or "No." If I held my hand at a certain spot

he would paw with his front foot. If a stranger came to see his performance and asked Prince different questions, he would answer them in horse sense. Questions like what would he do if he was tired, if I touched him behind his front leg, he would lie down and sometimes roll over on his back. If he was asked if he likes grass he would nod his head "Yes" if I touched him on his breast. If he was asked do you chew tobacco he would shake his head "No" if I touched him on top of his neck. If he was asked how old he is he would paw as long as I held my hand on his shoulder. I always tried to turn Prince in such a way that the curious person was on the other side and could not see me touch him at different spots. He was also a good riding horse. I wondered if he was trained for jumping. I took him back of the barn and fixed a rail for him to jump and sure enough he jumped over it with ease. He jumped a rail 3 feet high easily. He probably knew more but I needed him for his working ability. When he was 12 years old he got breathing problems and I had to get rid of him.

-*Gideon Fisher*

The Traveling Bible
Mrs. Dan M. Borntreger, 2015

The Amish have been involved in cleaning up at the storm site in Delmont. The Bible which belonged to the Delmont church was found twenty-five miles north close to Mitchell. It was still intact. A whole row of houses in Delmont lay in ruins. What a feeling that must be for the occupants. Christian Aid Ministries of PA has sent a groupd out here to help.

Ein Schönes Dank-Lied

1.

Wir danten dir, Herr Jesu Thrift,
   Dafz du ein Kindlein worden bift;
Des banft dir alle Chriftenheit,
   Und freut fich des in Ewigkeit.

2.

Wir danten dir, Herr Jesu Thrift,
   Dafz du ein Menfch geboren bift,
Bon einer Jungfrau rein geboren,
   Dafz wir nicht möchren fein verloren.

3.

Wir danten dir, Herr Jesu Thrift,
   Dafz du vom Himmel kommen bift,
Und haft als ein Römig gerecht,
   Gelöft das ganze memchlich Gefchlecht.

4.

Wir danten dir, Herr Jesu Thrift,
   Dafz du für uns geboren bift;
Daiz und der Teufel Tob und Sünd
   Wilt feiner Macht nicht überwind.

5.

Wir danten dir, Herr Jesu Thrift,
   Dafz du daz Lämmlein worden bift;
Daiz wir im Kreutz geduldig fein;
   Uns iröften beiner Schroeren Bein.

6.

Wir danten dir, Herr Jesu Thrift,
   Dafz du für uns geftorben bift,
Und halt uns burch bein teured Blut
   Gemacht vor GOTT gerecht und gut.

7.

Wir danten dir, Herr Jesu Thrift,
   Dafz du der rechte Mittler bift;
Nach deiner Gnad gedente mein,
   So mird ich ewig bei dir fein.

8.

Wir danten dir, Herr Jesu Thrift,
   Dafz du soin Lod aufg'ftanden bift,
Und haft dem Lod zerftört die Macht.
   Und und das Leben wider bracht.

9.

Wir danten dir, Herr Jesu Thrift,
   Dafz zu gegen himmel gefahren bift.
Und haft für mich und alle velt
   Bezahlt ein ewig's Löfe-Geit.

10.

Wir danten dir, Herr Jesu Thrift,
   Dafz du bei deinem Bater bift;
Und mo du bift ba will ich fein.
   Hilf Herr ben Fchwachen Glauben mein

11.

Wir danten dir, Herr Jesu Thrift,
   Du mein Heiland und Helfer bift,
Du weift mein elend und mein Mag.
   Biel beffer als ich dir es fag.

12.

Wir danten dir, Herr Jesu Thrift,
   Du ein rechter Noth-Selfer bift;
Befekie du die Geele mein,
   Go wird ich ewig bei bir fein.

13.

Wir danten dir, Herr Jesu Thrift,
   Ich weis dafz du mein Tröfler bisht;
Wer glaubt an GOTT und auf ihn traut
   Rein ftarter Haus ward nie gebaut.

Compiled by Moses B. Lapp

Once a Maid— Now a Mother

AS A YOUNG GIRL, I enjoyed the challenge of being a maid and I have many precious memories of the time I spent helping out in various homes. What compares with the feeling of satisfaction of having given a tired, busy mother a lift and knowing it is appreciated? I especially enjoyed taking over the household duties after the arrival of a new baby in the family. It was a challenge to step in and try to fill a mother's place for a few weeks. This was firsthand experience what a mother's life is like and I really enjoyed it, but I was always ready to turn everything over to the mother again when the time came to do so.

Working as a maid is a good experience for any girl, and especially for the younger girls in the family who do not have the chance to help with babies or small children. It is interesting and educational to observe the many different ways of doing something, and it is also enlightening to observe the methods that are used in handling and training children. All in all, being a maid is a very rewarding experience if it is done willingly and cheerfully. It is a privilege I'm glad I didn't miss.

But now the tables are turned and I find myself at the other end of the deal. Because of failing health I must depend on others to help with my work from time to time. It is not as I would prefer it, because I enjoy doing my own work. But since that cannot be, how thankful we are for girls who are willing to lend a hand in time of need.

I want to be considerate of my maids, so that working for us can be a rewarding experience for them. I want to trust my maid with my things and my work so that she can relax and feel at home with us. That is not always the easiest for me, as I would choose to do my own work and I like to do it precisely. But it won't hurt me to have things done differently for a little while.

What does it matter if the wash isn't hung up like I would do it—it can dry anyway. I love the satisfaction of watching the laundry flapping in the breeze, neatly hung up with like garments all in a row. Then I remember the time when I was the maid and to save space on a crowded line, I hung up a few hankies by the corner. Later, I happened to see my "mistress" hanging them up properly somewhere else.

"Just as if they couldn't dry like that for once," I thought. It was humiliating at the time, but I think it helps me to remember to be forbearing with the ways of my maid, as long as her way still works.

I want to be gentle with corrections and suggestions where they are needed, remembering that my maid does not yet have the experience that I do, but she is getting trained for her future by working for me and I want to make this experience a pleasant one for her in every way I can.

Maids are such an inspiration with their youthful vigor and enthusiasm. It is uplifting to watch them tackle a job, especially a long neglected one, and to hear them sing as they work. Indeed, are they not in a sense like "ministering angels?" So let us treat them respectfully and be sure to let them know that we appreciate their service. How thankful we are that our girls are available and willing to help out when someone needs help. May the good Lord bless them richly for their help and inspiration, both now and in their future.

-A Thankful Mother in Kentucky

Blacky the Crow
by D.B.

MY EARLIEST RECOLLECTION of Blacky The Crow was when he arrived at our house in a brown paper shopping bag with not a feather on his body. As close as I can figure I was around four years old. My father was a trapper and had caught a whole litter of baby foxes out of their den. This was in the spring of the year. We lived on a dairy farm, and the silo being empty, he kept the baby foxes in the silo. A neighbor saw them and offered to trade a baby crow for a baby fox. It was a deal. The trade was made. We got our crow and he got his fox. The crow was with us for the next fourteen years. The fox escaped his pen the very next week.

I don't remember exactly when or how Blacky got his name but it did seem to fit him well. I sometimes think he was black all the way through. The first while we kept him in the house and I remember feeding him worms, bugs, and bread with milk. He would open his mouth and gobble an unbelievable amount of "food" with a "num num num" sound. When he was older he could easily crack an egg open with his beak. He loved eggs.

When Blacky was big enough to fly he would go with my father to bring the cows from pasture at dawn. He was always glad to see us in the early morning. We thought he might start to associate with the wild crows and eventually leave with them but one morning he had a surprise. Evidently he had invaded another crow's domain because there was an aerial battle with feathers flying and when Dad got back to the barn with the cows, Blacky was already there. After that he was careful to stay away from wild crows.

He knew when we would eat supper in the evening and would come to the back porch where we would feed him. (One of his favorite treats was raw hamburger.) This was right outside the kitchen door. One evening we heard him out there and Dad say, "Hello, Blacky."

"Hello," the reply came. We looked at each other, thinking there must be someone out there. There wasn't. Blacky could talk. Suddenly Blacky was famous. He could say, "Hello, Blacky" just as plain as I could. Matter of fact he sounded a lot like me. Maybe because I spent so much time with him. We actually grew up together. Eventually he could say "Well, well," and "Whoa."

He could also laugh in a very haughty way. He would be very interested whenever we would turn the cows out of the barn, sometimes flapping his wings at them, hopping onto their backs and pecking them. This reminded me of a dog, helping to chase them out to pasture. What do you say to cows that you are chasing out of a barn? "Get out of here" of course. Blacky would never quite master that. It would come out "ka-wa-wa-wa." Quite comical.

He also seemingly thought he was human. So I would get up real close to him and talk to him saying, "Hello, Blacky" over and over until he would finally talk. It was great fun to watch people's eyes when they heard him for the first time. Especially the doubters. It was like "Am I really hearing this?" Sometimes Blacky just wouldn't talk, even for me, and then Dad would scold him and shout "BLACKY!" at him. If he felt like he was trapped or couldn't make a fast enough getaway, he would start talking. He would say "Hello, hello, he-llo, well, well" just as nice and friendly as you please.

Blacky could always tell who was afraid of him and would act accordingly. One neighbor boy often had to pass our house to run errands for his mother. Blacky would recognize him way up the street and start to jabber excitedly, flap his wings and strut and hop about. He would meet him at a certain point and harass him unmercifully, diving at him like a hawk. The poor boy started to carry a stick and walked way out into the field to try to bypass our house but if Blacky was home he wouldn't ever get by without an attack or two.

Sometimes when we would go visiting or to church with the horse and buggy, Blacky would go along. He would fly along ahead and sit on the light poles or wires until we caught up, then he would fly ahead again and that way we would arrive at our destination. Mother was always so embarrassed when that would happen. Blacky would very often cause a commotion, flapping his wings and hollering "whoa" at the horses.

Then when services would begin he would sit outside where he could look in and carry on as only he could. I remember Dad sending me out to see if could catch him or chase him home. He only went home if he wanted to go home. All he had to do was stay out of my reach until I tired or despaired of catching him and went back inside, then he would be right back as though he was the guest of honor. Blacky had no shame. He had an uncanny ability to detect a trick or attempt to catch him. He knew if we put the harness onto the horse we were going to go away and if he wanted to go along he would.

Blacky had a very playful side too. I've seen him go along the clothesline and pull the clothespins off mother's clean wash, letting them fall to the ground. He would also jump up and grab the bottom of the clean wash with his dirty feet and swing in the breeze like a child on a swing. In the winter time when we had high snow piles along the side of the driveway, he would get on top of them, then turn over onto his back and slide down much like a child on a sled. He would do that over and over.

Very often in the spring of the year, Blacky would wander away from home and sometimes be gone for a week or more at a time. Very often someone would tell us where he was. He would go to places like a school where there were lots of children or lots of activity and he could get the attention that he craved. He was very much a show-off. Usually when he got tired of it or hungry enough he would come back home. Sometimes we went and caught him and brought him back home. Then we would clip his wings so he couldn't fly for a while. The trouble with that was we always worried that some cat or predator would catch him when he couldn't fly so we never clipped them too short.

Blacky was a terrible pest when we would work on farm machinery. He would notice tools or parts lying around and would watch his chance to dart in and pick up anything small enough for him to carry in his beak and hop or fly away with it. It wasn't easy to get anything away from him if he thought you wanted it. The best approach was to act as if you really didn't want whatever he had and soon he would lose interest in it and drop it.

I can still see Dad scrambling out from under some machinery and pick up a hand full of gravel and fling it at him to chase him away or make him drop something he was trying to snatch. As far as I know he never had a treasure nest where he would take his plunder. He always lost interest in whatever he had if he thought you didn't want it.

Toward the end of his life he would spend most of his time in the barn close to his roost. He wouldn't talk much anymore and was very droopy. One day I moved some machinery out of the barn and found a bunch of black feathers. Blacky had either died and fallen off his roost or some stray cat was able to catch him because of his lack of mobility. That was the end of Blacky The Crow.

BIG BRUTUS

What is the biggest machine you ever saw? Just south of the little town of West Mineral, KS, stands a very large electric shovel. This machine even has a name. It goes by the name of Big Brutus. This shovel is taller than a 15-story building—160 feet from the ground to the point sheave at the top of the boom. Miles before you reach this retired giant you can see that huge boom rising above the horizon. During its working days it was used in the coalfields of southeast Kansas. Big Brutus did not dig coal. The huge bucket removed the overburden (dirt & rocks covering the coal seams). Yes, the bucket is huge. The size of the bucket is 90 cubic yards, approximately 150 tons of dirt and rock on one scoop or enough to fill three railroad cars. It took four cables, 3½ inches thick and powered by eight 500 horsepower electric motors to lift the bucket.

Big Brutus was erected on site in the minefields. The period of erection was from June 1962 to May 1963. A peak number of 52 men were employed to erect the shovel. 150 railroad cars were required to ship all of the component parts of the shovel. After the shovel was completed it ran 24 hours a day for 11 years. It ceased operations in April 1974. They quit using it because of high operating costs. The electric bill of Big Brutus last month of operation was 27,000 dollars.

Now it is retired on the bank of a strip pit, like an old ship, resting in its harbor—a place of its own making. Now it is open to the public as a museum. A memorial dedicated to the rich coal mining history of southeast KS. Visitors can go up inside the machine and inspect the many parts and components, as well as sit in the operator's seat. It makes a person feel small to stand beside it. Big Brutus dwarfs even the biggest farm equipment of today. West Mineral is located 7 miles north and 6 miles west of Columbus, KS. Have a good month!

-Henry R. Borntrager

THE MISSING PIONEER MAN

A pioneer man was spotted by Indians, so he quickly crawled up a tree to escape, where he found a huge hole partways up the tree. Having a rifle along, he got into this hole, but the hole was quite deep. He heard the Indians outside. He felt lucky to escape, but alas! He couldn't get up and out again. By using his hunting knife to cut steps inside he still could not crawl up out of the hollow tree. Eating sparingly of eats in his pocket hoping to hold off on his hunger till someone might come by so he could yell for help. By the scant light coming in through the upper hole he wrote in his diary entry for thirty days. The last entry was, "I am too weak to write anymore." Thus he starved a hard death and nobody knew what became of him. Many years later the tree was cut down. While sawing it for fire wood they hit steel, the rifle barrel. No trace of anything else except several bones. This was the answer for the community's lost man back in the pioneer days of early 1800's.

Our Growing Generation

1989

Due to the increase in population among the Amish people in Lancaster County, it is difficult to keep the younger generation occupied in farm work. Instead they find good paying jobs in doing carpenter work, masonry jobs, furniture shops, craft shops, etc. This holds true for young married men as well as single boys. The girls can also find employment in stores, market stands, and housework away from home.

We sometimes must wonder what this generation of today will experience in their lifetime if they are led away from the farm. The history of our nation has proven that there were always times of prosperity as well as recession or depressions. History has also proven that it is not best for a Christian nation to always live in times of prosperity as well as always in times of depression. Both of these issues have a bearing on Christianity. Sooner or later they will show up in our government office holders, and everybody will bear some effects from it.

In the last quarter century we have lived in times of prosperity. The younger generation has no idea what a depression would be like. To live in times when our food, clothing, and household goods would not be available, or limited to a minimum quantity for each family. We as older folks have some experience of how times were during the early years of the 1930's, and how it affected our nation. Most of the jobs that our younger generation are holding today are jobs of luxuries.

In our days we cannot imagine how times were when a man would come to our door, asking for a bite to eat, or ask if he may sleep in your barn tonight. Or if he would ask if the farmer could give him a few day's work for room and board. Or ask the missus for a bucket of warm water to take a bath. We who are living in a fast age can't imagine how such times could ever reach our doorstep. We hear people say that our government would not let such times enter our country. This nation is too strong for such a downfall.

In the writer's opinion, we are living in false prosperity. In the last 50 years our government has gone into debt to more than a trillion dollars so that the nation may enjoy prosperity. And every year it is going higher and higher. We are a part of the government, so that is part of our debt that we owe. In the U.S. there is a national debt of more than $12,000 for every man, woman, and

Growing Up—1903–1920

The last Lancaster-to-Intercourse stagecoach. It was operated by Coleman Diller and made a daily trip until 1910.

child. And we are enjoying prosperity. The jobs of luxuries will be the first ones to go under if a depression should follow. Farmers will be the last, for people will still eat as long as food is available.

The point that we want to stress is, the farther away that we get from farming, the more severe a depression will be. What can be done for the future generation if farm land is no more available in our area? There are any number of young families with school age children that would prefer farm life. And there is no better place to raise a family than on a farm where father and mother may work together with the children. It is the most enjoyable part in a person's life, where love and charity is shared with one another.

The question may be, who wants to be responsible for not doing what can be done to encourage our younger generation to start farming? And the question is, where? We well know that we can't do as our grandparents did, just by an adjoining farm close to our home farm. Most of the farms that were sold in this area are those that the non-Amish farmers did not want to be tied down to farm life. These were then bought by the Amish. This has been going on until today about 90% of the farms in Leacock Twp. are owned by the Amish. The same holds true in other areas. In our days it is almost impossible to buy a non-Amish farm because of developers buying up anything available. And the prices are out of reach for farming.

Now what is the next move to make?

In 1940 the first move of this kind was made to move to Maryland by a group who planned to start an Amish church and settlement. And it proved successful. It was well worth the effort.

From that time on a number of other settlements were started, and most of them proved to be successful. Now it has been 11 years since the last one started, with now a large increase in population. The feeling by most elderly folks is to search for a suitable area for Amish folks to settle. But there are a lot of questions that enter into starting a new Amish church settlement. There are also a lot of opinions on where to start and what to look for. Just to mention a few, it is very important to go with a group of like-minded people in order to form a church. Then there is the need to have a home to live in. The kind of soil, water resources, drainage, climate, market for products, school conditions, these are only a few that are important. There has no such step been taken for the last 11 years, and as fast as our population is growing, it is long overdue to start another settlement. Anyone who is looking for a new settlement has to sacrifice some things. But let us consider how much and for what our forefathers sacrificed.

At this time there is talk for a new settlement in Kentucky. Sure there are advantages and disadvantages in a move of this sort. There are thousands of acres of nice farming land available. But the buildings according to our way of living are a disadvantage. Houses are few and far between. But there are no zoning laws for out in the country in KY. The state has all kinds of land, rolling with good drainage, flat land, hilly and wood land, as well as mountain land. So it is a matter of choice. It depends on what a person is looking for.

But a disadvantage is the distance from here to Kentucky. It is approximately 800 miles. It depends on what part of the state. Their climate is similar to ours here in PA. It is a few weeks ahead of ours in the spring and a few weeks later in the fall. Average rainfall is about the same. So it depends very much on what the person is looking for. Kentucky has advantages and disadvantages the same as any other state.

-Gideon L. Fisher

The Power of Prayer

My mother was getting ready for a family reunion in our house and there was a lot to be done. My 12 year old brother, 9 year old sister, and I had to pitch in. "There are four loaves of bread in the oven," mother said, as she and dad got ready to go into town for last minute supplies. "Take them out when they're a nice golden brown, if you burn that bread we will be in big trouble." We all promised we knew how important the family bread was for that day. We settled on the couch to wait; finally we decided to wait outside. Surely a little playing to pass the time wouldn't hurt. Well we lost track of time until I smelled something burning. "The bread," I screamed, "we forgot about mother's bread." We rushed inside, as Richard opened the oven door there was the bread black and smoking. "What are we going to do?" I cried. Lucia said, "Let's pray, mother says all things are possible with God." So we all put a hand on the warm oven door and bowed our heads. "God please change this bread to a golden brown like she told us to in Jesus' name Amen." Then Richard opened the oven door again. <u>Four Golden-Brown loaves</u> we couldn't believe it they were perfect. At the reunion one of mother's sisters asked, "Where did you get the recipe for this bread?" "It's the same recipe we've used for years," mother said. "No this definitely tastes better," her brother said. "It's the best bread I've ever had." Everyone agreed. Finally we children brought mother into the kitchen and explained why the bread tasted so good, *answered prayers.*

-Fran-Alice Aberle
Tulsa, Oklahoma

Christmas Without Christ
Elizabeth A. Stoltzfus

It seems me, myself, and I can't think of any news to write. I might as well put an end to this. May God bless you all. Merry Christmas to you all and a prosperous New Year.

I most often think back to many years ago teacher had written Merry Xmas on the black board. Now I went to a public school at that time. It so happened that the state superintendent happened to come visit the school. Teacher had written Merry Xmas on the board. Teacher asked him to make a speech. He then talked about Merry Xmas on the board. He said Xmas is like having Christmas without Christ. Teacher never wrote it like that on the board since he mentioned it.

Last week's paper said a man, age 48, died and his weight was 867 pounds. His peak weight was 1,230 pounds. He was in bed for years as he couldn't walk. Due to health problems he had to go to the hospital. He had to be taken with a crane by emergency and civil defense workers.

-Barbara L. Smoker
2014

"A Recipe for Rest"

When at night you sleepless lie,
And the weary hours drag by,
Lift your thoughts to God above,
Bending down to you in Love.
Feel His presence by your bed,
His soft touch upon your head…
Let your last thought be a prayer,
As you nestle in His care.
Ask Him all your way to keep,
Then O, then drop off to sleep.

Haus Segen

Jesu wohn' in meinem Haus,
Weiche nimmermehr daraus;
Wohn' mit deiner Gnad' darin,
Weil ich sonst verlassen bin.

O du großer Segens-Mann;
Komm mit deinem Segen an;
Gieb, daß Friede, Glück und Heil,
Auch meinem Hause werd' zu Theil.

Gleichwie Hiob und Abraham,
Den reichen Segen überkam,
So schütt' auch gnädig über mich,
Deinen Segen mildiglich.

Jesu wohn' in meinem Herzen,
Wenn ich leide Kreuz und Schmerzen,
Wenn mich drücket Angst und Noth,
So hilf mir, O treuer GOTT!

Wenn ich nicht mehr Güter habe,
Bleibt mir doch die Himmels-Gabe.
Ob ich hier schon Trübsal leide,
Bleibt mir doch die Himmels-Freude.

A Bro's Spiritual Love

The true incident as I recall reading:
Date – 1ˢᵗ Decade of 1900
Place – Chinatown in Manhattan, NY

Two brothers, single and living at home—one living a Godly life, the other living in sin. His sinful life increased to the point of murder in a back alley one dark night during a knife fight.

He came home to change his bloody clothes for clean ones, and fled in fear of the law following him, being captured and prosecuted.

The righteous brother awakened at home, seeing his brother leave, understanding the guilt and what evidently happened, made a decision. Knowing his brother was not a Christian and not prepared to die, and expected his charge of death penalty, dressed himself with his brother's bloody clothing.

The officers came, as expected, and apprehended the brother in bloody clothes. Without defending himself he was eventually convicted of murder and placed on death row. He who was righteous gave his life for the sinful brother.

Many years later, under self-conviction and seeking inward peace, he came back to the town of his youth with the confession of murder to the authorities. Court records researched showed the truth.

The murder had been paid, the murderer released—even as Christ loved us that we also can be free.

-David King

Das Isht die Sinnflut

Jacob I. and Lizzie Ann J. Schwartz
Geneva, IN

Here is something that I have been thinking about. *Das Isht die sinnflut.* Just how high did this water raise in 40 days? If my calculation is right, the highest mountain in this world would of some less than 30,000 feet and it may have been around 15 elle higher. How much an elle is I really do not know. I read six hands or from the tip of your middle finger to elbow or around 21 inches. Anyways according to my calculation it would of raised around 750 feet every 24 hours, or maybe over 31 feet per hour, or maybe over five inches per minute. In my poor little mind that is something I just cannot comprehend with that much water going would that not of been very loud with all that rushing water. Now let's imagine this whole world being covered with water. Would there not only of been one shadow in the whole world? And that might have been where the ark was, from where Noah built the ark till it set down on Mt. Ararat. How far did it float! Would the fish and the likes be the only things that survived? Oh my, there would be many questions *aber das isht genug.*

A pupil asked his teacher if one should be punished for something he didn't do. "Oh no!" "Well," said the boy, "I didn't do my arithmetic."

"Rich Minister"

An old minister had unintentionally told of his wealth and fortune, and the fame of his possessions got to the ears of the tax assessor. So one day the government's representative came to his door to press him for a statement of his wealth.

"Is it so," began the official, "that you have much capital?"

"Yes," said the preacher, "I am a rich man."

"In that case," said the tax man, pulling his book out, "I shall have to assess you. So what are your possessions?"

"Well," replied the minister, "I am enjoying good health, and health is worth very much."

"What more have you?"

"I have a good wife, worth more than diamonds."

"Congratulations!" exclaimed the tax man. "But don't you own more?"

"Yes, I have healthy, intelligent, upright children and that is a possession of which any man can feel rich."

"Do you own anything?" he was asked next.

"Oh, yes, I own citizenship in the United States, and have an inheritance in Heaven. What more would a man want to own?"

"But don't you own any money or real estate?"

"No, otherwise I own nothing," said the preacher happily and joyfully.

"My Friend," said the assessor as he closed his book, "you are indeed a rich man, and your riches no man can take away, not even the government."

Riches maketh itself wings and fly away
as an eagle toward heaven. (Prov. 23:5)

"Mother Shipton's Prophecy"

This wonderful forecast in poetic form was written by Mother Shipton, who died at Clifton, Yorkshire, England in 1449. Some of the things mentioned were scarcely even thought of for hundreds of years, and other have been fulfilled only recently.

A carriage without horses shall go.
Disaster fill the world with woe.
In London Primrose Hill shall be,
Its center hold a Bishop's See.
Around the world men shall fly,
Quick as the twinkling of an eye.

Beneath the water men shall walk;
Shall ride, shall sleep, and even talk.
And in the air men shall be seen,
In white, in black, as well as green.
A great man then shall come and go,
For Prophecy declares it so.

In water iron then shall float,
As easy as a wooden boat.

Gold shall be found in streams and coined,
In land that is as yet unknown.
Water and fire shall wonders do,
And England shall admit a Jew.

The states will lock in fiercest strife,
And seek to take each other's life;
When North shall thus divide the South.
The eagle builds in lions mouth.
Then tax and blood and cruel war
Shall come to every humble door.

And now a word in uncouth rhyme,
Of what shall be in future time:
For in those wondrous far off days
The women shall adopt a craze
To dress like men and trousers wear,
And cut off all their locks of hair.

They'll ride astride with brazen brow,
As witches do on broomsticks now.
Then love shall die and marriage cease,
And nations wane as babes decrease.
The wives shall fondle cats and dogs.
And men live much the same as hogs.

More Help Wanted

To the Night Owl: Ben Franklin was noted for his wise sayings. One of these is: "Early to bed, early to rise, makes a man healthy, wealthy, and wise." Evidently he took his own advice, and therein might have been his wisdom. Medical authorities are proving that Franklin was right. They assure us that an hour's sleep before midnight is worth 3 hours after midnight. It seems that the Creator made darkness in which man should rest. Daylight is the time for work. This is the law of nature. When man violates this law, he must suffer for it. Arising to begin the day in that fresh new hour as the sun appears, gives one the joy of a new chance, a new world, a new opportunity. In health, in working habits, in cheerfulness, early rising pays!

THE FALLING STARS
1833

In those days there were no custom butcher shops. When people wanted to butcher, they did it at home with the help of an experienced butcher. On a certain day, my grandfather had plans to do his butchering with a neighbor. Like always, he went bright and early and started the fire to heat the water for scalding the hogs, while the farmer did his morning chores.

Something very strange happened that morning. The farmer came in, all excited and out of breath. He said, "Moses, the end of the world is coming. It is here! Moses, just come to the door and see for yourself."

My grandfather went to the door and looked out. To his surprise, the stars were falling—falling like rain! Some of the people in that community were not ready for the second coming of Christ. Some ran to the neighbors to make wrong things right; they asked to be forgiven, and they forgave one another. Some people could not stand the pressure. There were quite a few suicides. But the end did not come. The butchering was cancelled, and Moses went home to his family.

It is believed that there was a mass of falling stars several times in that century, but I cannot record the exact date of the happenings.

-David E. Huyard

WHAT IS COMMUNISM?

How would you like to live in a country where it would be unlawful to own anything except the clothes you are wearing and perhaps a few other small items? How would you like to have been taken away from your parents when you were about five years old and placed in a school most of the next twenty years? You might be allowed to live with your father and mother part of this time but the state, or government, whatever you might want to call it, would be your boss and you would have to do as they tell you, regardless what your parents would think.

During the time you went to school you would be taught that it is childish fairy tale to believe in God and that you must obey the state instead of your parents. Your teachers would drill into your minds that in countries like America and Great Britain there would someday be a revolution in which the workers, or the laboring classes would someday arise and kill or banish all the ruling classes such as governors, senators, and their President. Then they (the workers) would take over and soon the entire world would be a most pleasant place to live. You would not have to worry anymore where your food and clothing would come from. Then you would be working for the state and they would control everything you would do.

This would mean that they would tell you where and what to work and would pay you whatever they wanted to. They would tell you where to live, which might be in an apartment house shared by a few other families, or it might be on a large collective farm where a few hundred other people would live, laboring from dawn until dusk for barely enough money to buy food and clothing.

As long as you would be patient and take all that without grumbling you would get along fine with your bosses. But if you would speak up and tell them that you should get more money, or you think that the ruler of your land is a *"dumkopf"* you very likely would find yourself in jail or headed for Siberia.

The worst evil of Communism, as we have mentioned, is its theory that there is no God and no Eternal Life. We want to thank God that we can live in a land where we may live and worship as we feel is right.

-LF

In eigener Melodie.

222. Arme witwe, weine nicht! JEsus will dich trösten. Der dir hülf und trost verspricht, Wenn die noth am grösten, Der sieht auch dein elend an, Und die thränen-fluthen. O wie weh wird ihm gethan, Wenn die herzen bluten.

2. Arme witwe, weine nicht! Laß die sorgen fahren: Ob dir öfters brod gebricht In betrübten jahren. JESUS giebt dir mehl ins cad, Und dein öl-krug quillet; Denn durch GOttes weisen rath Wird er bald gefüllet.

3. Arme witwe, weine nicht! Wenn du bist verlassen: Der sein aug auf dich gericht, Kan dich ja nicht hassen. Der sich deinen Vater nennt, Weiß wohl, was dir fehlet, Und der deine thränen kennt, Hat sie auch gezehlet.

4. Arme witwe, weine nicht! Wenn die feinde toben, Und der satan dich ansicht, GOtt schützt dich von oben. JEsus ist dein schirm und schild, Ja dein stab und stecken: Ob die hölle noch so brüllt, Laß dich nicht erschrecken.

5. Arme witwe, weine nicht! Wenn du einsam sitzest, Und die kreutzes-hitze sticht, Daß du thränen schwitzest: Witwen-thränen steigen hoch, Bis zu GOttes herzen; Hilft er nicht gleich, hilft er doch, Der kennt die schmerzen!

6. Arme witwe, weine nicht! JESUS hört dein schreyen. Er, der deine krone flicht, Wird dich bald erfreuen. Senk den anker mit geduld Nur in seine wunden, Da wird lauter JEsus-huld, Lauter trost gefunden.

7. Arme witwe, weine nicht! Was willst du dich kränken? Denk an deine christen-pflicht, GOtt wird an dich denken. Ey vielleicht ists heute noch, Daß er dich befreyet Von dem harten kreutzes-joch, Und dir rosen streuet.

8. Arme witwe, weine nicht! Laß die welt nur lachen. JEsus, deiner seelen licht, Will dich selig machen. JEsus schließt den himmel auf, JEsus reicht die krone: Eil! beförder deinen lauf Zu des lammes throne.

Legend of the Flight Into Egypt
Vera E. Walker

Long, long ago, on the dark and sorrowful night when Herod had made up his mind to kill the Child born to be King, His father and mother stole out of Bethlehem and made their way towards the far-off land of Egypt for safety. The light of Joseph's lantern made strange shadows flicker along the narrow street as he led the little ass forward, and Mary drew her cloak closer round the babe as if to shield Him from evil. They went quickly, lest Herod's spies should be at work even now, yet not as if in fear. They went along the ridges of the stony hills first, and then climbed down into the plains and turned their faces towards the blue sea and the desert country that lies between Palestine and Egypt, choosing paths which travelers rarely followed. It was in these lonely places, full of dangers, that many strange and beautiful things took place…

They traveled by night mostly, for the day was too hot for walking, and as they went the wild creatures of the desert came out of their dens in search of food. The little grey jackals moved like swift shadows about them; the desert birds circled around their heads; lions roared in the distance. Yet all seemed friendly. The jackals would trot by their side without snarling; the lions walked with them as a bodyguard; the birds flew peacefully overhead. In the presence of the Babe of Bethlehem the creatures were at peace with one another and did no harm. . . .

Near Egypt they came to a dark place leading through a woods, and as they went a band of robbers rushed out to meet them. They were fierce, rough men, who thought nothing of killing an old man for the sake of his ass or the few goods he carried with him. But, as the young chief came forward he saw the babe smiling in His mother's arms, and he gave an order that checked his men, and spoke kindly to the travelers. Still looking at the babe he led them into his cave and begged them to rest there till morning. The robber's wife brought them cakes and honey and fruit, and they lay down peacefully to sleep. Next morning…the chief entered and taking them outside, showed them a good road which would take them where they wished to go. "Farewell," he said to them as they rode away, "and in whatever place you are remember me who have lodged you this night."

So the travelers passed on, and came quickly to the land of Egypt, where they lived safely till news of Herod's death reached them. For God is Lord of all creatures, of the wild beasts and the hearts of men, and He would let no harm come to His child.

Lamb Adopted by Cow
Edgewood, IA
Jonas and Lovina Hershberger
March 28, 2016

Greetings. A very nice clear spring day. Baby lambs with their mothers relax on the hillside soaking in the sunshine.

One little lamb is seen close by our Jersey milk cow. Its mother died so we started bottle feeding. Another ewe lost its lamb, both being about same age, so we tried to coax this ewe to take this little orphan lamb. The ewe just wouldn't show enough interest to satisfy this little lamb. It would come running to be fed till this Jersey cow adopted it. It now seems fully satisfied. Is seen following the cow sucking a little every once in a while as lambs do. If the cow is brought in to milk the lamb follows and rests by her head. If the lamb is out of the cow's sight she softly moos. The lamb looks well fed and a picture of health.

A True Story—The Underground Railroad

Henry Brown wasn't sure how old he was. Henry was a slave and slaves weren't allowed to know their age. Henry worked in the big house where his master lived. Henry's master had been good to him but Henry's mother knew things could change. "Do you see those leaves blowing in the wind? They are torn from the trees like slave children are torn from their families."

One morning the master called for Henry and his mother. The master lay in bed with only his head above the quilt, he was very ill. He beckoned them to come closer, some slaves were freed by their owners, Henry's heart beat fast. Maybe the master would set him free, but the master said, "You are a good worker Henry. I am giving you to my son. You must obey him and never tell a lie." Henry nodded but he didn't say thank you. That would have been a lie.

Later that day Henry watched a bird soar high above the trees. Free bird, happy bird, Henry thought. Henry said goodbye to his family thinking maybe never to see them again.

Henry worked for his new master. He was good at his job but he was lonely. One day he met Nancy who was shopping for her mistress. They walked and talked and agreed to meet again. Henry felt like singing but slaves didn't dare to sing in the streets. Instead he hummed all the way home.

Months later Henry asked Nancy to be his wife. When both masters agreed, Henry and Nancy were married. Soon there was a little baby then another and another. Henry knew they were very lucky. They lived together even though they had different masters. But Nancy was worried; her master had lost a great deal of money. "I'm afraid they will sell our children," she said. Henry sat very still. He worked hard all morning, he tried to forget what Nancy had said.

The next day his friend came and whispered to Henry, "Your wife and children were just sold at the slave auction." "No!" cried Henry. He couldn't move he couldn't think, he couldn't work.

At lunchtime, Henry rushed to the center of town. A large group of slaves were tied together. The owner shouted at them. Henry looked for his family. "Father, father," cried the children. Henry watched his children disappear down the road. Where was Nancy? He saw her the same moment she saw him. When he wiped away his tears, Nancy too was gone.

Henry no longer sang. He went to work. At night he ate supper and went to bed. He tried to think of happy times, but all he would see were the carts carrying away everyone he loved. Henry knew he would never see his family again.

Many weeks passed, one morning Henry heard singing. A little bird flew out of a tree into the open sky and Henry thought about being free, but how? At work, he was lifting a crate and the answer came to him. He asked James Young and Dr. Smith to help him. Mr. Smith was a white man who thought slavery was wrong.

They met early the next day at an empty warehouse. Henry arrived with a crate saying, "I will mail myself to a place where there are no slaves." James stared at the box then at Henry.

"What if you cough and somebody hears you?"

"I will cover my mouth and hope," said Henry.

On the box Henry was in, Dr. Smith wrote: "To William H. Johnson, Arch Street, Philadelphia, Pa." Henry would be delivered to friends in Philadelphia. Then he also printed on the box in big letters, THIS SIDE UP, WITH CARE.

The sun was not yet up when Henry climbed in the box. "Ready," he said. James nailed down the lid. Dr. Smith drove him to the station. The railroad clerk tipped the box over and nailed a paper to the bottom. Hours passed.

Henry was lifted up then thrown again, upside down. This must be the boat headed for Washington, D.C. The ship rode smoothly but Henry was still upside down. Blood rushed to his head, his face got hot and his eyes ached. He thought his head would burst, but he was afraid to move, someone might hear him.

Soon Henry heard voices. A man said, "Why don't we move this box and sit on it?" Henry held his breath. Could they be talking about his box? Henry was pushed and the box scraped the deck. Now he was on his right side, then on his left, then suddenly right side up.

"What do you think is in here?" said the first man. "Mail, I guess," said the other. Henry was carried off the steamboat and placed in a railroad car; this time head's up. He fell asleep to the rattling song of the train wheels. After a while he awoke to loud knocking.

"Henry are you alright in there?"

"All right," he answered. The cover was pried open. Henry stretched and stood up.

Four men smiled at him, "Welcome to Philadelphia!"

At last Henry had a birthday, March 30, 1849, his first day of freedom and from that day on he also had a middle name—everyone called him, *Henry Box Brown*.

Author's Note:

In the mid-1800's there were about four million slaves living in the United States. Slaves were owned, like tables or cows, or wagons. Historians believe between 60,000 and 100,000 slaves escaped to freedom, traveling on what was called "The Underground Railroad." The Underground Railroad wasn't a real railroad. It was all the secret ways from the South to the North. They hid in carts, rode on horseback, walked hundreds of miles through forests and swamps and crossed flowing rivers in summer and ice bound rivers in winter. Conductors and Station Masters hid them and helped them throughout their journey.

When Henry Brown climbed into his freedom box, he hoped he'd be carried to a safe world. He brought along a small tool to make air holes, a little water and a few biscuits. Henry arrived in Philadelphia having traveled 550 miles from Richmond, Virginia, in 27 hours. His story made newspaper headlines in America and Europe. Henry never found Nancy and his children. In 1850 he went to England and there are some reports that he married again. We do know with absolute certainty that Henry "Box" Brown became one of the most famous runaway slaves on the Underground Railroad. The man who mailed himself to freedom.

PLEASANTVILLE, TN
Mary Ellen Miller

A tornado hit about 12 miles from where we live on the last of December and a couple lost their lives. Man and wife, and also their home. Now the local paper states that 2 pages of the couple's Will were found 40 miles away in a lady's yard. She called the police and yes, the name on the papers were returned to them. It said, God must have had a hand in returning these papers to the family.

-2016

AMISH CHURCH SPLIT IN 1877

Now I will start with things that happened 20 years before I was born, but heard older *leit verzehl*. Christian Umble was Bishop, David Stoltzfus was preacher and Tennessee John Stoltzfus was Deacon. (David was the late Bishop Sam F. Stoltzfus's grandfather.) At that time, Deacon John's son, Gideon, seemed to make some problems in *gma mit ordnung*. He did not part his hair in the middle as was *ordnung*. They said when he was baptized he had to comb his hair different to be baptized, but after it was over, he gave his head a shake and his hair was as before.

Well, he got married and when he was about 33 years old, they wanted to make *diener* and Gideon, who always had caused some problems, was stimmed in the lot. The *diener* talked of not taking him along but were afraid it might make trouble as it was never done before. His Dad, Deacon John, said we would better take him along as he felt sure he would not be the chosen one, but when it was over he was ordained preacher.

Now it went as they had feared, he did not want to work with the other *diener*. Giedeon was ordained in 1868 and in 1877 things seemed to come to a head, and he was silenced. He was not to preach anymore for the Old Order Amish. They said, before the *gma* left out a brother, Joe Kennel stood up and said next Sunday we will have *gma* at our house for Gideon, so then the split was made. Now the sad part of it was, he took about 2/3 of *die gma* along. I think it sure would have looked dark for the little group, etc.

The Gideon group had *gma* in the homes for about 6 years. Then they built the Millwood Church House, which I was told this summer, by one of their *gma leit*, is only about 1/2 full when they have *gma*. I do not want to judge anyone,

but am thankful still that my father stayed with the Old Order. I wish them and us all *die Evig Ruh*.

-John K. Lapp
New Holland, 1978

MESOPOTAMIA, OH

In Jan. 2016, our local Giant Eagle Store had a power outage. Because the Dairy and Fresh Meat were without proper refrigeration for over four hours, everything was thrown out, yes all thrown away. They (the management) refused to sell it or give it away and the employees were forbidden to take any home. This was butter, cheese, eggs, milk, fresh meat, etc. They had a $60,000 loss because common sense no longer used.

-John & Sarah Miller
January 2016

TOUCHING INCIDENT OF 8 YEAR OLD

Lancaster County wedding season! Some days are rainy and some are very nice, typical fall weather, except for the first day of November when Hurricane Sandy was passing through. Some weddings were put off for a day or 2 later, I don't remember of hearing that before here in our area.

The tornado one week and Hurricane Sandy the next are now history, but left many memories, some almost too precious and too amazing to describe, like the 8 year old in a neighboring church who felt a hand on his shoulder and couldn't move while the tornado was passing close by.

-Henry & Rebecca King, 2013
Quarryville, PA

Reading in the Matter Spiegel

I think it would be impossible to fully realize what these people went through. It would be impossible to know just how many thousands and thousands of Christians died for their belief. I started to kind of keep track how many but you can't, sometimes it might say *unzahlbar* or uncountable. One place I read that in seven years' time they killed over 200 thousand Christians. That would average out approximately 80 people per day. Now where did they bury that many people? Or were they burned? That would be 80 people per day for seven years. Thanks to Eli S. Sensenig for the information you gave *ivverich und ender.*

-Jacob I. Schwartz
2016

A Sad Situation

Yes, the United States is in a bad shape—worse off than any other country in the world, in some respects. No other country is suffering political and economic troubles because of a surplus of food. No other country has traffic congestion because so many people own automobiles. In no other country does everyone make so much money and help is so hard to find and harder to keep. In no other country do people take so many holidays, and work so few hours, so they will have time to spend the money that keeps piling up on them. In no other country is overweight, caused by plenty of everything and high living, one of the chief medical problems.

Yes, it's a sad situation!

-Selected

Peace in the Church

The old folks used to say back in the 1800's the authorities came to the Amish to ask them if they have peace in the church claiming if they don't have peace in the church there won't be peace in the world. The Amish might have more to do with how affairs go in the world then we might think. Something to think about. *Gehabt euch wohl.*

Americans Waste Food

America's largest surplus food supply may be as close as our garbage cans, according to an Iowa State University extension nutritionist. In reviewing a Tucson, Arizona, study, it was found that households threw away seven to ten percent of the food they purchased. This means that the average household throws away at least $100 worth of food a year—without counting the wasted drinks—amounting to $4.5 billion nation-wide! This would be enough to feed about 7.5 million people for a year, according to the U.S. Department of Agriculture figures.

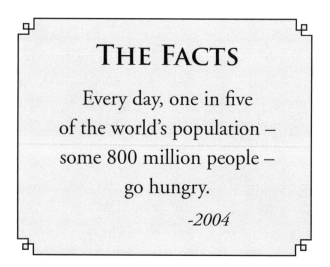

The Facts

Every day, one in five
of the world's population –
some 800 million people –
go hungry.

-2004

Priest That Disappeared

The other day there was a wreck in Quincy. A girl was trapped in her car and couldn't be released with the Jaws of Life. She asked people to pray with her and everyone was reluctant to. They were afraid she'd give up and die if they did. A priest walked up and said that he would like to pray with her. They said no; he would have been administering last rites. He said he wanted to just pray, so they consented. He prayed that they could stay calm and she could be helped, etc. Before long, another rescue squad showed up with more equipment and they managed to cut her free. The girl's parents wanted to know who the priest was, but he was nowhere to be found. The police say that he couldn't have passed through the road blocks and isn't in any of the many pictures taken at the site, yet they saw him and heard him pray.

-Mervin and Linda Yoder, 2013

A Waste

"Mr. Troyer," said a public school teacher a few years ago to an Amish farmer, "do you realize that your son Bennie has an exceptional mind. He always gets straight A's without even working. You should certainly see that he goes to high school and college. It would be a shame, a terrible waste if he didn't." The Amish father shook his head. The schoolteacher shook his too though for a different reason. He went home muttering to himself, "A terrible waste. All that talent, and all he'll ever amount to is an old-fashioned farmer, sweating in the field, tilling the soil with his hands like a common peasant when he might be a doctor or a dentist. Who knows, maybe even an artist or a poet." A waste? Yes, Bennie might get on in the world. He might well reach fame, wealth, and pleasure. But what if he lost his soul, would that not be the greatest waste of all?

-March 1975

A Florida Court Sets Atheist Holy Day

In Florida, an atheist created a case against Easter and Passover holy days. He hired an attorney to bring a discrimination case against Christians and Jews and observances of their holy days. The argument was that it was unfair that atheists had no such recognized days. The case was brought before a judge. After listening to the passionate presentation by the lawyer, the judge banged his gavel declaring, "Case dismissed!"

The lawyer immediately stood and objecting to the ruling saying, "Your Honor, how can you possibly dismiss this case? The Christians have Christmas, Easter, and others. The Jews have Passover, Yom Kippur, and Hanukkah, yet my client and all other atheists have no such holidays…" The judge leaned forward in his chair saying, "But you do. Your client, counselor, is woefully ignorant." The lawyer said, "Your Honor, we are unaware of any special observance or holiday for atheists." The judge said, "The calendar says April 1ˢᵗ is April Fool's Day. Psalm 14:1 states, 'The fool says in his heart, there is no God.' Thus, it is the opinion of this court, that, if your client says there is no God, then he is a fool. Therefore, April 1ˢᵗ is his day. Court is adjourned…"

You gotta love a Judge that knows his scripture!

A Change of Character

In 1490, Leonardo da Vinci set out to paint a picture of how he thought it might have looked when the disciples ate with Jesus in the upper room where Judas was exposed as traitor. This work resulted in a classic that is known throughout the world as *The Last Supper*.

The painting took a little over eight years to complete. He wanted the painting to be a study of gestures and emotion on canvas so he took much time in selecting the men who would pose for his characters.

The character of Jesus had to be first, so he set out to find a man with kindness in his eyes. This man had to look friendly, honest, and innocent. After weeks of searching he found the exact face he had hoped to find. He very carefully transferred what he saw onto his canvas so as to catch every detail. When he completed his work, he paid the man and began to look for the men who would pose as the other disciples.

One by one, he carefully inserted into his painting Peter, James, John and the others. The time finally came to paint Judas. He had been pushed to last because he was the hardest to portray. Leonardo had to find the face of a man who looked like a Judas. He searched all over for the man who could look like a traitor. He would have to look suspicious, his features traced by lines of stress. His countenance would have to be hardened like one who could betray Jesus.

Many would offer their services to him over several months but all were turned away. None had the troubled look that Leonardo required for this character called Judas. Frustrated, Leonardo set his painting aside and went to work on some of the many other things for which he is so widely known. A few years later, Leonardo picked up his unfinished painting and determined within himself to find the man that could help him complete his work.

He walked the streets at night looking for someone to pose. After a few unsuccessful tries, he began to search the alleys behind the bars. He studied the features of the homeless and the drunks. There, in the shadows, he saw a man in a pile of boxes. Leonardo offered the man a bath, a hot meal and some clean clothes if he would pose for his picture. Leonardo often caught the man's leery stare. It concerned him a little, but he had finally found what he wanted and he would not be turned away by fear. The man had a look of sorrow and of regret, a look of mistrust and of guilt. This man was the picture of Judas.

It took several sittings for the painting to be completed. When it was done, Leonardo offered the man payment but made him promise not to spend it on liquor.

The man looked at Leonardo and said, "You really don't know who I am, do you?" Leonardo looked at him trying to place him in his recollections. He answered him by saying, "No sir, I don't believe I've ever met you."

No sooner had he said it a shock coursed through his body as he realized that this man had posed for him before. The man then explained that he had been his first model several years before, the man he had used for his picture of Jesus.

With a grief stricken heart the man told Leonardo the sad story about his years with booze. How sad, that in just a few years, a picture of Jesus was turned into a picture of Judas.

"Wine is a mocker, strong drink is raging: and whosoever is deceived thereby is not wise."
(Proverbs 20:1)

-Millersburg

Mocking

Elisha was tired and weary but still trudged on. He had started off in Jericho that morning and had come almost thirty miles by now. The small cakes he had taken along to eat had long ago given out. For over an hour he hadn't come to a spring or brook so he could get a refreshing drink or bathe his feet in the cool waters. At Bethel there would be friends where he could rest for a day or so before he continued onward. But still, there was a certain anxiety in his thoughts. The people of Bethel weren't always very friendly to servants of the Lord. Most of them were worshippers of the golden calf and didn't like to be reminded of their sin.

Rounding a bend in the road, he came upon a group of children playing in an open space beside the road. He had almost passed them when one of the older ones recognized him and shouted, "Go away, you baldhead, go away!" They were mocking him.

Soon others took up the chant and started following him with abusive taunts. Wearily, the traveler pressed forward till suddenly a stone hit him between the shoulders. Turning around, he looked sternly at the faces following him. The children stopped, but kept up their chant, "Go away, baldhead; go away, baldy."

After standing there awhile, he noticed the bigger ones picking up stones. Suddenly the man lifted up his hands and looking towards heaven, asked God to take notice of his predicament.

Almost immediately a savage roar was heard coming from the woods. As the frightened faces turned to see where it came from, two she-bears came galloping out from among the trees and started ripping and tearing children to right and left.

When the two she-bears had finished, forty-two children lay mangled on the ground. How terrible! How frightening! A fairy tale you say? No, my dear fellow parents, sad to say, this is not a fairy tale, as you can see if you read the last verses of II Kings 2.

"Vacation"
Writings of John S. Byler

I seen in reading that a Pastor closed his church doors and wrote on the door: Off on Vacation. Why his members might erect a calf before he comes home, but I believe he had the calf erected before he left. I also read that Atheism is coming so fast. What is the reason? I seen in writing that young woman said, she did not read so much in the Bible yet, but she read so much that she sees that The Bible is false. I heard say they have schools that they learn the children infidelity. I believe that is Satan's school. Like we can read in the Scripture, I believe it is like I heard say already, "Wherever a Christian Church is built, the Satans build one alongside." I believe one reason Atheism is coming so fast, our Christianity is getting too weak, our churches are getting too careless, carelessness is our worst enemy. Too many of our church members are going out on vacations, they are getting out too much amongst the worldly things and worldly people. The world looks to us, confessing Jesus, to live as a Christian, and if we do not, they will lose their confidence for us. It is alright to travel around and visit our brethren but not go so much at so worldly places, just for sightseeing. I heard talking already when the end of the world will come, it will not come through the worldly people, but through destructive Christianity, the Fall will come before the End. When the salt will lose its Savior once then the end will come.

A FATHER THAT FAILED
(A True Story Recorded by Bona Fleming)

A young lady, just as intelligent as any young woman, went to a revival meeting. The power of God was upon the meeting. Sinners were being saved and Christians were being revived. The power of God struck this young girl and tears began to roll down her cheeks.

She took her handkerchief and wiped them away. Her father, a wealthy farmer, stood across the tent, he remarked to a friend, "If my daughter goes to that altar, I will wade in blood to my neck to take her out of there." She did not go that night.

The father got into his machine and drove home. The young man took the young lady home. When she got inside she saw him—a big 240 pound father—walking the floor. She knew that something was wrong. She said, "Papa, what is the matter with you? Why are you not in bed?" He answered, "I have stayed up to give you orders."

She said, "Papa, *what in the world have I done?*" He replied, "I looked across the tent tonight and I saw you weeping, saw you with your handkerchief up to your eyes. Mae, if you go to the mourner's bench, I will wade through blood up to my neck to take you out of there and when I get you home I will wear out a hickory over your back." He put it down so strong that she knew he meant what he said.

She began to weep and went to her room. There in the darkness she settled it that she would not go to God. She was a beautiful girl between 19 and 20 years of age. She clenched her fists and said, "O God, I will never seek thee! O God, take this feeling away from me, lighten my heart! I do not want to feel this way! Lord, I will never seek thee! I will never go to that altar! Take this burden away from my heart!"

She went to bed and went to sleep. The next morning this young lady got up and went to school, came back and went to the service that night. When the altar call was given, he looked across and saw her standing with a young man laughing. He took his neighbor by the arm and said, "Look at my daughter. I conquered her last night before I went to bed. She will never go to that altar." So the girl laughed and giggled while other folks wept and got saved.

But listen! The meeting closed on Sunday night and settled the destiny of dying men and women. The tents were taken down and the preachers left the grounds. The next Monday morning this girl went back to school as usual and went all week, but the following Monday morning as she started, she said, "Mamma, my head is hurting me."

The mother said, "Mae, go on to school." Mae went, but returned in two or three hours and said, "Mamma, my head is hurting me so that I couldn't stay."

She went to her room and went to bed. She had been in bed three days, when on Thursday afternoon, she sent for her mother to come up and said, "Mamma, I'm sure that you and Papa do not know my condition. I want you to send for a doctor. I am in an awful condition and I am going to die."

The mother was excited and she said, "I will, I will," and had the family physician come.

He felt her pulse and took her temperature. He touched the big strong father on the shoulder and asked him to come outside to the automobile. He loved the family for they had been so kind to him. He said, "You have called me too late. Your daughter may soon be in eternity, and if you have anything to tell her, tell her at once. It is no use for me to tell you that I can help her or call for more doctors. In a few hours she will be gone." The neighbors a mile away heard that father.

What do you suppose was the first thing that he thought of? It was the night he conquered his daughter and made her settle with God. He left the automobile and came in wringing his hands. He fell at her bedside and said, "Oh, Mae! Oh, Mae! Seek the Lord. Mae, pray. Give your heart to God. PRAY! MAE. PRAY!"

She put her hand on his face and said, "Papa, please do not taunt me with the name of God—please do not mention His name to me. My heart has been like stone since that night you gave me my orders. I went to my room and asked God to leave me, and God took me at my word." Then she told him that she was conscious that her doom was sealed and that from the beginning of her illness she knew she was going to die.

She said, "Papa, what time is it?" He answered, "Four o'clock in the afternoon." She said, "How slowly these hours are passing by! *But think,* I am going to a place where there will be no time." They had built a new home out on the pike and their old home stood back in the field, with the old moss-covered well and moss-covered bucket. She said, "Papa, go to the old moss-covered well and bring me a fresh drink of water, for I will soon be in a place where I can get no water."

He went and brought the water and put it to her lips and she drank it. Her mother was praying, and her two unsaved sisters were down on the floor praying. I have heard the loudest prayers from sinners praying for their loved ones, that I ever heard from anybody's lips. I have never heard louder prayers around a corpse—than around the altar.

The dying girl said, "Papa, put your arms under my arms and pull me up in this bed; my feet are on fire; my feet are slipping." He put his arms beneath her and drew her up in bed. Again she said, "Papa, my feet are slipping. Take my feet out of the fire."

He said, "Mae, I have done all I can do." She said, "Papa, go back to that old well again and bring your daughter another drink of water." He started for the water but before he got back his beautiful daughter had gone into eternity. Listen; friends! That father goes to town to buy hardware or groceries and he stands over the counter like a maniac and the merchant has to talk to him to find out what he wants. He goes to the field to plow but he does not plow. He goes to salt the cattle but forgets to take the salt. When he goes to market, he stands there and does not know what he wants. Everyone who knows the story knows what is the matter with the father; they know what is on his mind.

May this be a warning to parents, not to obstruct the way of their children and keep them from this free and full salvation that was purchased for us by Jesus Christ on the cruel cross of calvary, which fits and prepares us for heaven and the glory world.

-*Selected*

*"Be not deceived:
God is not mocked,
for whatsoever a man soweth,
that shall he also reap."*

(Galatians 6:7)

HORSE AND BUGGY DAYS

Back in the horse and buggy days—
The days of long ago—
When people had old-fashioned ways
And things moved on quite slow;
It seems we had more time to pray,
More time God's Word to search,
And quite a bit more time to stay,
In Sunday school and church.

We didn't have so much to do
To run us all day long;
We didn't see so much that's new
To lead us in the wrong.
We had no speeding cars back then
To take us far and wide;
We had more time to be true men
And in God's grace abide.

Back then the neighbors went about
To prove their love and grace;
They blessed and helped each other out
Along life's Christian race.
They visited from home to home
In sickness and in health,
And never sought so much to roam,
Or work and scheme for wealth.

Those far-off days, we know, are gone
And things have changed around,
But God's good grace continues on
In spite of sight and sound;
Therefore, in spite of all the rush
Let's tarry, pray and wait,
And when there is a blessed hush
Hear God from heaven's gate.
-Selected

THE FIRST BATHTUB

This took place the year the Amish had church services in spring on Easter.

In December, 1842, Adam Thompson of Cincinnati filled the first bathtub in the United States. The news of Mr. Thompson's tub was quickly spread. Newspapers said that the new-fangled idea would ruin the democratic simplicity of the republic; doctors predicted rheumatism, inflammation of the lungs, etc. the wise ones agreed that bathing in the wintertime would result in the decline of the robust population. Philadelphia, the cradle of liberty, tried to put a ban on bathing from the first of November to the first of March; Boston, in 1845, made bathing unlawful except on the advice of a doctor; Hartford, Providence, Wilmington and other cities tried to block the bath habit with extra heavy water rates. The State of Virginia took a slap at bathing by placing a tax of $30 a year on every bathtub brought into the state, but by 1922, there were manufactured 889,000 tubs a year. To think that but such a brief time ago man did not know that a bath was a good thing for him. This puts man in a class of absolute unreliability as to his judgment or thinking on any matter. Yet today, men all over the world are sitting in judgment on the Bible!

-Selected by Dan A. Hochstetler

My parents told me about COMMON SENSE early in my life and told me I would do well to call on her when making decisions. It seems she was always around in my early years but less and less as time passed by. Today I read her obituary. Please join me in a moment of silence in remembrance, for COMMON SENSE had served us all so well for so many generations.

Obituary
Common Sense

Today we mourn the passing of a beloved old friend, COMMON SENSE, who has been with us for many years. No one knows for sure how old she was since her birth records were long ago lost in bureaucratic red tape. She will be remembered as having cultivated such valuable lessons as knowing when to come in out of the rain, why the early bird gets the worm, life isn't always fair, and maybe it was my fault.

COMMON SENSE lived by simple, sound financial policies (don't spend more than you earn) and reliable parenting strategies (adults, not children are in charge).

Her health began to deteriorate rapidly when well intentioned but overbearing regulations were set in place. Reports of a six-year-old boy charged with sexual harassment for kissing a classmate; teens suspended from school for using mouthwash after lunch; and a teacher fired for reprimanding an unruly student, only worsened her condition.

COMMON SENSE lost ground when parents attacked teachers for doing the job they themselves failed to do in disciplining their unruly children. It declined even further when schools were required to get parental consent to administer aspirin, sun lotion or a sticky plaster to a student, but could not inform the parents when a student became pregnant and wanted to have an abortion.

COMMON SENSE lost the will to live as the Ten Commandments became contraband; churches became businesses; and criminals received better treatment than their victims. COMMON SENSE took a beating when you couldn't defend yourself from a burglar in your own home and the burglar could sue you for assault.

COMMON SENSE finally gave up the will to live after a woman failed to realize that a steaming cup of coffee was hot, she spilled a little in her lap and was awarded a huge settlement.

COMMON SENSE was preceded in death by her parents, Truth and Trust; her husband, Discretion; her daughter, Responsibility; and her son, Reason. She is survived by three step-brothers; I Know my Rights, Someone Else is to Blame, and I'm a Victim.

Not many attended her funeral because so few realized she was gone. If you still remember her, pass this on. If not, join the majority and do nothing.

-Author Unknown

Mocking is a serious offense, a sin. I could name a few such as a boy and his brother in their teenage years that were mocked. It was so bad that the one boy left the Amish for the rest of his life.

Another incident a teenage boy was noted for mocking a dwarf and not being nice to him. In later years after marriage and having children of his own two of them were dwarfs.

Gott lest sich net sputta.

The Powerful Fragrance of Love

Sheila Walsh

A FRIEND SENT ME A STORY THIS WEEK THAT beautifully illustrates the potential each one of us has to powerfully impact a life that we are brought into contact with. To protect her privacy I'll change the names, but the story is about a teacher I'll call Mrs. Brown.

One of Mrs. Brown's fifth-grade students was a little boy named Sam. The teacher quickly noticed that Sam didn't play well with the other children, that he performed poorly in his studies, and that his clothes were messy and his personal hygiene poor. She found herself actually taking delight in marking his papers with a broad red pen, making bold X's and then that devastating F at the top.

The school required teachers to review each child's past records, and Mrs. Brown put Sam's off until last. When she finally reviewed his file, she was shocked by the story it told. It seemed to be describing a different child,

"Sam is a bright child with a ready laugh. He does his work neatly and has good manners. He is a joy to be around," Sam's first-grade teacher wrote.

His second-grade teacher reported, "Sam is an excellent student, well liked by his classmates, but he is troubled because his mother has a terminal illness and life at home must be a struggle."

When Sam reached third grade, his teacher warned, "His mother's death has been hard on him. He tries to do his best, but his father doesn't show much interest and his home life will soon affect him if some steps aren't taken."

His fourth-grade teacher said, "Sam is withdrawn and doesn't show much interest in school. He doesn't have many friends, and he sometimes sleeps in class."

Mrs. Brown, seeing the larger picture, was ashamed of her attitude toward this broken boy. Her empathy for him was further heightened when her students brought their Christmas presents for her that year; wrapped in beautiful ribbons and bright paper—except for Sam's, which was wrapped in a brown-paper grocery bag. Some of the children started to laugh when she opened his gift and found a rhinestone bracelet with some of the stones missing, and a bottle that was one-quarter full of perfume. But she put the bracelet on and dabbed some of the perfume on her wrist. Sam stayed after school that day just long enough to say, "Mrs. Brown, today you smelled just like my mother used to."

After the students left, she cried for an hour. She now says that on that day, she quit teaching reading, writing, and arithmetic and began teaching children, paying particular attention to Sam. As she worked with him, his mind seemed to come alive. The more she encouraged him, the faster he responded. By the end of the year, he had become one of the most accomplished children in the class. A year later, she found a note from Sam under her classroom door, telling her that she was the best teacher he'd ever had.

Six years later she received another note. Sam wrote that he had finished high school, third in his class, and she was still the best teacher he had had in his whole life. Four years after that, she got another letter, saying that while things had been tough at times, he'd stayed in school, had stuck with it, and would soon graduate from college with top honors. He assured Mrs. Brown that she was still the best and favorite teacher he had ever had. Four more years passed and another letter came. This time he explained that after he had achieved his bachelor's degree, he decided to go a little further. The letter simply stated that she was still the best and favorite teacher he'd ever had. But now his name was a little longer. The letter was signed, Sam F. Stone, M.D.

That spring brought yet another letter. Sam said he'd met a girl and was going to be married. He explained that his father had died a couple of years ago, and he was wondering if Mrs. Brown might agree to sit in the place at the wedding that was usually reserved for the mother of the groom. She accepted his invitation and wore the bracelet with the missing rhinestones. She also made sure she was wearing the perfume that reminded Sam of his mother. They hugged each other, and Dr. Stone whispered in Mrs. Brown's ear, "Thank you for believing in me. Thank you so much for making me feel important and showing me that I could make a difference."

Mrs. Brown, with tears in her eyes, whispered back, "Sam, you have it all wrong. You were the one who taught me that I could make a difference. I didn't know how to teach until I met you."

Father, I ask that today you will give me your eyes to see, your ears to hear, arid your heart to love. May the fragrance of your Son, Jesus, be so sweet in me that other people will dare to dream that they can be all you've created them to be. Amen.

SHOW HIM YOUR HANDS

Bishop Woodcock of Kentucky has told a touching story about a young girl whom he knew. She was left motherless at the age of eight. Her father was poor, and there were four children younger than she. She tried to care for them all and for the home. To do it all, she had to be up very early in the morning and to work very late at night. No wonder that at the age of thirteen her strength was all exhausted. As she lay dying a neighbor talked with her. The little face was troubled, "It isn't that I'm afraid to die," she said, "for I am not. But I'm so ashamed."

"Ashamed of what?" the neighbor asked in surprise.

"Why it's this way," she exclaimed. "You know how it's been with us since mama died. I've been so busy, I've never done anything for Jesus, and when I get to heaven and meet Him, I shall be so ashamed! Oh, what can I tell Him?"

With difficulty the neighbor kept back her sobs. Taking the little calloused, workscarred hands in her own, she answered: "I wouldn't tell Him anything, dear. Just show Him your hands."

LIEBER FRIEND LEVI!

Greetings of Best Wishes. We wish you the brightness of the morning star in this darkest evening of time (2 Peter 1-19). Wir haben deinen welcome brief enfangen. Es ist bedenklich von die alte leut 101 jahr mit einander im ehestand. Wir haben eine alte deutch Bibuel von 1770. Die sagt die flood von Noah ist gekommen im jahr 1657. Von die flood, bis Christes gebarnen ware im jahr von 3,947 jahr gezt sind wir 2013 site Christus gebornen ware. Was ein total macht von Adam und Eva wo sie erschaffen waren 5958. Nur 42 jahr bis des jahr 6000 Der Heiland sagt. Ein 1000 jahr sind wie ein tage vor dem Herrn. So leben wir im abend von lezten tag vor dem ewigen Sabbot. Niemand weist wen der Herr kommt aber der Heiland sagt. Er wirde die tagen verkurzen oder es wird niemand selig wirden. Und Er kommt in eine stund da wir nicht meinen. Er sagt. Er kommt nicht es kommt zuvor den affalt. Im Wandle Seel buch sagts die leute haben der Noah gefragt wie ware es vor die flood. Noah antwortet. Groze schrecke. Schelle tod. und ungewohn lich wetter. Wie ist es yezt? Machte der Herr uns gnade sein.

-Titus and Fannie Hoover

Questions Asked at Baptism Service

(1) Könnet ihr auch bekennen wie der Kämmerer bekennt hat? Antwort: Ja ich glaube daß Jesus Christus Gottes Sohn ist.

(2) Erkennt dir es auch für eine christliche Ordnung, Kirche und Gemeinde Gottes worunter dir euch jetzt begebet? Antwort: Ja.

(3) Saget dir auch ab der Welt, dem Teufel, sammt seinem anweisenden Wesen, wie auch eurem Fleisch und Blut, und begehret Christo Jesu allein zu leben, der für euch am Stamm des Kreuzes gestorben und auferstanden ist? Antwort: Ja.

(4) Versprechet dir auch vor dem Herrn und der Gemein daß dir diese Ordnung wollet helfen handhaben, raten und arbeiten in der Gemein und nicht davon abweichen mit des Herrn Hilf, es gelte euch zum Leben oder zum sterben. Antwort: Ja.

Dann wird das Gebet getan, die Täufling knieend, die Glieder stehend.

Auf deinen Glauben denn du bekennt hast wirst du getauft im Namen des Vaters und des Sohnes und des Heiligen Geistes, Amen.

Im Namen des Herrn und der Gemein wird dir die Hand geboten, stehe auf. Hand und Kuß.

Questions Asked at a Marriage Ceremony

Erkennet und bekennet dir es auch für eine christliche Ordnung daß ein Mann und ein Weib sein soll, und kennet dir auch hoffen daß dir diesen Stand so weit angefangen habt wie dir sind gelehrt worden? (Ja.)

Kannst du auch hoffen, Bruder, daß der Herr dir diese unsere Mit-Schwester möchte zu einem Eheweib verordnet haben? (Ja.)

Kannst du auch hoffen Schwester, daß der Herr dir diesen unsern Mit-Bruder möchte zu einem Ehemann verordnet haben? (Ja.)

Versprechst du auch deinem Eheweib daß wenn sie sollte in Leibes Schwachheit, Krankheit, oder einigerlei solche Zufällen kommen, daß du willst für sie sorgen wie es einen christlichen Ehemann zusteht? (Ja.)

Versprechst du auch gleiches deinem Ehemann, daß wenn er sollte in Leibes Schwachheit, Krankheit, oder einigerlei solche Zufällen kommen, daß du willst für ihn sorgen wie es einem christlichen Eheweib zusteht? (Ja.)

Versprechet dir auch beide miteinander daß dir wollet Lieb, Leid und Geduld mit einander tragen, und nicht mehr von einander weichen bis euch der liebe Gott wird von einander scheiden durch den Tod? (Ja.)

Dann wird das Gebet getan.

So finden wir das Raguel die Hand der Tochter nahm und schlug sie Tobias in seine Hand und sprach: Der Gott Abrahams, und der Gott Isaaks und der Gott Jakobs sei mit euch, und helfe euch zusammen und gebe sein Segen reichlich über euch, und das durch Jesum Christum, Amen.

HAVE BUFFALO, WILL TRAVEL

VERNON PATTERSON of Wichita Falls, Texas, says his mom snapped this photo after a man traveling from Wyoming to the East Coast in a buffalo-drawn wagon spent the night on their Missouri farm. That's Vernon on the buffalo and his brother, E.J., holding the lines.

-1932

OLD AGE BAPTIZED

In the year of 1931 in Lower Pequea, 20 youth were baptized including a retarded single lady named Annie Glick, daughter of David and Katie Glick. Her parents were born in the 1840s and were no longer living at that time. Annie was asked if she would like to join the church and be baptized. Her answer was yes. She was baptized at age 56. She lived another 12 years after that. They were baptized by Sam M. Stoltzfus of Morgantown. Old Sam M. Stoltzfus was was pretty able yet, but slow. It was 3:00 when church left out.

-John Glick

HUNGER FOR AMISH CHURCH SERMON

In the year of 1966 a 53-year-old Amish man from the Gap area went with the New Order Church split. It was not long until that church allowed cars, which this man also did. After a while he was a mail carrier. Some years later on his mail route north of 340 the Amish had Communion church services in a house that was right along the road. With the mailbox right outside the house and with the windows open he could easily hear the sermon, which was just what he wanted. The sermon was by old Aaron Esh of Monterey. The date was Easter Monday, April 23rd, 1973. He was there one whole hour listening to the sermon before he moved on. If anybody wondered why the mailman was late that day that was the reason.

-L.F.

GOTT LAS SICH NET SPOTTA

Dear Readers,

A few lines in the name of our Lord. Just a few lines to let you know that I did find out how it was about those two boys, about the one that just turned around in his casket.

There were three boys who did not listen to their parents and went out in the world. They were buddies with each other and after a while the one boy decided that he was going to settle down, go home and join the church. But he asked his other two buddies what they would do if Jesus came today. The one boy said that he would hang his soul on the fence and the other boy said that he would turn his back.

Not long after that they were in an automobile accident and both boys were killed. When they got to the accident they found the one boy hanging on the fence, and when the undertaker brought back the other boy's body in the casket, when they opened it up, his back was turned up, so they turned him around. But the next morning when they went to view him, his back was turned up again. On the day of the funeral when they were lowering the casket into the grave, they heard a rustling going on inside the casket.

(Bedenklich) We have to be careful of what we say, *As Gott las sich Net spotta.*

-Amos Petersheim

Yonie Esh, Georgetown,
wrote it took the children of Israel
nine days to cross the Jordan River.

As Ye Sow…

by D. J. Stutzman

A certain husband said to his wife, "Mary, what have you done? Do you really think that was the thing to do? After all, he is your father." Clair Moody's eyes filled with tears as he spoke thus to his young wife.

"I cannot help it, Clair," she retorted, "I've stood him long enough. I've given him every opportunity to do better and to show me that he appreciates the home I've tried to make for him, and Clair, you know how he returns ungratefulness for every kind thing I do for him."

"But still, was it right to turn him out into the night? And oh, what a night it is." Clair drew back the curtains and shuddered as the howling wind drove the sleet in fury against the pane.

"Where will he go, Mary?" Clair asked.

"I don't know and care less. Please, Clair, let's talk about something else now. He is gone, and for the first time in years we are alone with the children. Let us have a happy ending."

Clair said nothing. He picked up a book and settled down into his favorite chair. But he read little. He thought only of an old man just turned out into the cold, stormy night with nowhere to go. No one to care for him, and scarcely enough clothing to brave the storm long. Mary put the baby to bed and then entertained Jimmy on the floor for half an hour. Mary Moody was going to be a real mother to her children, she vowed, and early in their lives she sought their companionship. She would lead them and teach them so that she might always have their confidence.

Jimmy soon tired of his exercise, and sought the comfortable lap of his father, where he begged for a story until bedtime.

"I can't tell any story tonight, sonny, Daddy's story machine isn't working."

"Is it brokted?"

"Yes, it is brokted! Suppose we go straight to bed tonight and be glad we have a nice warm bed to sleep in."

"O, Clair!" Mary reproached him, "Is that statement necessary? Remember, Jimmy has been a good boy today. Grandpa was not."

"Grandpa cried, Daddy," Jimmy said.

"He did? Why?"

"'Cause mother scolded him."

"She shouldn't have done that! Grandpa didn't mean to be naughty."

"Mother should have spanked him! Why Daddy, he spilled his water on the table cloth, and made it all wet! Grandpa was bad!"

"And Clair, that wasn't all," Mary added, "you know, I just can't stand his continual coughing around the place. I've asked him dozens of times to please leave the room when he is seized with a fit of his coughing, but he'd stay right in his big chair, too lazy to move. He has no consideration at all for the children!"

"I saw Grandpa coughing, Daddy! He was bad."

Clair arose from his chair and took his son upstairs to bed. In gentle tones he tried to tell him he must be respectful toward old people. But at the same time he knew that his words would have little effect, since the child's mother was teaching him more by example, than he (the father) ever could by precept. His gentle words were almost meaningless to the boy, who insisted strongly that "Grandpa was bad." Clair himself did not feel that Mary's father fully appreciated the comfortable home they were trying to give him, nor did he seem to have, as Mary had said, proper consideration for the children when he coughed.

But at the same time, Clair knew that Mary's duty was not fulfilled until she had gone to the uttermost in caring for her own father. Old people are old people, and perhaps they do act unreasonable at times. And often insist upon having their own way at the expense of other person's rights. Nevertheless, these would be no reasons for any woman to turn her aged father out of her home on a cold, stormy night, with no place to go, and without anyone to care for him.

So after he had kissed Jimmy goodnight, Clair Moody returned quietly to the first floor where he dressed quickly in his warm street clothes. He was buttoning his overcoat close to his chin, when Mary peeped out of the sitting room and saw him.

"Why, Clair, where are you going this time of the night? Surely, you do not need to go out in this storm, do you?" she asked.

"Mary, see here," Clair replied, "I cannot stand it to think that your Father is wandering around somewhere in this storm. Where would he go to? I am going out to find him."

"But Clair, why are you so concerned about him? Cannot you rejoice that we no longer have him to bother with? Oh, Clair," she sobbed now, "he was so unreasonable! I just can't keep him! Please don't bring him back here."

Clair looked at his wife. He pitied her. No one knew how much she had to put up with during the day when she had the training of the children to do, and a man she considered disagreeable, to annoy and vex her, while she tried to do her best with the little ones. But yet, that old man was her father!

"Well, Mary, if I find him, I will not bring him back here, but I will try to find a place for him to stay. Don't wait up for me."

"Clair, he won't go with you anywhere. He's stubborn. You know how he acted when we wanted to place him in the Old People's home. He wouldn't go!"

The door closed. On the inside, Mary Moody tried to interest herself in a fascinating piece of embroidery to while away the time until Clair returned. On the outside, her husband raised his eyes beseechingly to heaven with a whispered prayer, that God might direct his footsteps in finding his aged father-in-law, and in locating a place for him to stay. He drew his warm fur cap close over his ears and then plunged out into the storm.

For an hour he wandered about, peering into every corner where he could see, half expecting to find the old man frozen in the snow. There were few pedestrians on the street, and the flickering lamps afforded poor light. At length an idea came to him. He would go to the minister who came to see Grandpa so often. Perhaps he could tell him what to do.

In another half hour he reached the Parson's humble abode. He stepped quietly up on the porch, and then, just as he was about to knock on the door, he stepped back, for through the window he saw the minister and his family gathered around an old man, who gestured pathetically as his lips moved and tears streamed down over his wrinkled cheeks. Occasionally he was interrupted by a fit of coughing, but he continued to hold the sympathetic interest of his listeners. It was Grandpa!

Clair's first impulse, after he recognized Grandpa, was to knock at the door and explain why it was that Grandpa was turned out into the night. But on second thought, he dreaded the humiliation of facing them all, even though the fault had not been his. So he tiptoed off the porch, and started again for home, facing the storm, and feeling assured that Grandpa would be safe through the night.

Mary ran to meet him when she heard his steps on the porch. "Did you find him?" she cried as soon as the door opened.

"Yes, he is over at Mr. Brinkman's."

"Oh!" Mary blushed. "What did they say? And how did you think of going there?"

"I think the Lord led me there. But I did not go in, nor even call anyone to the door. Through the window I saw him sitting among them as I was about to knock. I left, not especially caring to face anyone in that family circle. We have certainly disgraced ourselves."

"I don't see why you think that! Oh, Clair, have you no sympathy for me at all? Is it all for him?" And again she burst into tears.

"Of course, Mary, I have much sympathy for you," Clair said as he put his arm affectionately around his wife. "I know life was a trial with him here. But I cannot believe that the right thing to do was to expel him from our home as you did this evening. In his physical condition he may not live long. Perhaps if we could be patient a little while longer, God would see fit to call him home. And we could rejoice that we had done the best for him until the end."

"But he may live ten or twenty years yet. And in the meantime, shall I keep my children in such environment until they are grown?"

"I cannot say, Mary. I know of no other way to solve the problem."

"Doubtless, the Brinkmans will put him in a home somewhere, if he will go."

"They have no money, and he would probably not go."

They discussed the situation no further.

The next afternoon Mary was not altogether surprised to find the Brinkmans at her front door when she answered the bell. When she had seated them in the parlor, Mr. Brinkman said: "Mrs. Moody, we had a caller last evening. It was your father. He said you have refused to shelter him any longer."

"Quite true," Mary replied tersely, "I have come to the place where I positively refuse to shelter him any more. I cannot stand him here. I have my children to consider first, and it is impossible to train up children in the way they should go, with him about as an example of everything that is wrong."

"But he is your father."

"Yes, he is. But that does not give him liberty to act in my home in a disorderly manner and always have his own way."

"He is ill, Mrs. Moody, I fear his cough will kill him if he is not properly cared for," Mrs. Brinkman said.

"Can't you people let him stay there?" Mary asked.

"I'm sorry, but we cannot," Mr. Brinkman replied. "Our home is small and crowded. Besides, we could not afford to take in our own members of the church in that way. You see the obligation is not ours, it is yours."

"Yes, I know," Mary admitted. "But isn't there some place you could put him?"

"We cannot afford to send him to a home for the aged, but if you folks meet his expenses there, we can help you admit him."

"Oh, no. I could not pay for him in such an institution. Besides he would not go."

The Brinkmans pleaded with her a while longer, but when they left there was no decision made as to what should be done with the old man.

Several weeks passed by, and then one day Clair learned that Grandpa had been taken to the Poor House. It hurt him, so he did not tell Mary for several days. When he did, her pride was crushed, but she determined not to recant in her resolutions not to take him back into her home. She tried hard to forget him as she busied herself daily with her wonderful task of mothering her children. She would train them to be obedient and considerate and loving. She would teach them to be the best Christians and citizens she knew. She would be proud of them when they were grown.

One evening as she sat about her fireside with her husband and babes, she recalled that it was just three months since she had last seen her father, when she had commanded him to leave her home forever, because she thought he was a bad influence in the lives of her children. Jimmy talked less of Grandpa, and she felt sure he was forgetting him. Just then there was a knock on the front door. Clair answered the call, while they both wondered who would be calling this time of the night. The man at the door was a stranger. In a few brief words he spoke his mission. He was from the Poor House. Grandpa had died.

Instantly, Mary's heart filled up with remorseful grief. She was crushed. She remembered Clair's words of a short time ago. "Perhaps if we would be patient a little while longer God would see fit to call him home, and we could rejoice that we had done the best for him until the end," but she had rebelled. She had cast him out, and now he is dead. He had died, neglected, in the Poor House, because she had refused to do what she could. And he was her father!

Years passed by. In them Mary Moody had mothered her children just as she wanted to do. She taught them the ways of life as only a careful mother could do. Clair stood by her and took his place as a father in a noble way. Gradually, the grief and remorse that had overcome her after her father's pathetic death, wore away, and she now seldom thought of him anymore. One by one her children married and started homes of their own after they had been educated in the best schools. Prosperity had favored the Moodys, and they now lived on the "fat of the land." But in the years that followed after the children had all started for themselves, Clair became involved in unwise investments, and in a short time practically all his hard-earned possessions were gone.

Last of all, he died, too, leaving Mary in her old age a widow with almost nothing on which to live. All that was hers was a small mortgage on a little place in the country where Clair's nephew was living. Her own home gone, Mary expected her children to take her into their homes. But none of them offered to do so. At last she entreated Jimmy to provide shelter for her.

"Impossible, Mother," he returned, "I could not ask Marjorie to look after you. She already has too much to do to keep our children in society. You'll have to provide for yourself, I fear."

Heartsick and disappointed, she appealed to each of the children. But they all had excuses of some kind. At length, almost in desperation, she went to the farm where Clair's nephew lived, and offered to let them have the mortgage if they would give her a home the rest of her life. They consented, only because they were glad to be free of debt.

But none of the Halleys ever really appreciated having Aunt Mary live with them. In recent years things had gone bad with her health and now in old age she suffered much. However, she bore her suffering with remarkable fortitude. The years had taught her to love and trust the Saviour and on Him she leaned in full assurance of faith.

The country folk around about all learned to love her, and to every one she was known as "Dear Aunt Mary." Only the Halleys were unkind to her. She received an abundance of bitter words and harsh treatment from them. In it all, she continued to be patient and quiet. Deep in her heart she remembered, and knew why she must suffer all these things in her old age. Often now she thought of her father, and his last days. Oh, that she had been more kind!

One evening when she was too sick to be on her feet, and yet had to keep going somehow, she sat with the family in their comfortable living room. She longed to go to bed, but wondered if she could attempt the long climb up the stairs. Once she had asked to occupy a little, unused room on the first floor, so that she need not have the steps to go every day. But Mrs. Halley had stormed furiously. She would not have an old woman sleeping on the first floor, her place was upstairs.

Tonight she was told, after awhile, to "get to bed," for the family wanted to be alone once in a while. Aunt Mary approached the stairs feebly, and began the long weary climb. Priscilla Halley, the only one in the family who ever showed any sympathy at all for her, and that was seldom, went to her side and helped her up the steps. But when they reached the top, Aunt Mary remembered she had left her much needed pills in the kitchen. She looked at Priscilla beseechingly, as she mentioned her negligence, but Priscilla would not go.

"Do you think I am going to go all the way downstairs and back again just for you? You are most ungrateful," she said, "after helping you up these steps!"

Aunt Mary turned toward the steps. There was no other way but to go herself, for she must have her medicine. Just as she started down the steps, she seemed to have lost her balance, or tripped, Priscilla could not tell which, and fell the whole length of the stairs. Everyone was at her side the moment she landed in a pitiful heap on the living room floor. They picked her up carefully, but she only moaned, and her spirit fled its house of clay.

Aunt Mary was dead. Her days of suffering were over. Her harvest was reaped, but what a sad and sorrowful reaping she had! Her children she had trained beautifully, but in one thing she had lacked. Too late she learned the bitterness of the awful truth, "AS YE SOW, SO SHALL YE ALSO REAP."

We gratefully acknowledge the permission of Andrew D. Stutzman for the use of this story.

POWER OF PRAYER

(A true happening of a tornado that struck the towns of Kennard, Indiana, and Rochester, Indiana, the same day.)

A couple once saw a tornado
With funnel reaching the ground.
It was coming straight toward their home
And making a terrible sound.

The lady then said to her husband,

"Oh, what do you think we should do?"
"Let us go to the house and pray"
Was the only answer he knew.

They hurried to the house and prayed
That no one in town be killed,
And that the Lord would watch over them,
Nevertheless whatever He willed.

The tornado raged-down buildings,
Took their house lean-to off its base,
Then lifted up and over their home—
Down, across the street, on it raced!

It moved on across this little town—
Not another building was left
Besides the one where the couple prayed;
Many were injured, but **no** death!

God answered the prayer of this couple
When all lives in town He did spare;
This is just one thing that we heard of,
Of the wonderful power of prayer!

A Child's Prayer Answered

The following touching incident which drew tears from my eyes, was related to me a short time ago by a dear friend who had it from an eye-witness of the same. It occurred many years ago in the city of New York, on one of the coldest days in February.

A little boy about ten years old was standing before a shoe-store in Broadway barefooted, peering through the window, and shivering with cold.

A lady riding up the street in a beautiful carriage, drawn by horses finely caparisoned, observed the little fellow in his forlorn condition and immediately ordered the driver to draw up and stop in front of the store. The lady richly dressed in silk, alighted from her carriage, went quickly to the boy, and said: "My little fellow why are you looking so earnestly in that window?"

"I was asking God to give me a pair of shoes," was the reply. The lady took him by the hand and went into the store, and asked the proprieter if he would allow one of his clerks to go and buy half a dozen pairs of stockings for the boy. He readily assented. She then asked him if he could give her a basin of water and a towel, and he replied: "Certainly," and quickly brought them to her.

She took the little fellow to the back part of the store, and removing her gloves knelt down, washed those little feet and dried them with the towel.

By this time the young man had returned with the stockings. Placing a pair upon his feet, she purchased and gave him a pair of shoes, and tying up the remaining pairs of stockings, gave them to him, and patting him on the head said: "I hope my little fellow, that you now feel more comfortable."

As she turned to go, the astonished lad caught her hand, and looking up in her face, with tears in his eyes asked her: "Are you God's wife?"
-Parish Register

Iraq

Here are some facts just in case you think of Iraq as only an oil rich nation ruled by an evil dictator. According to the information I ran across: 1. The garden of Eden was in Iraq (it sure doesn't look like Paradise on earth today). 2. Mesopotamia which is now Iraq was the cradle of civilization. 3. Noah built the ark in Iraq. 4. Abraham was from Ur, which is in southern Iraq. 5. Daniel was in the lions den in Iraq. 6. Belshazzer, the king of Babylon, saw handwriting on the wall in Iraq (hopefully Saddam will, too). 7. The events of the book of Esther took place in Iraq. 8. The three wise men were from Iraq. Where are the wise men of today.

Recipe for a Good Marriage

Was told of this one couple who were having the best marriage. Man and wife each wrote their grievances about the other on paper then exchanged the papers and read them then went outside and burned them. Next they wrote the good things they like about each other on paper and put them on the wall above the bed.

-Leola, PA

The Animals' Story

Edna Hochstetler

Donkey:

My master is a good man,
He takes care of my life.
One day he called me to him
To carry his chosen wife.

"We're going on a journey
To Bethlehem," he did say.
"A lot of folks are going,
We are leaving right away."

My burden was not heavy,
Sometimes she walked awhile.
My master was so careful,
I heard she was with child.

Up hill and down we traveled,
Some days were long and dreary.
Although my back was strong,
By nighttime I was weary.

At times it was exciting,
Their talk was strange to me.
What was registration?
What was that meant to be?

When we arrived in Bethlehem
Where I never was before,
People looked for shelter—
It was a scary uproar   .

My master stayed nearby,
In this place where I was led.
His wife grew heavy on my back
Or I might have up and fled.

At last we found a stable,
Here we could be alone.
I was thankful to relax;
This was more like home.

Sometime in the night
I heard a baby cry.
They made a manger bed
And crooned a lullaby.

They said it was foretold
Where this birthing was to be.
I'm glad we got them here on time,
My master and me.

Cow:

Here in my warm stable,
Some voices I could hear;
Many people all around
Someone was coming near.

Two came into my stable,
I heard this couple say:
"We're so thankful for this place."
Then they laid down on the hay.

Sometime in the night,
I do not know what time,
A baby cried—they made a bed
In the manger that was mine.

I heard it was foretold,
This is how it was to be
I'm glad they came to Bethlehem
To share this place with me.

Sheep:

The night began as usual,
From activities of the day;
We lay on the grass listening
To what the shepherds had to say.

As the night was passing
And resting by the fire,
Some to sleep, some to watch—
So the flames would not expire.

They were very good to us,
I always stayed nearby.

This night there came so suddenly
An angel from the sky.

We were all so frightened,
It never happened so before,
The angel said, "Fear not."
They there were many more…

Saying, "Glory to God in the highest,
Peace and goodwill to all.
In Bethlehem the Savior's born
In a lonely, stable stall."

When the angels disappeared,
We grew quiet in the grass.
The shepherds said, "Let's go and see
What they said has come to pass."

This birth had been foretold,
I heard the shepherds say.
They found the child and coming back,
Told to all along the way.

I was glad to be a part of this,
But do not understand or see,
When they say He's the Lamb of God;
How can He be like me?

Camel:

My master studies stars;
One night he saw one—new.
He searched what may have been foretold,
Then pondered what to do.

It seemed to move and beckon,
My master's a wise man.
He called his friends together,
Then decided on a plan.

They got each a camel ready,
This journey might be far.
And, they had no experience
In following a star.

We traveled many days
From our country in the East.
Up and down, over hill and plain,
Each wise man with his beast.

When we entered Jerusalem
They asked, "Where can He be,
The One born King of the Jew?"
Priests searched the Book to see.

They found it would be Bethlehem,
That news caused quite a stir.
In Bethlehem they found Him
Gave gifts of gold, frankincense & myrrh.

Then my master had a dream
To go home another way.
This all had been foretold,
In a long, long bygone day.

I was glad to be home again,
We had journeyed far.
I'm glad I helped my master
In following that star.

Those animals all had a part,
Why, they did not know.
They just did their master's bidding,
Where they were told to go.

These events all came to pass
Two thousand years ago.
That baby grew to be a Savior,
For all the world to know.

As we celebrate His birthday,
Let's remember, if we can…
As gifts are given and received,
Jesus is God's gift to man!

CORNER BALL

Gideon L. Fisher, 1978

There was a large number of farm dispersal sales from 1925 to 1955. They were usually held between February fifteenth and March fifteenth. It was a custom for farmers to attend these public sales. It was a season when most farmers were relieved from being real busy, tobacco stripping was well underway, and spring work had not yet started. Besides doing their morning and evening chores, they found time to buy machinery or livestock, but mostly for social gatherings, and curiosity, and as the saying goes: "To see and be seen." Late news and social problems were discussed at these afternoon farm sales.

One event which drew a large crowd and much attention was the ball game. Quite often the ball game had more spectators than the sale itself. People traveled from far and wide to see a special game. In those days most homesteads still had the Swiss type barnyard, where the manure was covered with a good layer of clean straw. It made an ideal place to have a four cornered ball game. Where the game originated is unknown.

Six players were chosen for each side, quite often boys on one side, and young married men on the other. After playing the best out of three games, the losers were relieved, and another six players were chosen to play the winners. Occasionally old-timers from forty to fifty years of age were pushed into the game to loosen up stiff muscles. These old-timers often showed the young men some cunning stunts and old tricks in playing ball.

Occasionally players came to the sale from other areas. There were Mennonite boys from Chester County, and the Team Mennonites from Weaverland, who had practiced corner ball playing since the cradle. Quite often these boys left for home with the honor of winning most of the games. If it happened that they had farm sales in their area they would notify the Amish, and invite them to their sales. At times the Amish also went home with the same reward. These ball games always drew large crowds. It is not unusual for two or three hundred men and boys to take an afternoon off to watch a well-matched ball game. The spectators often gave the players a boost by cheering for their respective sides.

Corner ball games have special rules, the same as all other games. These were handed down by our forefathers, and no basic rules are published. At these farm sales no one received a special reward except perhaps a ten cent hot dog, or an oyster stew from a friend.

After the men and boys watched and cheered for three or four hours out in the fresh air, battling a brisk wind, it stirred up a good appetite. To solve this problem, some people had a business of providing a lunch counter at the sale. They served their customers a variety of food. To quote a few prices: in the early thirties oyster stews sold for 15 cents, hot dogs 10 cents, large chocolate bars 5 cents, small bars 2 for 5 cents, ice cream sandwiches 10 cents, and peanuts 5 cents a bag.

In 1950, a man who came home from attending a farm sale was asked by his wife about prices of the items being sold at the auction. After hesitating a bit, he finally said, "Oh, well, hot dogs still sell for 15 cents." This proved that he was not interested in the livestock and machinery, but had watched the ball game.

Die Heilige Woche...

Als Jesus von seiner Mutter ging
Und die heilige woch anfang,
Da hatta Maria fiel herzileid,
Sie fragte den sohn mit traurigkeit...

Auch sohn, du liebster Jesu meun,
Vas virsht du am heilige Sontag sein.
An Sontag verd ich ein Konig sein.
Da vird man kleider und palmen stein.

Ach sohn, do leibster Jesu mein.
Vas virsht du am heilige Montag sein?
Am Montag bin ich ein vanders mann,
Da virgenda ein ablach finden kann.

Ach sohn, du liebsther Jesu mein,
Vas wirsht du am heilige Dinnshtag sein?
Am Dinnshtag bin ich die velt ein prophait.
Verkinde der himmel und erde fergeht.

Ach sohn du liebshter Jesu mein,
Vas virsht du am heilige Mittwach sein?
Am Mittwach bin ich arm und gring,
Verkauft um dreizig silverling.

Ach sohn du liebshter Jesu mein,
Vas virsht du am heilige Donnershtag mein?
Am Donnershtag bin ich speise sall,
Das Oshterlamm bie dem obendmal.

Ach sohn du liebshter Jeus mein,
Vas virsht du am heilige Freitag sein?
Ach mutter, ach liebshte mutter mein,
Kann dir dan Freitag verboren sein?

Am Freitag liebshte mutter mein,
Da verd ich ans kreitz ge'naggelt sein.
Drei naghel gehn mir durich hand un feez,
Verzage nicht, mutter, das end iss seese.

Ach sohn, du liebshter Jesu mein,
Vas virsht du am heilige Somshtag sein?
Am Somshtag bin ich ein veitzen korn,
Das in der erde vird neugeborne.

Un am Sunntag frei dich, O mutter mein,
Dann verd ich todd ershtanden sein.
Dann traag ich das kreitz mit die nagelmal in die hend
Dann siesht du mich vieder in Gloria Land...

The passing of bro. Aaron closes a chapter for that family. My mind goes back to my mother, who grew up in Amishtown, back of New Holland. In the 1890s, she walked across the fields to the Amsterdam School. The Lapps said she walked through the woods. They had Bachelor Hoffman who taught school for many years.

He later had 2 boys who did not take to schooling, made poor grades. He said he does not know what will become of Eddie Nolt and Ivan Martin. Eddie invented the world's first automatic pickup baler, and brought New Holland Machine out of shambles to grow big. And as for Ivan, he had Martin Limestone, and was said he finally sold most of his holdings for 11 million.

-Andrew Hertzler, Maryland

The Oldest Brother

It was in the days of persecution
When the secret preaching in the outdoors was
     being conducted
That men were actuated with a noble spirit,
despite the enemy's rage.

During that time a preacher had arrived
Who would preach in the forests.
A woman came from far
Because she really wanted to hear him.

She had heard that first he would preach.
Usually in front of a great assembly,
Then he would administer the Lord's Supper.
She, too, wants to participate there.

She, too, wants to proclaim the Lord's death.
Despite the fact that she has to walk far
And brave many dangers,
Yet, what happens to her is good.

Very early she starts her journey,
Well over fifty miles she has to go.
When she has come to the edge of the forest
She is being commanded to stop.

There are soldiers, who watch there.
They have formed a circle around the forest
To so prevent the people
From listening to the preacher.

The old mother is being stopped.
"Where are you going?" they ask her.
Will she come up with a lie
To still be able to go there?

But, no, she will tell the truth.
You don't know what I am going to do there?

My oldest Brother has died
And now, I am going there.

We are planning to divide the inheritance
Which this Brother left behind.
My brothers and sisters will be there also.
This is the reason of my journey, you see.

"Go right ahead, that is not forbidden"
And when they let her pass
She had spoken the truth, certainly,
But yet, they didn't understand her.

If things were lovely all the time
And all our days were good
We never could appreciate
God's blessings as we should.

To the Jasper, NY, Diary Scribe Jonas B. Byler about the girl that was stopped by authorities and said her brother had died and his Will will be read today. A number of years ago a Dutch couple was here from Holland and I inquired about this. He said he's got a copy at home. When he got home he couldn't find it so he got in touch with his brother in another village and his minister had a copy. Only this wasn't a young girl, but an older woman. This was sent over in the Dutch language and our Dutch neighbor girl translated it over in English.

-Roman Miller, Ontario

The Story of Dorothea

1. A pious Christian maiden
In heathen lands did dwell;
God's Word, the Holy Bible
She read and pondered well.

2. Her name is Dorothea,
Was known both far and wide;
Her father and her mother
To her this name supplied.

3. Translated, Dorothea,
Denotes a gift from God.
Which from His throne in heaven
To earth was sent abroad.

4. A calm and quiet nature
Oft follows a good name,
If parents use their children
They'll likely do the same.

5. She in her youth quite early
Would often go to hear
The preaching of God's Holy Word
In faith and truth sincere.

6. She loved her parents dearly,
And gave them honor due,
And followed their instructions
As far as she might do.

7. These things the fierce old dragon
Determined to prevent;
This maid was apprehended
And into prison sent.

8. The heathen priests determined were
To make her serve their gods,
She loved her Saviour better
Than to fear their threats and rods.

9. With words both sweet and sour
They sought to astray
From God the heavenly Shepherd
This maid on error's way;

10. But firm, like rocks and mountains
She stood like saints of old,
Like Daniel in the Lion's Den
Or in the fire of gold.

11. When they could not accomplish
Their purpose they were filled
With fury, like their master
Because she would not yield.

12. A sentence was accrued by them
That she would have to die;
She threw herself upon her knees
And thus to God did cry:

World Figures

Haven't much local news so will copy some interesting articles got somewhere. 20% of the world is Chinese, 18% from India, 22% from the rest of Asia, 15% from Africa, 12% from Europe, 8% from Central and South America and 5% are North Americans. Only 33% of all the people in the world are Christians and 51% Roman Catholic. Of theses Christians only 0.1% are Anabaptist-Amish, Mennonite, Hutterite, or related groups. 20% of the world is Muslim. 16% of the people in the world don't have clean water for drinking or cooking. 17% of the world live on less than $1.25 a day. 48% live on less than $2.50 a day. 80% live on less than $10.00 a day. Only 1% of the world lives on more than $34,000 per year. Let us count our blessings!

-John Byler, 2015

13. "Into Thy hands Lord Jesus,
My spirit I commend,
Be with me with thy spirit
Grand me a happy end;

14. For thy great name and honor
I as a Christian die,
Oh, help that these blind people
May all converted be."

15. Theophilus, a chancellor,
This maiden pitied sore;
He said, "Have mercy on thyself,
Despise our gods no more;

16. Renew their dear young life again."
But Dorothea saith…
"A better one my God will give
When I have gone through death;

17. To Paradise my soul will go
When here my body's dead,
Where to my Saviour's honor
Stand many roses red,

18. From which my Lord and Master
Will make for me a crown;
Death is to me more welcome
Than all above the ground."

19. Theophilus in sport did say,
While she before him stood:
"My dear young Dorothea,
When you come to your God,

20. Send me some roses, apples, too
From Paradise so fine."
"Yes," answered she, "just wait a little while,
Your wish you shall obtain."

21. Now when this pretty maiden
There with the sword was slain
A little lad, most beautiful,
With a basket did remain,

22. Who said, "See here Theophilus,
Come take theses roses red,
They're sent by Dorothea
From Jesus' flower bed.

23. Her soul in joy and happiness
Eternally shall live,
With a body bright and glorious
Which God to her will give."

24. Theophilus was quite amazed
This wonder for to see.
He said, "I truly can rejoice
From error I am free."

25. He instantly began to praise
Christ Jesus as his Lord,
And left himself instructed be
In God's most holy word;

26. The Christian baptism he received,
Himself a Christian named
To martyrdom he also went
Was not of Christ ashamed.

27. Just like a fruitful flower
Is the true martyr's blood,
Much good it may accomplish
If blessed with help from God;

28. Through pain and tribulation
The church will live and thrive,
Through death to life eternal
Will pass who this believe.

When the Stars Fell

There was nothing unusual about the morning of May 19, 1780. The sun rose in a cloudless sky. It was calm, a handsome spring day. By noon, however, darkness cast its deepening shadows over Prince Edward Island. The fisherfolk, fearing a major storm, headed their small vessels to ports of refuge.

By one P.M. the darkness deepened, all work was put aside, and candles were lighted in homes. Nothing like this had ever been experienced before and the inhabitants began to be uneasy. What could it mean? The sun was blackened out and the entire heavens took on a frightening aspect. The wind rose to a fiendish shriek. Was something dreadful about to fall upon the frightened people? The barnyard fowl had gone to roost some hours before, and the livestock left the pasture fields for the protection of the farm buildings.

Now the storm broke in all its fury. Rain fell from the clouds in torrents. Thunder fairly shook the earth, while awesome flashes of lightning stabbed through the blackness, lighting up the countryside as though the sun shone in the fullness of its glory. Now settlers left their homes and gathered in little groups here and there and spoke only in whispers. Neighbors who had not spoken to each other in years dropped their differences to embrace as old friends. Toward evening bonfires were lighted across the country and the settlers gathered about the fires for comfort and companionship. This was no-time to be caught indoors. Nor was it a time for sleep except for the very young and the feeble oldsters.

About six P.M. patches of blue sky began to appear. When the moon struggled through a cloud bank, it looked like a blood-red disk. To add to the terror of the inhabitants, the stars began to fall in showers. Some reached land while others dropped into the sea and were entirely extinguished. At sight of all this, the dogs set up a mournful howling that no amount of scolding could stop. Children clung to their fathers and mothers and sobbed while the older people actually trembled in fear of they knew not what. Many believed the Great Day of Judgement had arrived and they prepared themselves and went to their knees in penitent prayer, believing that soon they would be face to face with their Maker. It was a time of great anxiety for those that witnessed the phenomenon which was observed through the Maritime Provinces and most of the New England states. The stars continued to fall most of the night, but towards morning the storm abated, the wind died down, and a full moon rode across the cloudless sky. The dreadful fear that had gripped the people gave way to joy and thanksgiving, and the people once more took up their various tasks.

Local historians in chronicles of the time, referred to May 19, 1780 as "The day of the falling stars." It was, they wrote, like a Fourth of July celebration in the heavens.

There was much discussion, conjecture, pondering, and ado about the shower of stars for many years, but no reasonable explanation was ever given. To this day it remains one of the mysteries of one of Canada's oldest provinces.

-Taken from old newspaper clipping.

A Woman's Apology

Many items of interest and gadgets quite queer
have been in our farmhouse since we're living here.
But the worst combination I ever have seen,
is my husband and me with the broom in between.
Now there is no argument, nor any big spat,
for we love each other dearly, so it cannot be that.

There are no big problems in our marriage at all—
if we have disagreements, they are usually just small.
We work hard together, we take time to pray.
We're true to each other, and faithful each day.

If we're not picking fights, then what's with the broom?
Well…this woman detests to have dirt in the room.
As many a woman in the countryside knows,
there's dirt wherever the good farmer goes.
He brings it in with his shoes and his boots;
it grows in the house as if it had roots.

I have learned through the years that my farmer man,
does not like all his dirt put in the garbage can.
He's much more at home on a messed-up floor—
that way he feels safe to bring in some more!
I no longer trail him behind his back
to sweep any straw that might drop in his track.

He has teased me so much, and I'm glad that he did—
for this habit of mine I'm trying to get rid.
While sweeping is something that most women dread,
my urge for the broom must be put down instead.
Sometimes I feel guilty…for as soon as he's out,
I've grabbed that old broom and swished it about.

I'm not from the city, as by now you might have guessed.
I was raised as a farm girl, and wouldn't want less.
I have my own daily round of chores that I do,
so I bring in dirt and some barn odors, too.
I know that some twine or pieces of dirt on the floor
should not bug me—they'll do me no hurt.

It's just a bad habit I've got myself in,
to let hay or straw bits get under my skin.
If I suddenly would have my dear husband no more,
I'd yearn every day for his dirt on my floor.
My goal is to set a moderate line—
sweep often enough, yet not all the time.
I must not complain about dirt in the room,
as long as I've got my old-fashioned broom.

-Ontario

The Other Dollar

Here is one for the very brightest boys and girls, or even for the brightest adults. Don't get addled if you have trouble, because it will trick almost anyone—at first.

Three men went out to dinner one evening. The bill for the dinner was $30. Since it was a Dutch Treat, each one gave the waiter $10. The waiter gave the $30 to the manager, who was at the register. The manager said, "Those boys are good customers, and $30 is a lot of money for what they got. Here is a $5 rebate with my compliments." The waiter thought $5 was too generous a rebate, so he gave each of the men a $1 rebate, and pocketed the $2 himself.

So, each man paid $9, making a total of $27 for the dinner, and the waiter had $2. What became of the other dollar? Think hard, find the other dollar, and then read on…

The confusion is caused by adding the $2 the waiter has to the $27 the men paid, to make up the $29. The $2 are part of the $27, and so cannot be added to them. To further confuse the problem, they assume that the $30 is still involved, and ask for the missing dollar, when the men have only spent $27 in all. The equation is, $30 = 25 + 3. When the $3 are returned to the men, they must be deducted from both sides, making 27 = 25 + 2.

With Wings Like Eagles

-by a Pennsylvania parent

Our family was thrilled and overjoyed that Thanksgiving Day, for a little girl had arrived to bless our home. Our youngest was five years old, so it was with great rejoicing that we welcomed this new baby.

We were an ordinary family with the usual trials and blessings. In the weeks before our baby's birth, I had pondered often over the bygone years. Were we worthy of the many blessings that were ours? We had had a happy marriage of fourteen years and four healthy, little children. Both sets of parents were still living and in fairly good health. Yes, we had much to be thankful for. Would our married life roll on so smoothly into old age?

I had an uneasy feeling that soon this would all change. Maybe tomorrow we would experience sickness, trouble, or death. We this in mind, I counted our many blessings and breathed a sincere, special thanks to God for our healthy family.

And now another baby had arrived and we named her Martha. Again, I said a heartfelt prayer of thanks for another healthy baby. I had no way of knowing what troubled and uncertain days lay ahead.

For a week Martha was the contented, perfect baby she appeared to be, but from then on she went backward and became more and more fussy. At four weeks of age we knew something would have to be done to ease her restlessness. We made an appointment with our doctor. He would probably check her, give some medication, and soon things would go better. We were not really alarmed and therefore wholly unprepared for the shocking news. After examining her, our doctor looked grave and told us gently, "Your baby appears to have some serious problems. You had better take her to the hospital for more tests."

With troubled hearts we hurried to the hospital. There we were informed that our baby would not live longer than seven months. They told us to take her home and care for her and love her as long as we could.

It was hard to break the news to our unsuspecting family, but we determined to accept it bravely and prayerfully for their sake as well as ours.

In spite of our resolve, our household was thrown into chaos. Baby always came first and she cried for hours at a time. For many days and nights, I did not get much rest. During this time, I often repeated my favorite Bible verse, "But they that wait upon the Lord shall renew their strength; they shall mount up with wings like eagles, they shall run and not be weary, they shall walk and not faint."

With each new day and each new night, He provided the strength I needed and His grace was sufficient.

Often we held or carried Martha around on a soft pillow, for that was what she loved most. With God's help, we were able to walk almost all night and not faint or grow weary.

Then came the morning when Martha was very quiet, yes, too quiet and her cries grew weaker and weaker. Soon the death angel came for our dear little beloved Martha. Her birth had filled us with happiness and now her death had filled us with sorrow. Why had she been born, only to die again so soon? But oh, the blessings that were ours because she had lived. It was better to have loved and lost than to never have loved. Our hearts were at peace when we thought of her spirit mounting up with wings like an eagle and that her failing strength had been renewed.

Now I often wonder how we were able to continue caring for Martha day and night and not grow weary, but I think we have learned the meaning of that beautiful verse. "They that wait upon the Lord shall renew their strength, they shall mount up with wings like eagles, they shall run and not be weary, they shall walk and not faint." (Isaiah 40:31)

LUTHERAN CHURCH BOY JOINS AMISH

My ancestors came from Switzerland and France and from a colony of Huguenots. Their family name was Huyett. My grandfather Moses Huyett was a respected person. As the story goes, he had a brother who lived a life very embarrassing to my grandfather. So strong were his feelings that he decided he could not go through life with the same name as his good-for-nothing brother. So he had his name legally changed from Huyett to Huyard. My grandmother Lydia was a midwife. She vaccinated children against smallpox. At that time, it was called "planting pox germ."

My grandparents were very poor. There were times when the neighbors would take some of the children and care for them. An Amish couple, Jonathan Lapp and his wife, Barbara (they were called Yonie and Bevely), who had no children of their own heard about the poor family. One day Yonie told his wife that he would like to contact the Huyards and perhaps "get a cheap hired boy and also help out the family by raising one of the boys." Yonie approached Moses Huyard, saying that he would give a boy a home, plenty of good food, a good bed, and good clothes to wear. The father turned to his two sons and said, "Boys, what do you say?" When Isaac, the oldest boy, heard "plenty of good food" he was ready to give it a try. He knew what it meant to go to bed hungry.

The lad climbed into the carriage. The Amish man seemed strange to him, but he was cheerful. After the evening prayers, Yonie took the boy to his bedroom. Feeling the separation from his family and brothers, he cried himself to sleep. There were many nights like that, but he was pleased that Yonie and Bevely were nice to him. The farm activities interested him.

One morning Yonie said, "Today Bevely and I are going to visit my brother. You can sweep the spider webs in the entire downstairs of the barn and clean out the hog pen. When you are done, go to the house, read a chapter from the Bible, and when we come home I want you to tell me what you read."

Isaac completed his work in a short time, for he was minded to plan his work and work his plans. He quickly finished the work and went into the house and got the family Bible. On opening the Bible, he was shocked. The Bible was loaded with genuine paper money. There were ten dollar bills, fives, and ones. He was not tempted in the least to take the money. But he was afraid some of it might get lost and he would then get the blame.

When Yonie and Bevely returned home they asked, "Did you find time to read the Bible?" He told of the passage he read and recited some of it. He never mentioned the money, nor did Yonie. The lad was sure the money was placed there for a reason. Young Isaac had proved himself faithful.

Isaac was given a horse and buggy to attend his own (Lutheran) church. Here he had been baptized in infancy. He also sang in the choir and was a Sunday school teacher.

One day Isaac explained to his foster parents that he wanted to get an education, and go into business or become a teacher. Yonie said, "That is no problem." Yonie paid for his education at Millersville State Teachers College. Because the Lutheran church had service only every two weeks, he attended the Amish church every other Sunday. He began teaching in the country schools and taught all eight grades. He worked for Yonie on the farm in the summertime.

There was one girl in the community who was very special to the schoolteacher. Her name was Mary, the daughter of David and Rebecca

Zook. In busy seasons the farmers helped one another, for they worked together. Isaac and Mary learned to know each other. Mary was very attractive and had a sweet personality. She was special. One day Isaac got the courage to ask Mary if she would accept him as her husband and life companion. Mary replied that she sure would accept him as a life companion but that she would not leave the Amish church. She said: "This would break my mother's heart, and I would not have a clear conscience to make such a change."

Now it was Isaac's turn to speak. He said: "Mary, I sincerely appreciate your respect for your church and your parents. I certainly would not ask you to leave. I will leave my church for yours. I can worship God in the Amish church. I will certainly join the Amish if they accept me." Mary's parents approved, as did also Christ Beiler, the respected father of Bevely.

Isaac tried hard to do his part. He let his hair grow extra long, and also let his beard and mustache grow. Isaac used to dress up quite a little, often wearing a white cowboy hat. But no more. He got a bottle of black ink and dyed his white hat and telescoped it. He also gave up his earlier desire to become a businessman. Now he would be an Amish farmer.

All went well until the Amish bishops said, "Isaac, we will not marry you, you are not a member of the Amish church." Isaac and Mary then had John Graybill, pastor of the German Baptist Church, perform the marriage ceremony on December 8, 1891. Because Mary married a nonmember, she had to be excommunicated. Then both Isaac and Mary were received into the Amish church together. Although Isaac had been baptized as an infant, he was rebaptized in keeping with the teaching of "believer's" baptism.

The couple worked on the farm of Mary's mother, but later took over Yonie and Bevely's farm, which became "home sweet home" for them. They enjoyed their new home, where Yonie and Bevely also lived in the grandpa house. They were blessed with five children, two girls and three boys.

My parents were conservative and saved wherever they could. They demonstrated that grandfather Christ Beiler was wrong when he told them before their marriage, "You are poor and will always stay poor." But they were cheerful givers and highly respected as honest and upright persons in business both with their neighbors and with the public. My father was chosen to be in the "lot" when a minister was selected, though he was never ordained.

He enjoyed his sausage and eggs. After the death of my mother, he often came and helped us boys on the farm. When he walked home he often repeated the poem "Alone and Yet Not All Alone":

Alein, und doch nicht ganz alein
Bin ich in meiner einsamkeit.
Dann wann ich ganz verlassen schein
Vertreibt mir Jesus selbst die Zeit,
Ich bin bey ihm, und er bey mir
So kommt mirs gar nicht einsam für.

(Alone and yet not all alone
Am I in my loneliness.
Although I do seem forsaken and lonely
Jesus is near and helps me pass the time,
I am with him, and He is with me
Then to be alone doesn't seem to heard
to bear.)

-David Huyard

Do Not Compromise

In 1992, Andy Kinsinger wrote about a meeting years before Washington officials when an old, gray-haired U.S. Senator with tears in his eyes said, "Encourage your church leaders to be firm in punishing and to have the Amish stay within their rules and Amish regulations . . . <u>do not compromise</u> but hold on to your Amish regulations; we well know that when the salt of the earth becomes weak there will be an end to this world." The forefathers and old bishops said to be thankful for and to value our many privileges and exemptions or we will no longer have them.

A List to Live By

The most destructive habit: Worry
The greatest joy: Giving
The greatest loss: Loss of self-respect
The most satisfying work: Helping others
The ugliest personality trait: Selfishness
The greatest shot in the arm: Encouragement
The greatest problem to overcome: Fear
The most effective sleeping pill: Peace of mind
The most powerful force in life: Love
The most dangerous pariah: A gossiper
The world's most incredible computer: The brain
The worst thing to be without: Hope
The deadliest weapon: The tongue
The two most powerful words: "I can"
The greatest asset: Faith
The most worthless emotion: Self pity
The most beautiful attire: Smile!
The most powerful channel of communication: Prayer
The most contagious spirit: Enthusiasm

247 Hot Peppers

It is amazing what some people will do for attention! Can you imagine a man gulping down 247 jalapeño peppers in eight minutes? That is what Richard Lefevre, age 62, accomplished in a contest in Nevada.

If any of our readers do not know what jalapeno peppers are, let me describe them. We have grown jalapeños commercially for many years. They are a cone-shaped hot pepper varying in size from an inch to three inches in length. They are much too hot for most people to eat except as a seasoning.

In the Nevada contest, some of the other participants needed medical help even though they had not eaten nearly as many as the record-setting Mr. Lefevre. One man who ate only fifty peppers, said his face was numb for hours afterward.

Again we wonder, what would provoke a man to do such a ridiculous thing? Did he want his name in the Guinness Book of World Records? Did he lack purpose in his life and craved some recognition? Did he wish others to admire him?

No doubt eating a tub full of jalapeño peppers is an extreme example. But the desire to be noticed, to draw attention to oneself, to seek a name or fame—this is a desire that is more common than we may care to admit. Usually the desire is more subtle than by trying to set a new world record. Yet it may show up in unexpected ways in the lives of all of us.

-Selected

Road Walkers

Sent in by: Stutzman

A common childhood remembrance for those who lived a half-century or more is the occasional visit of a wayfaring man or "tramps" as they were called.

Since these wandering men needed to eat and to rest as well as others, they would rely on handouts along the way. Perhaps the Amish got more than the normal share of such visitors because of the traditional idea that the poor man may be an angel unawares. Since one so taught would not want to be caught offering an angel inferior provisions, they often got the best one had to offer, especially in the way of food. Many however, refused to give them a bed in the house since they were suspected of carrying lice. More commonly they were put up in the wash house, the workshop or in the haymow in the barn. In fair weather, their meals were usually served on the porch rather than at the kitchen table.

I remember when, back in the forties, a faint knock on a porch post brought mother and myself to the front door to see a bowed man with one hand held to his failing heart and the other cupped to his ear. His voice was so soft and frail that it hardly carried the eight feet of distance between us. His request was for a dime and a loaf of bread. When my mother offered him better food left over from our meal, he insisted on his dime. Fascinated by the frail stranger and wondering how much farther his failing heart would take him, I slipped around the barn to observe his departure. To my surprise, as soon as he had passed our barn, his stooped body straightened up, the hand held over his failing heart was now counting dimes and his faltering gait became quite brisk. My father, plowing the field, had stopped to rest the horses several hundred feet from the roadside. The man's voice was now strong enough to call to him from the road to inquire about directions. His hearing had also returned. Apparently we had not entertained an angel that time.

Good Advice from Son to Father

Back in the year 1890 an issue came up in the Amish church here in Holmes County, Ohio, that caused quite a controversy. Like it usually goes, truth and gossip were mixed together. The overall issue caused a deep concern. The problem was there and had to be dealt with. So with a prayerful attitude and taking into consideration the welfare and the future of the church and also the souls of those involved, some older leaders worked on it.

It came to a point that Jacob Schrock was expelled and placed under the "Bann." He was an elderly man who had the reputation of having a strong will and of being easily hurt. Therefore, it was very hard for him to accept this verdict, and he allowed himself to get very worked up about it.

Jacob was retired and lived in the "Daudy Haus." His son Emanuel (often known as Monie) lived at home and did the farming. He was a young man about twenty-two years old at the time.

One Sunday evening while doing the chores Monie was in the feed aisle, feeding the horses, when his father came to him, burst into tears and said, "What has been done to me today is far too much. I cannot bear it. I know there are others that feel the same way. If you stand by us, we can make a big thing out of this."

After a pause, Monie said to his father, "*Ach, Daudy, mir welle net so denke. Mir welle des uf uns nehme. Es kann uns zum Guten dienen. Denk mol an Jesu, was er gelitten hat und huts alles gedulitch an-*

genommen, und war doch ganz unschuldig." ("Oh, Grandpa, don't think like that. We want to take this upon ourselves. It can work for our own good. Think of Jesus, how he suffered, and took it patiently upon himself, even though he was completely innocent.")

Jacob seemed reluctant to accept this advice, and expressed a "let down" mood. However, after some time had elapsed, he changed his views and was taken back in full fellowship with the church.

Years passed by. Monie moved about eight miles away. Old Jacob's health began to fail, and Monie often went to visit and help care for his ailing father. One of the last times he was there before Jacob's death, the old man said, "I do not think my time on earth will be long anymore. I want to thank you for that advice you gave me that Sunday evening in the feed aisle. It has helped me more than anything else I can think of. I have a good feeling toward the ministers and the church, and have no ill feelings toward anyone. I have hopes that God has forgiven me, and that I can die in peace."

Jacob died soon afterwards. How this story would have ended, had his son supported him in his rebellion, we do not know.

-Roy L. Schlabach

A Miracle of God

On December 5, someone stopped at the shop and said the day before something happened that amazed him. Eleven-year-old twin girls attended Bible school in Tennessee somewhere and the last day of Bible school all the students were given helium balloons and they put in a request that they would like to be adopted by Christian parents. They were foster girls. Then this fall, a childless couple in northern Maryland were out raking leaves and they saw this balloon in top of their tree. So the man got a ladder and got it down and here was the request or prayer of the 11-year-old twin girls. So on December 4, the judge granted the adoption of these girls to the childless couple, stating on TV, it was a miracle of God.

-Delbert R. Schmucker, 2013
Mio, Michigan

Unusual Horse Story

In White Horse area a family with four boys running around takes another horse once in a while. In 2011 a horse was bought and driven by one of the boys. Two years later, 2013, he was sold again as they had a horse that they liked better. Then a few years after that the father needed another driving horse for one of the younger boys, so he goes to the New Holland horse sale to see what they have. After a while a horse came through the ring that he thought looked pretty good so he bought him and took him along home. After he was unloaded something went through his mind—something familiar—there he was the same horse that was in that barn a few years ago. **Welcome home, Smokey.**

STRETCHING A DOLLAR

They tell me you work for a dollar a day;
How is it you clothe six boys on such a pay?
I know you think it conceited and queer
But I do it because I am a good financier.
There's Pete, John, Jim, Joe, Bill and Ed;
A half dozen boys to be clothed and fed.
And I buy for them all, good plain victuals to eat,
And clothing—I only buy clothing for Pete.
When Pete's clothes are too small for him to get on,
My wife makes them over and gives 'em to John.
When for John who is ten, they have grown
out-of-date
She makes them over for Jim who is eight.
When for Jim they get too ragged to fix,
She makes them over for Joe who is six.
And when little Joe can wear them no more,
She makes them over for Bill who is four.
And when for young Bill, they no longer will do,
She still makes them over for Ed who is two.
So you see if I get enough clothing for Pete,
The family is furnished with a wardrobe complete.
But when Ed gets through with the clothing,
and when
You'd call them worn out, what do we do with
'em then
Why, once more we go around the circle complete
And begin to use them for patches for Pete.

> "Every father should remember that one day his son will follow his example instead of his advice."
> -*Charles F. Kettering*

SOUTH CAROLINA FLOOD
David J. Stoltzfus, 2015
Honey Brook, PA

Greetings to all in *Botschaft* land. This morning finds me in the chilly north once again after a week of enjoying the warm, southern South Carolina sunshine. A group of sixteen of us plus two drivers and one of the driver's wives headed for SC last Sunday afternoon to do some volunteer work where they had major flooding back in October. We went through MDS and worked from a base that they had set up in the town of Andrews, SC.

It was an eleven-hour drive and we arrived at the United Trinity Methodist Church where MDS had set up their early response base at around 12:30 a.m.

At 7:30, we were up and headed for a restaurant where we had a good southern breakfast. We found the food in the south was good and very reasonably priced.

Afterward, we split in two groups. One group was working on trim, drywall, and painting. The group that I was with went to a larger house where we installed wainscoting, trim, drywall, flooring, and paint.

The homeowner's name was Mike Cox. He stayed at the house all week and went for supplies as we needed them. He was an interesting man and spoke in that slow southern drawl that is so common in the south. He said that it rained for twelve days straight and one day it rained twenty-eight inches in twenty-four hours. He raised Walker hunting dogs and between him and his friend they had about thirty dogs. Six of them were in the kennel behind his house when the storm began. Mike and his family weren't at home when the rain started, and by the time that they found out that their property was underwater they couldn't drive to their place anymore. He had to use a boat to rescue the dogs. The kennel was covered with about three feet of water and the dogs were swimming when they rescued them. He said it was unreal. The water at its highest point came up about three feet in their house all in about twelve hours. There was little warning and some houses lost everything. One place where the road crossed a stream, the water level rose twenty-eight feet. At thirteen feet above sea level and rain every day for twenty-eight days, it took a while for all the water to recede leaving behind a huge area of flood damaged houses. There will be work there for several years to restore the flood-damaged homes.

By the end of the week, we had most of the flooring in, the painting almost done, the drywall was up, and Mike seemed to be relieved that so much got done. The Good Book says it is more blessed to give than to receive and I honestly believe that. The gratefulness that was expressed by the homeowners, the friendships that were built more than made up for the time and effort it took to plan the trip.

The Amish are reported to be doubling their population about every 20 or 22 years. By the year 2040 there will be more than one million Amish in North America.

But do not expect the world to stand that long.

-Elmer S. Yoder

A PRAYER ANSWERED IN TIME OF NEED

In the early 1800s a remarkable happening centers around this Hertzler baby, Caroline. Her paternal grandparents, Christian and Nancy Hertzler, Sr. of Berks County, had raised ten sons but no daughters. Christian was sixty-eight and Nancy fifty-eight when they decided to raise their baby granddaughter, Caroline. Riding horseback, they went to fetch her from her maternal grandparents in Mifflin County. On their way they had the following experience:

Mile after mile was covered in silence as they rode along the mountain trail. It is a beautiful valley in summer in which to behold the handiwork of God; but now it was bleak and cold, covered with a deep blanket of snow. The milk was diminishing alarmingly fast, when Nancy said, "Where can we get more milk? We will need it soon."

I wonder what you or I would have done under similar circumstances? Didn't God say, "Call upon me in time of trouble." And "God shall supply all your need." After asking God to supply this need, (I suppose if they ever prayed earnestly, they did now) they traveled on. They soon came to a wooded spot by the way where they found a cow fast in the underbrush. Christian said, "This is nothing else than an answer to our prayer, for why should this cow be out here when there is so much snow on the ground?" Christian milked the cow, released her, and she immediately turned around and walked back into the woods. This called for a prayer of thanks. The remainder of the journey was made in safety.

The First Amish Church in America

by Ivan H. Byler

Many of our pioneer forefathers fled from their home in Europe to escape persecution and martyrdom, migrating to America for religious freedom. They suffered unbelievable hardships in the unbroken PA wilderness, having no homes and no money. According to records, the first Amish church was found in Berks Co., PA, from 1714-1740. A widow, Barbara Yoder, is said to have been the first Amish family to arrive in America, in 1714 with her 9 small children, all under 17 years of age. Her husband, Christian Yoder, died on the ship en route from Switzerland to America.

Thousands of men, women, and children perished on the European shores from hunger and exposure while waiting months for a chance to board a ship for America. Other thousands died on the ships from hunger diseases and overcrowded conditions on the ship, which were usually on the voyage from 3-4 months. Records show over 30,000 perished on ships between the year 1727-1736 and their bodies were lowered into watery graves in the sea.

Sometimes they suffered terribly in severe storms on the sea which tossed their ships to and from for periods of 6 to 9 days. In this time they could not sleep, they could not sit or stand but were tossed about on top of each other. Many of them were vomiting and could not eat for days. Other times they ran short on food. All these terrible hardships and sickness brought great numbers of painful deaths. Many a mother left the European shores with 6 to 10 children and arrived here in America with not one living child.

Some of the saddest funerals among our Amish people were held by our forefathers as they lowered the bodies of their loved ones into the sea. Fathers and mothers were separated. Many lonely widows and orphans arrived here in the strange wilderness with no home or anything in their possession, but they had something greater than riches, RELIGIOUS FREEDOM.

One of the greatest sorrows that any mother in the world could endure would be to see her family of loved ones suffer and die of starvation, and then cast them out of a ship into the sea where no marks of their graves can ever be found.

Many later suffered terribly from Indian attacks, not one had a desire to return to their native land and live under the Romish rulers. They found far more mercy among the uncivilized Indians than from the hands of the rulers of Europe.

It is because of these terrible sufferings and hardship that our ancestors came to America and now we have what we have. Are we thankful or do we take our way of living for granted?

Mystery of the Roast Meat

More than a century-and-a-half ago there lived near Lowick in Northumberland, England, a man of the name of Thomas Hownham. As far as this world's goods are concerned he was very, very poor, but he was rich in faith. He lived very close to God, and was favoured with many wonderful experiences of definite answers to prayer, and also of God's provision in times of need.

His only means of livelihood, for the support of his wife and two children, was by keeping a donkey, on which he used to deliver coals from the local coalmine, or by making brooms of heath, which he sold round the country. He often found it hard to make ends meet. After one particularly discouraging day, when he had received no money at all, he came home to find to his great distress that there was no food in the house. His wife and children were hungry, the latter having cried themselves to sleep. Finally his wife fell asleep also from sheer exhaustion and anxiety.

Being a fine moonlit night he went out to a sheltered spot some way from the house, a familiar trysting place for him. There he pleaded with the Lord on behalf of his wife and children, asking Him to meet their need in their sore plight. As he did so, a wonderful time of liberty in prayer followed.

He returned to the house, and saw something on a stool beside the bed—chairs they had none—and found it to be a roast of meat, and a loaf of bread. He went to the door to see if he could see anybody, but there was no sign of anyone. He immediately woke his wife and children for a good meal. Where the food came from in the middle of the night was a complete mystery.

Nearby lived a young fellow, who knew Thomas Hownham. They met the following day, when this story was related, but he was able to throw no light on it. Occasionally his parents used to help the Hownham family but they had not done so recently.

Not long after this event the young man left the country. Returning some twelve years later, on a certain evening the conversation took a turn about an old miser, who had lived at Lowick Highstead, but had since died. The young man enquired as to what had become of his property, adding that it did not appear that he had done one generous action in his whole lifetime.

An elderly woman in the company then spoke up, and told him that he was mistaken. She could tell of *one*. She had been with him as a servant, and about twelve or thirteen years ago he had ordered her one day to roast a joint of meat, and to bake two loaves of bread. He then went to Wooler market, taking a bit of bread and cheese in his pocket as usual. He came home later in the day in very bad humour, and went to bed. After a couple of hours or so he called up his man-servant and ordered him to take one of the loaves and the joint of meat to Thomas Hownham's and to leave them there. The man did as he was told, and finding the family asleep he left the loaf and the joint on the stool by the bed and came away.

The following morning her master sent for her and the man-servant. Greatly agitated, he told them that it had been his intention to ask some neighouring farmers in for supper the night before. They were always taunting him for his meanness. It was for this the food had been prepared. But they left the market early, before he had time to ask them, and so he missed the opportunity. On going to bed he did not rest well. Three times he dreamed that he saw Hownham's wife and children starving. On sudden impulse he sent his servant with the food. He much regretted having been so foolish, but it was too late now to do anything about it. He charged her and the man never to speak of it on threat of instant dismissal. She then added that since he was dead, she felt at liberty to tell the story as a proof that he had done *one generous action*, even though he regretted it afterwards.

The above incident was well authenticated at the time, and illustrates how easy it is for God who feeds the ravens to care for His people even in the most mysterious ways.

-Selected

A Strange White Bird

Clarence & Susie Schlabach
Dalton, Wisconsin

Liebe Freund,

Ein grusz in GOTTES Nana received your letter about the story of our son Orva that was killed deer hunting on November 19, 1994. I will try and give an account of the happenings as good as I can. It was probably close to a week before this happened that one day my wife saw a strange white bird sitting outside the window of her sewing room, so she walked outside to look then the bird flew over the fence into the chicken yard, she then went back in the house. Then after a while the bird was sitting in our lawn again.

When I came in she said something to me about it so I went out to see what it was but I did not know what kind of bird it was. It stayed at either our place or at the children's place. Then the morning after our son was shot that bird sat on the elevator where Orva was standing when he was hit, it stayed sitting on the elevator up to the morning of the funeral, when we got back from the cemetery it was gone and we have not seen it since.

On the day that this happened there were nine hunting together and one of the men shot at a deer running and when he got to the deer he had got two deer with the one shot and both were does and they had only one doe tag, but they knew that son Orva had a few doe tags for crop damage but Orva wasn't hunting with the ones that were hunting on our land, so one of the boys went to Orva's to see if he would want to come and get the deer, so he said, "Sure, I will come right away," and did. When they had loaded the deer he was planning to go home, then the others said they want to walk through the cornfield to see if they can find the deer that they had seen go in the cornfield that was limping so Orva said he would stay and help.

So they decided some of them would walk to the north end of the field, then walk through the corn and Orva and his brother Homer would stay at this end of the field and watch as the others walked through the corn. Orva decided that he could see more if he stood on this old elevator that was standing by a small grove of trees so he got on the elevator and the ones that were walking through the woods did not know that he was standing there, they thought that they were at the corners of the field. Then one of them said he sees the deer laying and is it safe to shoot and the others said as far as they know so he shot and right away they heard Orva holler and when the one that had shot looked he saw Orva fall off the elevator. *Gott sie mir sinder gnadich.* So they all ran into where he was and saw right away that life was gone. They then called the police and they looked for about two hours to see where the bullet had glanced off of and could not find anything. All were questioned separately and the District Attorney said they will report it as pure accidental. He then said to the one that had shot that before he shot he had control of the gun and the bullet but the minute that he pulled the trigger GOD TOOK CONTROL OF THE BULLET. He said Orva's time was up and GOD had a plan and you were part of his plan, why we will never know but just accept it as God's plan and that is all we can do, still after 21 years. It happened on Nov. 19, 1994.

We had the funeral here at our place on the day before Thanksgiving with close to 1,000 people attending. He left a family of 7 children who are all grown up now and all married except the youngest one.

"High Chair Days"

I like to see them at the table
With the high chair in its place.
And I like to see the baby
With a spinach smeary face.
There's no music quite so soothing
As the banging of a spoon
For the baby at the table
Is a joy that ends too soon.
I like those pudgy fingers
Reaching out for Mother's sleeve
And the stains of crimson jelly
Which at supper they leave.
And I like that rush for towels
After every sad mishap
When a cup of milk has landed
In the middle of her lap.
Some feed them in the kitchen
Where there's no one near to see
But I like them at the table
For it's where they ought to be.
And the accidents that happen
I am always glad to share
For too soon the day is coming
When the high chair won't be there.

True Story of Andy the Horse

Andy wasn't much of a horse to look at. A standardbred about 15^3 hands with a chestnut color. When Crist was 15 years old his father shopped for a horse that would fit Crist's needs—not too strong and fast, not too slow and old—as Crist had open heart surgery at age 15. The perfect one was found at Katie er Amos's. Crist and Andy bonded immediately. When Crist wanted to travel slow the horse went slow. When a race was on Andy was up there with the best of them. With Crist's heart condition his best time for resting was in the morning. He wanted nobody else to feed his horse. The jangling of harnesses and the work horses being hitched was heard by Crist at his bedroom window. "I'll be there soon," he called to Andy, a return whinny answered from the barn.

But first the horse had to work for his oats. When his stall door was opened for him to get a drink Crist took Andy for a jaunt around the pine tree of the circle lane. This was a regular routine and Andy soon did this by himself. When the trash barrel was full his father loaded it on the back of the spring wagon. Now Crist hitches Andy to the traces and away we go. A small incline had been made into the sinkhole to make unloading easier. Crist crawled over the seat to dump the contents. What a banging and clanging of tin, broken glass, jars, and pieces of wire. Andy wasn't patient—he pranced and danced, showing his discomfort. The family watched from the house thinking surely sometime Andy would take off quickly upsetting his cargo, but no, he always waited until Crist was ready. The next day mom needed things at the greenhouse, a three-mile drive down the valley. So down the road goes Crist and Andy. The Zook boys see him coming. Crist drives in and

Andy stays standing. "Now is our chance to trick Crist," thinks Sam and Ben. "C'mon Andy get up. Come on go," clucking and clinking trying to make Andy go past the window so Crist thinks he ran away. A back up boy had been there to head him off before he hits the road. But to no avail Andy solemnly shook his head up and down but stayed standing until Crist came back with the greenhouse purchases for his mother.

Crist bragged about Andy being so smart, no need to use the lines to guide him, just tell him where you want to go. Usually his errands took them west into town to the bank, the grocery store, etc. Mom decided to try this test. She hitched Andy to the carriage and said, "We want to visit Steff's today." Sure enough, he turned east and took her there without any guiding. "On the way home we will try something else. Get the mail, Andy, get the mail." He drove past the lane made a U-turn on the road and stopped at the mailbox. Crist told his parents Andy knows about everything. He understands my time on earth is limited.

October 30, 1993, Aunt Nanny from Big Valley was buried. Crist's parents had gone to the funeral that day mostly because Crist wanted them to. Aunt Nanny had a special place in her heart for this young boy and had often written him letters of encouragement. She also had heart problems and felt sympathy for him. The parents came home rather late that evening. Crist said Andy wasn't fed that day yet, he felt too tired to go to the barn. His father offered to feed him, but nobody had thought to take care of that. As his father was helping Crist to bed he peacefully passed away. He was almost twenty-two when he died. Andy the horse was all but forgotten until a day later when father went to the barn. Andy held such a mournful expression in his eyes. He put his nose on father's shoulder and pushed him down, "What is it? What can I do for you? Yes, we will miss Crist." Extra horses were needed to take friends to the graveyard. Unknown to the family the buddy boys decided to hitch Andy for the graveyard. As Crist's body was taken out of the carriage, Andy brought forth a long shrill, wrenching cry of pain. It was a cry from the heart of a dear friend. After the funeral the coffin was opened for the last time for one last viewing. Andy stretched his neck to look again upon the face he loved so well.

Sunday morning the neighbor man came to say his horse lost a shoe, would Andy be available. Father answered, "Crist always felt the horse knows what you want, ask him." Quill went to the barn to ask Andy and he shook his head "yes." After this the family would ask Andy questions and he would shake his head yes or no. Andy was useful to the family for nine more years. A brother of Crist's married and moved into the neighborhood. Notes and other things were exchanged with Andy and his wagon. "Andy take this to Jonathon's," the nephew at 3 years old would ride along sometimes holding onto the lines. Andy became old and was no longer being used. Father decided the horse could spend the summer days in the upper pasture with the young colts. Andy did not want to go. "Yes Andy, you have everything in the meadow you could wish for. Green grass, blue skies, shade under the trees, other horses for company." Father went to check on him after a few days, and Andy almost broke down the gate in his want to get to the barn. He wanted closer to the house and people. Father felt worse than before as he had promised to take good care of Andy. He reconsidered to bring him to the barn the next day. But by the next day he was no longer living, perhaps he had died of a broken heart.

-Jonas Yoder, Brush Valley

THE CHRISTMAS STORY

A tiny tree began to grow
beside a flowing stream
And as it grew he began to
dream of what he'd like to be.

As years went by, the tree grew tall
as well as his hopes and dreams
Made into a cradle for a child
is what he longed to be.

Then one day a man came
into the forest all alone
And with an ax chopped down the tree
and he carried it back home.

With craftsman's tools and skillful hands
he scraped the bark away
But as he worked he never heard
a word the tree would say.

He cried, "All I ever wanted to be
was to be a baby's bed
All I ever wanted to do
was to rest a small child's head.

I never wanted to be stacked away
in the corner of a shed
So please take my wood
and make me into a baby's bed."

The man got up and put away
his tools for he was done
But sadness came upon the tree
when he saw what he'd become.

Filled with hay he then was placed
in the corner of the shed
For he'd become a manger
for the cattle to eat some hay.

And he cried, "All my life I couldn't wait
to see my dreams come true
For cradling a newborn child
was what I longed to do.

But look at me, my dreams are gone
and never to come true
God must not care, I'm worthless now
I guess my life is through."

He cried, "All I ever wanted to be
was to be a baby's bed
All I ever wanted to do
was to rest a small child's head.

I never wanted to be stacked away
in the corner of a shed
But I guess I'll never get the chance
to be a baby's bed."

Then one night the door was opened
and filled with lantern light
Shadows played across the walls
as a man came with his wife.

There's not a room left in this town
that's vacant anymore
But my wife's great with child
and she can't go on no more.

The night wore on, then suddenly
a child cried in the shed
But wrapped in swaddling clothes
he had no place to rest his head.

With lantern high, the man searched
every corner of the shed
And spied a manger filled with hay
a perfect baby's bed.

As he laid him in the manger bed
the tree began to sing
Of all the children in the world
tonight he held the KING.

He cried, "All I ever wanted to be
was to be a baby's bed
All I ever wanted to do
was to rest a small child's head.

I thought my hopes and dreams were gone
in the corner of this shed
But God didn't forget my dream
was to be a baby's bed.

For tonight I held the King of Kings
tonight I held the Lord of Lords
Tonight I gave the Baby Jesus
a place to rest His head."

THE HEREAFTER

    The preacher came to call one day. He said at my age, I should be thinking about the hereafter. I told him, "Oh, I do that all the time. No matter where I am, in the parlor, upstairs, in the kitchen, or down in the basement, I ask myself, what am I hereafter??"

CHILDREN OF ISRAEL

I want to share a letter someone shared with us about the children of Israel. An older man that goes to FL in the winter, has plenty of time and figured this out. The Title is: "The Enormity of the Exodus of the Children of Israel." The Israelites' journey from Rameses to Succoth. There were about 600,000 men on foot, besides women and children. Also many other people went with them. Estimated number of people 2½ million. That would equal 2 times the size of Phila., PA, or 45 times the size of Lanc., PA. Marching 10 abreast that procession would have been approx. 236 miles long. That would roughly be from here to Pittsburgh. Or if they had 100 wide that would still have been over 23 miles long.

BIBLE POINTS OF INTEREST

Adam was 930 years old when he died and Noah's father, Lamech knew Adam and was 56 years old when Adam died. Noah's lifespan overlaps 18 generations from Adam's grandson Enos, all the way to Abraham. Noah's father and grandfather was alive while the ark was being built. His father died five years before the flood and his grandfather, Methusaleh, died at the age of 969, the year of the flood. Noah died in 2006 B.C. at the age of 950 and Abraham was a young man of 58 at that time!

A FRIEND IN JESUS

In 1857, Joseph Scrinen was a young man in Ireland. His fiancée accidentally drowned on the evening of their wedding. Soon after this he sailed for Canada. He wanted to live alone with Jesus as his closest friend. He never intended to publish this hymn. He sent a letter to his mother in Ireland when she became ill. He sent her a reminder that the best friend is Jesus himself. A friend visiting him noticed a scratch pad near his bed and asked, "Did you write this?" "Well, not completely," he answered. "The Lord and I did it togehter." It was the song, "What a Friend We Have In Jesus."

THAT WAS NO HAND TOWEL!

We used feed and flour sacks for bed sheets, pillowcases, curtains, towels, and all our apparel, including underwear.

On one memorable occasion, our washing machine broke down and it was beyond repair. An enterprising young salesman brought a Maytag washer out to demonstrate its merits. My mother sorted the wash and asked him to start with the sheets and towels, which were all made of feed sacks.

At one point, the salesman wanted to wipe his hands. He reached down into the laundry pile and grabbed some white material he thought to be a towel.

Much to my mother's embarrassment, he was wiping his hands on her bloomers! They just happened to be made out of the same material as the towels and sheets. My sister and I laughed so hard our sides ached!

-Dorothy Paterick,
Shawano, Wisconsin

A Brother's Gift of Life

Original story by Al Hirshbergin, 1955

When his twin lay dying, doctors told Ronald, he alone, might save him by making a vital sacrifice at the risk of his own life.

At precisely 8:00 a.m., two days before Christmas, in the amphitheater of Boston's Peter Bent Brigham Hospital, surgeons bent over the wasted form of 23-year-old Richard Herrick. On the table in an adjacent operating room lay his twin brother, Ronald. Richard was a victim of nephritis, a disease which causes inflammation of the kidneys. His had ceased functioning. Uremic poisoning coursed through his body. He was dying. His twin brother, Ronald, on the other hand, was in perfect health and he had two functioning kidneys.

Doctors had long ago discovered that normal life could be maintained with one kidney. (One person in a thousand is born that way.) If one of Ronald's could be successfully transferred to Richard, Richard might live. True, in all medical history no such transplant had ever been completely successful, but here there was a chance.

On the morning of December 23, 1954, Richard was wheeled into the amphitheater, Room 2 of Peter Bent Brigham Hospital's operation section. Ronald was taken into Room 1, separated from the amphitheater only by a small scrub room where surgeons prepared themselves for operating.

Dr. Joseph E. Murray, specialist in plastic surgery at the hospital, was in charge of the surgical team in the amphitheater. Dr. J. Hartwell Harrison, head of the hospital's urological service, headed the team in Room 1.

Both teams worked slowly, carefully, methodically. The spectators could hear every word, but few were spoken except for an occasional low-pitched, clipped order, a brief comment or question about progress in the other room.

In the spectators' balcony, tension mounted. Medical history might be in the making.

In spite of his weakened condition—he weighed less than one-hundred pounds, his blood pressure was high, his heart faltering—Richard, under a local anesthetic was standing his ordeal remarkably well. In Room 1, Ronald lay on the table, his kidney exposed and ready to be taken out.

The kidney, pink when first removed from Ronald's body, began to lose color as the blood drained from it. Even as the surgeon in the amphitheater picked it up to study it, the kidney took on a bluish tinge, like the lips of a child who has been in cold water too long.

The kidney was to be placed within Richard's abdominal cavity—just below and behind the appendix—instead of where his diseased kidneys were. It was a natural enough location. There was room, and connections to artery, vein and ureter could all be made from there. The diseased kidneys would then be removed later.

For fifteen breathless minutes the surgeon studied the kidney. Then he nodded his head. He had decided. "All right," he said quietly. For the next 45 minutes, the team in the amphitheater worked on the grim jig-saw puzzle, following the plan that had been formulated.

During the 45 minutes it took to connect Ronald's kidney to Richard's body, the only sounds in the amphitheater were the gentle hum of the electric clock on the wall, the brief, calm instructions of the operating surgeons, and the occasional clicking of instruments.

Then the surgeon straightened wearily. He was done. "Now you're going to see this pink up," he said. As he spoke, the kidney, now receiving blood from Richard's heart through the newly connected renal artery, began to lose its blue tinge. Seconds later, it was a healthy pink. The tension relaxed.

From the depths of the operating table, in a startlingly clear voice, Richard said, "I knew it was going to help."

The five and a half hour operation was over. Richard had a kidney that worked.

As the weeks passed, Richard grew stronger every day. All evidence of uremic poisoning and heart failure disappeared. His blood pressure dropped dramatically.

He left the hospital at the end of January, and returned in April for the removal of one of the two diseased kidneys still in his body. Two weeks later, he was back home, well on the way to recovery.

The final step in the series of operations was taken when the other diseased kidney was removed. Only after that had been accomplished did the doctors concede that the twin's transplant was a complete success.

Ronald and Richard were identical to the point that each had only one kidney. Inseparable and devoted, they found it unnecessary to put their feelings into words.

Perhaps doctors at Peter Bent Brigham expressed it for them when they released a statement which read: "The Herrick twins have been an inspiration to us all in their unflinching willingness to share their lives in such a vital way. No better example of the spirit of Christmas can be found."

"When the Banks Closed, Our Hearts Opened…"

I was 9 years old in the Depression days when the banks closed in our little Illinois town. I believe Roosevelt called it a "bank holiday." Some holiday.

You might wonder why a third grader would have any memory at all of a financial event. What could a kid have to lose?

Well, I lost my life's savings. It amounted to something on the order of $8 and change, as best I can remember. But it was pretty serious to me then. Fact was, the bank had closed and I was wiped out.

A Lesson in Thrift

The only reason I even *had* a savings account—rather than the bicycle I really wanted—was because the bank and our school promoted a savings program. It was supposed to teach us the virtues of thrift.

It had taken me quite some time to amass my fortune, small though it was. I carefully kept track of my money, dropping it dutifully into the little bank that my parents had given me.

Then, on every Monday morning throughout the school year, I would bring my saved-up nickels and dimes (or whatever I happened to have in my pockets) to school.

Sometimes it was the savings from my bank. Other times it was money I'd earned doing chores over the weekend. Still other times, it was a handout from a benevolent aunt or charitable uncle. Or maybe a birthday gift from Grandpa and Grandma.

My deposits were recorded each week in my trusty passbook. The entries seemed to fill the book fast, but my savings grew slowly. Twice a year the accrued interest (no princely sum, either, at the 3% rate common in those days) was entered.

Never Became Junior Tycoon

Watching my savings and interest accumulate, it slowly entered my mind that my chances of becoming John D. Rockefeller were somewhere between slim and none. By my calculations, it appeared that my personal fortune might pyramid to as much as $50 by the time I graduated from high school. It seemed like scant reward for a childhood of deprivation. To me a nickel saved was, well, a Clark Bar not enjoyed.

Then came the day the banks closed. Preposterous! A bank was a place with guards and expensive furniture and brass bars in front of the tellers and an enormous steel door guarding a vault where, insofar as I knew, my $8 was under safekeeping.

I was wrong. And now I was ruined.

Eventually "my" bank reopened. The first depositors to be repaid were us school kids. Whether this was an uncommon stroke of public relations genius or simply a case of paying off the smallest depositors first is something I never found out.

As you might suspect, my money did not go back into the bank. I put my life's assets into a mason jar, which I hid above some rafters high up in the corncrib. For years I had considerably more faith in mason jars than I did in banks.

Given the course of economic events in more recent times, it appears I may have been wise beyond my years.

-Clancy Strock

Run for your Money: Widespread rumors drove many depositors to withdraw their life savings before the banks closed. Others chose to wait…and lost everything they had.

"DEPRESSION HIT US LIKE A TORNADO"
by Cecile Culp
De Soto, Kansas

Everyone had their radios tuned to the news when the bottom dropped out of the stock market. They listened closely that day, and for many days to come.

The wealthy were hit first, but it wasn't long before the Depression came sweeping through our little town of Lenape, Kansas, like a tornado. The banks went broke and closed their doors. It was hard to believe the money we'd saved there was really gone.

My father owned a general store, the kind where the sugar and beans came in barrels and were weighed out on scales. I remember standing on the store's porch, watching the Union Pacific freight train roar through. Men filled the boxcars, sitting side by side, all seeking a new life somewhere, anywhere. Some men traveled by walking the tracks; others walked the roads.

Many of these men came into the store to ask for food. My father always fed them. As I watched those men, driven by the forces of self-preservation, I thought about how lonely they must be, alone and remembering the loved ones back home who were depending on them.

Soon there were bread lines—hungry people standing in lines a block long just to get a bite of food. Some of the missions offered one free meal a day, but they soon ran out of money, too.

Meanwhile, more businesses were closing. Smokeless factories carried "for rent" signs, and the doors were closed.

My father's store began to look like a gold mine with all the food lining the shelves. Some of my friends' families had been hit hard; they thought we were rich, and that we had all the food we wanted.

Grandma Kept Table Set for Travelers

I was far luckier than most during the Depression. I was being raised by my grandparents in a small Alabama town on Route 80, then the only coast-to-coast highway in the nation.

Granddaddy was the depot agent for the Southern Railway, and Grandma (who we called Nannie) ran a gas station and general store on the highway. For a long time, the worst thing that happened was when the railroad cut Granddaddy's pay.

Others weren't as fortunate. We'd see whole families walking on Highway 80 past Nannie's store, their few possessions on their backs, with pieces of old automobile tires tied onto their feet in place of shoes.

Nannie had a warm, loving heart, and she couldn't bear to see hardship; she had to do something to help. Whenever she spotted those wanderers, she'd send them to our house 2 blocks away for a hot meal. She and Priscilla, our cook and housekeeper, kept a big table set up in the backyard, and there was always a big pot of beans on the stove and hot corn bread in the oven.

Nannie also told Bailo, our hired man, to find something for the men to do, even if it was just cutting wood for the fireplaces, she they could feel they'd worked for the food and weren't getting a handout. Nannie was a wise woman; she knew those people had needs that went beyond hunger. Their spirits needed to be fed, too.

There was somebody eating at that table almost every day. When the weather was bad, Priscilla fed our guests on the long screened porch that ran alongside the house.

Thankfully, food was no problem for us. We kept chickens, raised a couple of litters of pigs each year and kept several milk cows. Pear, cherry and peach trees provided us with jams, jellies and preserves, and we could easily find persimmons, wild plums, dewberries and blackberries in the woods near the house.

Granddaddy and Bailo produced a bumper crop of vegetables each year, which Nannie and Priscilla preserved in shelf after shelf of fat mason jars. Much of that food was shared with others who were less fortunate.

Nannie's generosity eventually cost her the store. She let many of her customers charge their purchases, and continued extending their credit even when she knew they couldn't repay her. She just couldn't bear to see those people do without.

I don't know if Nannie ever collected the debts that were owed to her, but I do know that she and Granddaddy paid off every penny *they* had owed, bankrupt or not. They were both fiercely honest people.

My grandparents taught me a lot about life. They taught me not to judge a book by its cover, and that money means nothing compared to decency and character.

-Evelyn K. Martin
Lakeland, Florida

No one who lived through the Depression can forget the terrible toll it took on the nation. Those who survived it remember the hard times all too well—but they're more likely to speak of the courage, strength, and the love that saw them through.

Tricks Kept Food Bills Down

Parents learned tricks that cut the food bill. You parked outside the grocery until 10 minutes before closing time on Saturday night and then hurried in to snap up bargains on fresh produce. It was priced for quick sale because it wouldn't keep over Sunday in those unrefrigerated times. I remember Dad buying an entire grocery sack full of bananas for 10¢. We feasted on them for nearly a week.

During the summer I was dispatched at dawn on my bicycle to scout country roads for wild asparagus. After a while you knew where it grew, so in a half hour you could collect enough for a couple of meals.

In the fall the whole family went with gunnysacks to a heavily wooded county park that had dozens of walnut and hickory trees. In a few hours we had enough nuts to last us until the next autumn.

Most people had gardens. *Big* gardens. They not only provided vegetables and berries and rhubarb for the summer months, but also the raw material for canning. The measure of a dedicated homemaker was how many hundreds of jars of vegetables, fruit and jelly she "put up" for the winter. No social visit was complete without a trip to the basement to admire shelf after shelf of mason jars filled with string beans and corn, red beets and tomatoes.

There were other tricks. In our family we still make "Depression syrup." The process is a simple matter of cooking down a mixture of white or brown sugar plus water, and perhaps some maple flavoring. It's not Karo syrup, of course, but tasty, warm and cheap.

People who lived on farms had a big advantage, and in the '30s, 20% of all Americans *did* live on farms. You had cows that gave milk and chickens that laid eggs (or else were the featured attraction at Sunday dinner). Your orchard produced apples and cherries and plums and pears.

Days of Riding the Rails Remembered

by Raphael P. Magelky
Eugene, Oregon

The 1930s were tough years. There were no jobs to be had—even the farmers weren't hiring. Thousands of us rode boxcars from place to place in hopes of earning a few pennies. Sometimes, when there weren't any boxcars, we rode *on top of* the trains, no matter what the weather was like.

Anyone who remembers those days can vouch for the "yard bulls" who worked in the railway terminals.

We'd keep out of sight and wait for the "highball," which signaled the train was about to leave. That was the time to climb aboard. If the "bull" caught you, you were herded into a special housing area at the rail yard and then put on a "work train" and sent out to repair the tracks. The railroad still owes me a few cents for some of the work I did!

On one occasion, about 300 of us climbed aboard an eastbound freight train in Laurel, Montana. Those riding with us through the dark night included a man and his wife and their young daughter, who was perhaps 10 years old. On that trip, I found a few days' work somewhere in the Bitterroot Valley of Montana, bleaching celery (Yes, celery was bleached in those days!).

A TOUGH WAY TO TRAVEL

Riding inside a boxcar or on top of the train was a dangerous way to travel. All of us were looking for work, but some were more desperate than others. If you had any money, you had to be careful; there was always the chance that other hobos might team up and overpower you so they could take it. A hobo also had to guard against the theft of his "bindle," a bedroll consisting of a piece of canvas wrapped around some blankets.

When there was no work to be found, we had no money for food. We sometimes went to the back doors of cafes and restaurants (no one ever went to the front door for a handout) to watch for the floor-sweeper. Getting a word to him could help us get a sandwich, which was usually just a bit of leftover meat and two thin slices of bread, but it was usually enough to tide us over for a few hours.

We never went through garbage cans for food. The cans usually contained only ashes and a few empty tin cans. It was better to try a home in an outlying area of town and ask the lady of the house for a few sandwiches.

I remember one very generous lady who had just served a meal but hadn't cleared the table yet. She asked me to come in and wash up, and then served me chicken, potatoes, and homemade gravy. It reminded me of the days when I was living at home and my own mother cooked food like that. When you were riding the rails, such meals were few and far apart.

Still, thanks to the generosity of those who shared their food with us, I can honestly say I never went hungry.

AN EMBARRASSING "SLIP"

My mother made a number of things out of feed sacks, including undergarments. She always bleached the sacks until they were white, but once in a while she'd have trouble getting the printed words out of them.

One day, she was dressing for a meeting of her church circle and put on a thin voile dress—over one of her homemade feed sack slips.

I looked at her, all dressed up, and said, "Mom, you can't wear that dress over that slip. You can read the print right through it." It read: "100 Lbs. Net Weight." We sure got a laugh out of that!

-Dorothy Kyes
Valparaiso, Indiana

MEMORIES BRING MORE LAUGHTER THAN TEARS

Some things in life must be experienced for one to truly grasp their meaning—like the Great Depression. Although I was very young at the time, my memories of those years bring more laughter than tears. I remember...

It was rare to be able to afford a meal in a restaurant in those days, but when you did go, you always looked for a seat by the window. The proprietor always gave larger portions to the diners with window seats so passersby would think it was a good place to eat!

SEASONS DETERMINED MANY FAMILIES' MENUS

by Juanita Killough Urbach
Brush, Colorado

Group gardens were popular in many communities, with several neighbors pitching in to tend one large plot. And, as the photo indicates, everyone in the family had his or her own row to hoe!

Our eating habits in the 1930s were regulated by the seasons. The grocery bill always had to be kept to a minimum because our only reliable source of income came from selling eggs and cream.

We welcomed spring each year. It was a time of hope. We searched the fence corners for lamb's-quarters, added winter onions to our scrambled eggs, and pulled tender rhubarb shoots for pies.

Soon there would be leaf lettuce, radishes and green onions from the garden. Topped with a sweet-and-sour cream dressing, they would become tasty salads.

The meat supply would be running low as spring approached, so whatever we had left was alternated with stewing hens.

In summertime, since we had no refrigera-tion, we cooked only enough food for one meal. Excess vegetables were preserved in a variety of ways. Green beans and tomatoes were canned. Sweet corn was cut from the cob and spread on a white sheet to dry. Cabbage was shredded and put into stone jars with salt for sauerkraut.

When fall came, we bought a few bushels of peaches and pears for canning. Baskets of grapes were bought for jelly. Potatoes, carrots, and onions were dug up and stored in the cellar.

Winter was soup season. A meaty bone boiled with vegetables made a tasty appetizer. Thicker, meatier stews were meals in themselves. Chicken noodle soup was a favorite, as were potato soup, and navy bean soup with bits of ham or bacon.

Tomato soup was a Depression specialty. Home-canned tomatoes and milk were heated separately, and a little soda was added to the tomatoes to keep the milk from curdling when the two were combined. It had a unique flavor unmatched by any other tomato soup.

Food preparation required more work then, but the cooks were creative. If they were out of one ingredient, they substituted another: Flour replaced cornstarch, honey or syrup took the place of sugar, and soda and baking powder were used interchangeably. The changes were rarely detected, and the food was just as delicious and filling.

We might have felt poor during the Depression, but we ate like kings!

DANDELION DISH WAS FREE FOR THE ASKING

At age 10, I didn't know we were poor. It seemed we had just as much as everybody else. We didn't eat much meat in those days. What we did eat was fried potatoes—and lots of them.

One day my mother decided we needed something a little different. She handed me a small knife and a paper sack.

"Go up to the telephone company and ask if you can pick the dandelions from their lawn," she told me.

I came back with a whole sackful. Mother cooked the dandelions in bacon fat, and they were *delicious*. I was so proud to have made a contribution to our meal!

-Gracie Thomas
Flagstaff, Arizona

HOBOS THANKFUL FOR FOOD AND CONVERSATION

Although I was a young housewife home alone with my babies, I was never afraid of the men they called hobos. They were just down on their luck, looking for work, and hungry.

My husband kept a sawhorse where the hobos could see it, with a railroad tie ready to be cut into lengths to fit into the stove.

On most occasions, while I was fixing my guest a big beef sandwich, he'd go to work sawing the railroad tie. Afterward, I'd bring a basin of warm water, some soap and a towel. The men seemed to appreciate having a chance to wash their hands and face.

Sometimes I'd send the men off with an extra sandwich and cookies. Sometimes they'd just sit on the steps and visit for a while. Most of them were family men trying to make a few bucks to send home.

I had no money, as those were hard times even with my husband working, but I could share what food we had. God bless those dear souls for carrying on.

-Pauline Clark
Helena, Montana

Food was a precious commodity during the Depression, and many families produced much of it themselves. No matter how humble the meal, they savored whatever they had.

"WE HAD EVERYTHING BUT MONEY"

"We May Have Been Poor, But We Had Plenty of Food"

Priceless Memories of the Great Depression…from strong people who tell *in their own words* what it was like when banks closed and hearts opened.

This book is the chronicle of a remarkable era in our history—the Great Depression. It also is the story of a remarkable generation of people born just about the time the 20th century began, somewhere between the presidencies of McKinley and Teddy Roosevelt.

We are their sons and daughters, grandchildren and great-grandchildren. Much of who and what we are was shaped by them.

It was their fate to be afflicted by wars, plagues, famines, epidemics, droughts and floods of near-Old Testament proportions. Yet they did much more than survive. These ancestors of ours stubbornly and bravely endured, sustained by their Bibles, their patriotism and their determination that things could be made better than they were.

WHAT A CHANGE THEY SAW

Theirs was the generation that went from outhouses to outer space, from kerosene lamps to computers, from straw mattresses to supersonic jets.

They made do during the bad times and adjusted to monumental changes in the world around them. They persevered through it all, anchoring their happiness and fulfillment on the belief that *family* was what mattered most.

Feed Sacks Helped Stretch the Family Budget

by Margie Landegard,
St. Olaf, Iowa

During the Depression, when I was growing up, we couldn't afford many "store-bought" things. I didn't mind that at all, because I knew there would always be plenty of clothing for Mom and me, made from those pretty sacks that our feed came in!

Mom sewed aprons, nightshirts, pajamas, dish towels, tablecloths, sheets and pillowcases from those feed sacks. If we were lucky enough to get quite a few sacks with the same color and pattern, Mom would make curtains and comforters, too. When there was material bearing any print Mom didn't like, it went into a special box for use later in weaving rugs.

Not all feed sacks were printed, though. When Mom got the plain ones that were light tan, she bleached them. The whitest, softest ones were made into warm petticoats and bloomers.

Flour sacks were usually white with a simple plaid design. These had a softer weave and were very absorbent, so they were packed in the back of our kitchen drawer for use as special "Sunday dish towels."

Sugar sacks were smaller, plain white, and made of thinner fabric. They were ideal for straining "crackling" from fresh-rendered lard. We also used them for straining milk, as drip bags for jelly and as bandages.

We made good use of seed bags, too, in those days. Seeds usually came in cloth bags printed with a bright company logo. Those labels were stubborn and wouldn't always bleach out, so Mom turned them into hand towels for the men.

With repeated washings in strong soap, the print eventually faded.

Factory-made bags were sewed together with sturdy cords that could be unraveled and saved.

So we even made secondary use of that string—we used it for mending, patching, tying sausages and even securing bandages.

Those sacks were precious to the farm wife, and if she had any she didn't need, she saved them. Even when she and her husband retired from farming and moved to town, any remaining feed sacks went along with her. You can still find them at estate sales, but the bidding is always brisk!

Worn With Pride

My folks raised hundreds of chickens, so we had plenty of feed sacks, and my mother used them to make most of my clothes. She used the prints for items like dresses, and saved the white ones or those with lettering on them for undergarments.

One day at a family picnic, we kids were turning somersaults on the grass. Suddenly, everyone began laughing!

I stood up, wondering what was going on. An uncle asked me, "So, you're the Pride of the Rockies?" I didn't understand what he meant until he explained, "That's what it says on your underpants!" Embarrased? You bet!

-Joyce A. Coleman
Hotchkiss, Colorado

MAKE IT LAST, WEAR IT OUT

LOOKING FOR WORK

JOBLESS MEN lined up three deep outside the employment office in downtown Milwaukee, Wisconsin in the mid-1930s. For many men, the wait in line was a daily ritual.

"I Like the Depression!"

I like the Depression. No more prosperity for me. I have had more fun since the Depression started than I ever had in my life. I had forgotten how to live, and what it meant to have real friends, and what it was like to eat common, everyday food. Fact is, I was getting a little too high-hat.

It's great to drop into a store and feel that you can spend an hour, or 2, or 3, or even half a day just visiting and not feel that you are wasting valuable time.

I like the Depression. I am getting acquainted with my neighbors and following the Biblical admonition to love them. Some of them had been living next door to me for 3 years; now we butcher hogs together.

I like the Depression. I haven't been out to a party in 18 months. My wife has dropped all her clubs, and I believe we are falling in love all over again. I'm pretty well satisfied with my wife and I think I will keep her.

I am feeling better since the Depression. I get more exercise because I walk to town, and a lot of folks who used to drive Cadillacs are walking with me.

I like the Depression. I am getting real honest-to-goodness food now. Three years ago we had filet of sole, crab Louie, and Swiss steak with flour gravy. We had guinea hen and things called "gourmet" and "Oriental." Now we eat sow bosom with the buttons still on it!

I like the Depression. Three years ago I never had time to go to church. I played checkers or baseball all day Sunday. Besides, there wasn't a preacher in Texas that could tell me anything. Now I'm going to church regularly and never miss a Sunday. If this Depression keeps on, I will be going to prayer meetings before too long.

Oh, yes! I like the Depression!

> L et us be more thankful and not abuse the prosperous times we are in.
> -LF

"Our Parents Were Our Greatest Gifts"

We didn't have much during the Depression, but we learned how to get by. During the leanest years we usually had oatmeal with diluted canned milk for breakfast. I can't remember ever having fresh milk; I guess the canned variety was cheaper.

For lunch or dinner, we ate a lot of what Mother called "poor man's dish," which consisted of macaroni, tomatoes, and some ground beef.

Greens were there for the taking in the spring. We often went out to look for dandelions before they bloomed, then Mother would cook them like spinach, mixing them with mayonnaise sauce and serving it over potatoes. If she had any bacon, she'd add bits of that, too.

Our parents never complained, nor did they expect anyone to give us anything. The government was giving food away then, but my dad was too proud to take it.

I'm happy I lived during that time; it taught me that material things aren't what's important in life. The greatest gifts we had were our parents and the example they set for us. They taught us that you can accomplish anything if you believe you can, and if you work hard enough.

-Dorothy Rhoads Ness
Annapolis, Maryland

Wagons, Ho!

My parents were just kids of 18 and 16 when they married in 1927. They moved to an Iowa farm, where Dad made $55 a month—a very good start.

But within a year, my young dad found himself supporting a household of five—my grandmother had moved in with them, and shortly afterward, my twin sister and I were born.

Then the Depression hit. Mom had relatives in California who urged us to come West, and they decided to go. It was a "burning your bridges" decision; they knew once we arrived, we wouldn't have the means to come back. We left Iowa in 1931 with $85 cash and all our possessions packed in and on our stage coach.

Like pioneers of old, we set up roadside camps each night, where we prepared the evening meal and the next morning's breakfast. Lunch was never elaborate; we simply pulled off the road and ate wherever we happened to be at noon. Travel was much different then; traffic was light, and towns and accommodations were few and far between.

Some farm families moved cross-country in covered wagons. This caravan was photographed near Clovis, New Mexico, in 1932.

BREAD LINES *sometimes stretched out for blocks. This crowd lined up for bread at the McAuley Mission under the Brooklyn Bridge in New York City in 1931.*

MILK LINE: *The Salvation Army provided milk for needy children, who lined up with their own containers. This photo was taken in 1932.*

HOBOS CAME FROM ALL WALKS OF LIFE

"They were searching for any job to be found…"

TOUGH TIMES DELAYED WEDDING

By Marie Jenkins
Porterville, California

I WAS "courted" during the Dust Bowl days. While the billowing black clouds hovered overhead, my husband-to-be and I went to dances, rode horses, worked the fields and enjoyed life. We planned our wedding for the autumn of 1932. But it was not to be.

The Depression worsened, and our parents begged us to wait another year. My father wanted to give his only child a nice wedding.

So we waited. In March of 1933, all the banks in the country closed, and I knew without asking that there would be no wedding that

year, either. At the end of the crop season, my fiancé and my father divided their profits. Each had made $17.

Times were hard, but we were happy. I made clothing out of gunnysacks, and stitched a stylish skirt and jacket set on my old treadle sewing machine.

On Dec. 23, 1934, my fiancé stopped by to see me with a somber expression on his face.

"I'm going to ask you just one more time," he said. "Are we ever going to get married, or do you want to call the whole thing off?" I looked long and hard into his honest blue eyes and knew he was serious.

Before I could answer, he went on. "I have $8. That's all I could get to save my life. I love you and will do the best I can."

I didn't have to think very long about my answer. "Let's try it," I said.

A happy smile came over his face. "When?"

"Now," I replied.

"Do we tell our parents?" he asked.

"No," I said firmly.

I rushed to my room and jumped into my knee-high lace-up boots and gunnysack suit, and we headed for town. We were married in the courthouse. The license and the ceremony cost $2 each, so we started married life with $4 to our name.

The hard times of the 1930s may be legendary, but those years also gave me some of the most beautiful memories of my life.

DEPRESSION YEARS

We were married December 5th, 1918, and started farming and housekeeping in the spring of 1919. We had good years until the year of 1930 then the bottom seemed to drop out of everything. Carpenters were glad if they could find work at 25 cents an hour, farmers also had a tough job of making ends meet. Hogs sold for two cents a pound, steers 4.5 cents a pound, potatoes 25 cents a bushel, and milk 80 cents a hundred. In 1934 it got better and about 1936 things leveled off, and supply and demand took care of itself. In 1939-40 when Hitler in Germany started to invade countries prices started to rise and have risen ever since. During the Depression, church members needed one another, and church affairs went along nicely. But now things have changed because there is so much money that comes easily and buys so many worldly things.

-Jonathan Zook, Aug. 1971

Jacob Bitschy Jr.

My father Jacob M. Bitschy was thirty-eight years old when he passed on to his eternal reward. He was a deacon in the Amish church of one and a half years. There were nine of us children, the oldest being sixteen and the youngest not being born yet. So mom was left with ten of us children.

Money had been borrowed from an Amish minister by the name of Bill Beachy. This was in 1935 during the time of the depression and money was very scarce. My uncles who meant well advised my mother to farm us children out into different homes. My mother refused to have us children separated. To this day I cannot thank God enough for this decision. Although my mom sacrificed her life unselfishly for us children.

Shoes were just worn when it was too cold to go barefoot. Clothes were patch upon patch. Our cereal in the morning was a small bowl, etc. I now know why mom taught us things. I could never teach my children, because of this poverty.

I still cherish the many good memories of seeing mom kneeling with us children with the prayer book or Sunday afternoons reading to us children out of the Bible. She was very fluent in reading German.

In later years when we had grown up, someone related to me that they heard her loudly praying for us children. This was late at night when someone passed by her window.

Timing for Sunday Trip Was Eggs-actly Right!

One Sunday we wanted to take our new baby to see her grandma, but we didn't have the 25¢ needed to buy a gallon of gas.

We did have hens, though, and 11 eggs. At that time, eggs sold for 25¢ a dozen. So we all got dressed up, and then we sat and waited for one of the hens to lay an egg! Finally one of them cackled, my husband put that egg with the 11 others, we took them to the store and exchanged them for a gallon of gas. Off we went to see Grandma!

-Cora M. Johns
St. Charles, Missouri

She Knew How to Count Her Pennies!

Dad lost his job early in the Depression, and we turned our backyard into a garden and sold the produce from house to house. My most vivid memory is the day my mother sold a 3¢ stamp so we could buy bread! She only had 2¢, so she sold the stamp to our neighbor. Then she was able to send me to the bakery for a nickel loaf of bread.

-Jane Hutchins
Yakima, Washington